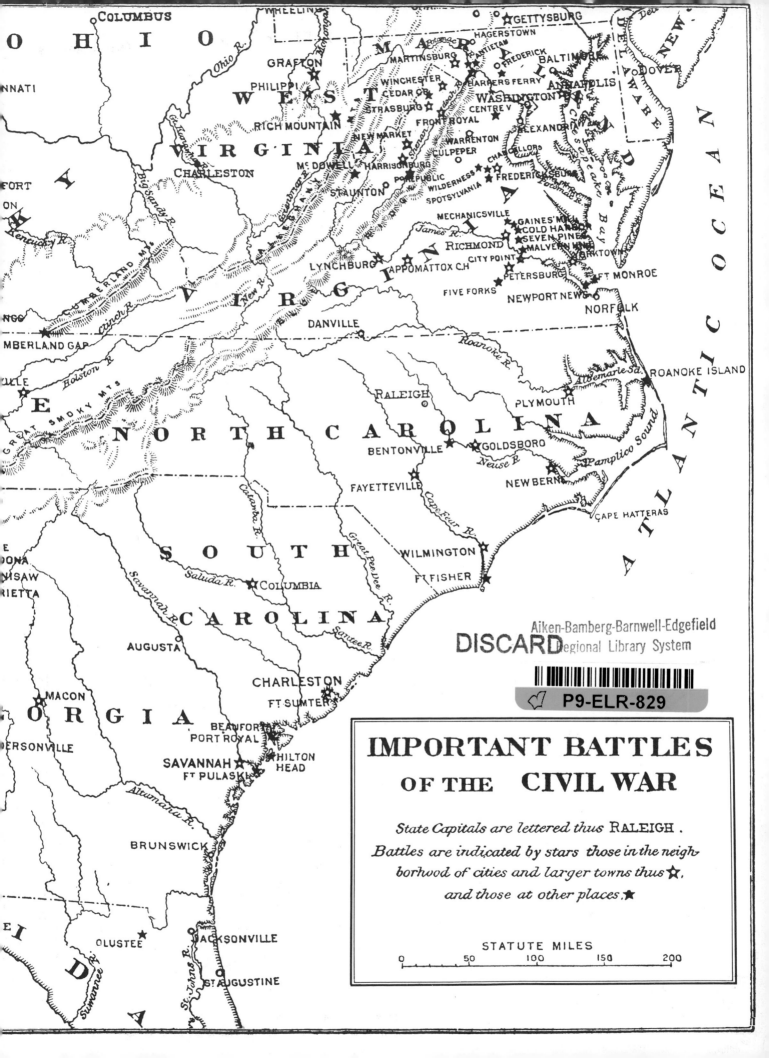

IMPORTANT BATTLES

OF THE   CIVIL WAR

State Capitals are lettered thus RALEIGH.

Battles are indicated by stars those in the neigh-
borhood of cities and larger towns thus ☆,
and those at other places. ★

STATUTE MILES

0   50   100   150   200

BATTLE CHRONICLES
OF THE
CIVIL WAR

LEADERS

INDEX

JAMES M. McPHERSON, Editor

Princeton University

RICHARD GOTTLIEB, Managing Editor

Grey Castle Press

MACMILLAN PUBLISHING COMPANY
New York

COLLIER MACMILLAN PUBLISHERS
London

Text © 1989. *Civil War Times Illustrated*, a division of Cowles Magazines, Inc., Box 8200, Harrisburg, PA 17105.

Introduction, Transitions, Index and Format © 1989. Grey Castle Press, Inc., Lakeville, CT 06039.

Published by Macmillan Publishing Company
866 Third Avenue, New York, NY 10022

ILLUSTRATION CREDITS—Some sources are abbreviated as follows: CWTI Collection (*Civil War Times Illustrated* Collection), FL (*Frank Leslie's Illustrated Newspaper*), LC (Library of Congress), NA (National Archives). Illustrations without credits are part of the *Civil War Times Illustrated* Collection.

Library of Congress Cataloging-in-Publication Data

Battle Chronicles of the Civil War.

   Includes bibliographies and indexes.
   Contents: 1. 1861—2. 1862—3. 1863— [etc.]
   1. United States—History—Civil War, 1861–1865—
Campaigns.   I. McPherson, James M.
E470.B29   1989   973.7′3   89-8316
ISBN 0-02-920661-8 (set)

Printed in the USA

Contents

ABRAHAM LINCOLN

The Military Strategist by T. Harry Williams
Commander Lincoln at Norfolk by Robert H. Joynt
"A few appropriate remarks" at Gettysburg

by Robert H. Fowler
The Man, the Myth by Stephen B. Oates
Photographs of Lincoln: The Burden of Years

The Military Strategist
by T. Harry Williams

If a modern poll organization had existed at the beginning of the American Civil War in 1861 and if it had asked which President of the rival governments would make the greater war director, what answer would it have received? Undoubtedly the average informed observer would have predicted that the head of the Southern states would outshine his Northern opponent. Such a judgment seemed justified by the backgrounds of the two men.

Jefferson Davis, President of the Confederate States, was a graduate of the United States Military Academy at West Point, then the only advanced military school in the country. He had served as a combat officer in the Mexican War, and he had been Secretary of War in President Franklin Pierce's Cabinet. Abraham Lincoln had had no military education and no military experience, except for a brief and inconsequential interlude as a militia captain in a small Indian war.

And yet Lincoln turned out to be a great war director and Davis a mediocre one. The war records of the two executives demonstrate better than any other example in history the truth of one of Clausewitz's dicta. The great German had said that an acquaintance with military affairs was not the principal qualification for a director of war but that "a remarkable, superior mind and strength of character" were more important. Fortunately for the cause of American nationality, these were qualities that Lincoln possessed in eminent degree.

The American Constitution clearly states that the President is the commander-in-chief of the armed forces. Thus Lincoln's authority to direct the Northern war effort was almost unlimited. But the command system with which he had to work was loosely and inadequately organized; in fact, in the modern sense it was not a system at all. In the entire military organization there was no agency charged with the function of planning strategy or of integrating strategy with national policy.

The army possessed a body known as the "general staff," but it bore little resemblance to a modern staff. The members were the heads of the bureaus in the War Department: the quartermaster general, the chief of ordnance, the adjutant general and others. Its work was completely technical and administrative, and each bureau head went pretty much his own way with little supervision from above.

Presiding over the staff and the rest of the army organization was the general-in-chief, the general officer with the senior commission. In 1861 the occupant of this position was Winfield Scott, who was 75 years old and in such bad health that he could hardly walk.

Scott was one of the two officers in the service who before the war had commanded men in numbers large enough to be called an army; the other was John E. Wool, who was two years older than Scott. And the army that Scott had led in the Mexican War (1846) numbered only 14,000. Small as this force had been, it was the largest aggregation of troops that the younger officers—except a few who had visited Europe—had ever seen. Not one of the junior officers had directed the evolutions of as large a unit as a brigade.

Most members of the officer corps were able, after the war began, to adjust their thinking to the requirements of the mass armies that came into being. But they had great difficulty in altering their concepts of strategy to meet the realities of modern war.

If there had to be a decisive engagement, American soldiers thought it should be fought by the maxims laid down by Henri Jomini, the brilliant Swiss who had served under Napoleon. According to Jomini, or more accurately, according to the American interpretation of him, the largest possible force should be concentrated at one point for one big effort against the enemy.

Most of Lincoln's generals could not understand that many of Jomini's ideas did not apply to their war. In a country as large as the United States and with the North enjoying a distinct numerical superiority, it was possible to mount two or more big offensives simultaneously. And

Abraham Lincoln upon his return to his residence in Springfield, Illinois, following his victorious 1860 presidential campaign. The artist erred in showing Lincoln bearded at this time. (National Archives)

the first Northern generals failed to realize that in a democracy and in a modern war the civilian authorities would insist, and rightly so, on having a voice in the conduct of the conflict.

Almost immediately Lincoln demonstrated that he possessed great natural powers as a strategist. His very first acts were bold and imaginative moves for a man dealing with military questions for the first time. He grasped the importance of naval warfare, and proclaimed a naval blockade of the South. He saw that human and material resources were on his side, and called for the mobilization of over 400,000 men. He understood the advantage that numbers gave the North, and—contrary to Jominian strategy—urged his generals to maintain a constant and relentless pressure on the whole line of the Confederacy until a weak spot was found and a breakthrough could be made. And departing from eighteenth-century concepts, he realized that the principal objective of his armies was to seek contact with the Confederate armies and not to occupy Southern territory.

During the first three years of the war, Lincoln performed many of the functions that in a modern command system would be assigned to the chief of the general staff or to the joint chiefs of staff. He framed policy, devised strategy, and even on occasion directed tactical movements. For this he has been criticized by some writers, who contend that he "interfered" too much with matters outside his proper sphere. But in judging Lincoln's actions, it must be remembered that he operated in the absence of a formal command system. If Lincoln had not acted, no action would have resulted.

Moreover, it was fortunate for the Union cause, in most cases, that he interfered. Many of his alleged interventions were nothing more than attempts to force his generals to fight, to execute the role for which generals and armies supposedly are created. Sometimes Lincoln erred —because he lacked technical military knowledge or because he neglected such mundane problems as supplies and transportation. But the vital point is that even when he was wrong he acted from a sound military basis: to make an offensive strategy more offensive. Conversely, it

Gen. Winfield Scott. (*Library of Congress*)

may be said that Davis's great error was to interfere from a faulty basis: to make a defensive strategy more defensive.

In the beginning months of the war, Lincoln naturally turned to old General Scott for strategic counsel. He soon discovered that Scott lacked the qualities required in a general-in-chief. Asked by Lincoln to present an overall plan, Scott came up with a design that called for a naval blockade of the Southern coast and the occupation of the Mississippi River line. The South would be enfolded in a gigantic circle—and with the drawing of the circle Scott would stop. The North could then sit back and wait for the besieged South to yield.

This was the famous "anaconda plan" to squeeze the Confederacy into submission. Although it had obvious merits (the blockade and the Mississippi line became staple items in Northern strategy), it also had basic defects. For one thing, the plan would be a long time in making its possible effects felt. More important, it represented, as Lincoln the civilian saw, the one-weapon or the one-service idea of war. No single strategic procedure was going to win the Civil War.

By November of 1861 Scott had been persuaded to retire. To the post of general-in-chief Lincoln named George B. McClellan, who was also the field commander of the principal Federal army in the Eastern theater. The 35-year-old McClellan demonstrated almost immediately that he did not possess the abilities to plan and direct the movements of a number of armies. At Lincoln's request, he too prepared a strategic design. He proposed that an

army of 273,000 men be placed under his command in the Eastern theater. The Navy would land this host on the Virginia coast, from whence McClellan would march inland and capture Richmond, the Confederate capital. In a series of similar operations, the army would conquer and occupy the entire Eastern seaboard of the Confederacy.

On almost every count, the plan was defective. It demanded too much of available resources. The government could not have assembled that many men in one theater, or housed and fed them if assembled. Nor did the sea transport exist to take the troops where McClellan wanted to operate. McClellan's scheme, calling for a supreme concentration of effort in one theater, was a complete example of Jominian strategy. Lincoln must have been amazed when he read the document, which he filed safely away without comment.

Outside of this proposal, McClellan indulged in no general strategic planning worthy of the name. When he took the field in the spring of 1862, Lincoln relieved him as general-in-chief on the grounds that one man could not direct an army engaged in active operations and at the same time plan moves for other armies. The President did not appoint another officer to the position until July.

In the interim Lincoln acted as his own general-in-chief. There can be little doubt that by this time he had come to have serious misgivings about the professional soldiers. Inclined at first to defer too much to their opinions, he now felt a growing confidence in his own powers to decide military questions, and he was perhaps a little too ready to impose his opinions on the generals.

Maj. Gen. George Brinton McClellan. (*Library of Congress*)

Nevertheless, in this period Lincoln did not presume to dispense completely with expert advice. Secretary of War Stanton had convened an agency known as the Army Board, consisting of the heads of the bureaus in the War Department. This was only the general staff brought together under a chairman, but the transformation of the bureau chiefs into a collective body was a forward step in command. Lincoln frequently consulted the Board before arriving at an important decision.

Lincoln seemed to sense that there was something wrong in the existing arrangement. He, a civilian, was doing things that should be done by a military man. Again he decided to fill the post of general-in-chief. In July, 1862, he named to the position Henry W. Halleck, who had been a departmental commander in the Western theater.

General Halleck seemed to be the ideal man for the job. Before the war he had been known as one of the foremost American students of the art of war, the translator of Jomini into English and an author in his own right. Moreover, he had been a capable departmental administrator. Lincoln intended that Halleck should be a real general-in-chief, that he should, under the authority of the President, actually plan and direct operations.

At first Halleck acted up to his role—but not for long. His great defect was that he disliked responsibility. He delighted to provide technical knowledge and to advise, but he shrank from making decisions. Gradually he divested himself of his original function and deliberately assumed the part of an adviser and an informed critic.

Halleck's refusal to perform the requirements of his position forced Lincoln to act again as general-in-chief, but he kept Halleck as titular head of the office. The President had discovered that Halleck could do one valuable service for him—in the area of military communications. Often Lincoln and his generals had had serious misunderstandings because, almost literally, they spoke different languages, Lincoln the words of the lawyer-politician and the generals the jargon of the military. Halleck had lived in both the civil and the military worlds, and he could speak the language of both. Increasingly Lincoln came to entrust the framing of his directives to Halleck.

In those years of lonely responsibility when Lincoln directed the war effort he grew steadily in stature as a strategist. Usually he displayed greater strategic insight than most of his commanders. But he was willing, as he had been earlier, to yield the power to frame and control strategy to any general who could demonstrate that he could do the job—if he could find the general. By 1864 both he and the nation were certain they had found the man—Ulysses S. Grant. And in that year the United States finally achieved a modern command system to fight a modern war.

In the system arrived at in 1864, which was the joint product of Lincoln and Congress, Grant was named general-in-chief, charged with the function of planning and

Gen. Henry W. Halleck. (*Library of Congress*)

directing the movements of all Union armies. Grant, because he disliked the political atmosphere in Washington, established his headquarters with the field army in the Eastern theater, but did not technically command that army. In the new arrangement Halleck received a new office, "chief of staff." He was not, however, a chief of staff in today's sense of the term. Primarily he was a channel of communication between Lincoln and Grant and between Grant and the 17 departmental commanders under Grant. The perfect office soldier, he had found at last his proper niche.

As general-in-chief, Grant justified every belief in his capacities. He possessed in superb degree the ability to think of the war in overall terms. But his grand plan of operations that ended the war was partly Lincolnian in concept. Grant conformed his strategy to Lincoln's known ideas: Hit the Confederacy from all sides with pulverizing blows and make enemy armies the main objective. The general submitted the broad outlines of his plan to Lincoln, and the President, trusting in Grant, approved the design without seeking to know the details.

The 1864 command system embodied the brilliance of simplicity: a commander-in-chief to lay down policy and grand strategy, a general-in-chief to frame specific battle strategy, and a chief of staff to coordinate information. It contained elements that later would be studied by military leaders and students in many nations. Abraham Lincoln, without fully realizing his part, had made a large and permanent contribution to the story of command organization.

Commander Lincoln at Norfolk
by Robert H. Joynt

Abraham Lincoln shouted above the roar of the naval gunfire. He motioned his tug captain to follow in the wake of the Union ironclad *Monitor* to within range of the Rebel land batteries. The steam tug dutifully transported the President of the United States across the James River to the rear of the crescent of bombarding Union naval vessels. Starboard of the tug, the lead vessel *U.S.S. Seminole* belched another puff of gray smoke. One of her crack gunners blew away the Confederate flagstaff atop the Sewell's Point batteries defending Norfolk, Virginia. An enterprising Confederate mounted the parapet and began replacing the flagstaff. The *Seminole* opened fire again. The Rebel, flag, and flagstaff disappeared in a red mass.

A mile behind the president and the Union naval attack line, the single recoiling Parrot gun aboard the ironclad *E.A. Stevens* lobbed shells over the president's head into the Confederate batteries. On the island of Rip Raps, a mile to the east of President Lincoln, the huge Sawyer gun at Federal Fort Wool fired her 100-pound shots into the Rebel works. The James Gun at the Union's Fort Monroe on the James River's north bank opened up from a range of four miles.

Rebel guns rarely replied to the lethal Union pounding. Some of their shots fell short of the fleet; most of the rest passed overhead. Shots from some Rebel Parrot rifles and Washington ordnance glanced off the forward-positioned *Monitor*. It was up to the Union's *E.A. Stevens* to cause the greatest damage to the fleet. A few of her shells exploded prematurely, one blowing through a spanker on the *U.S.S. Susquehanna*. Other errant shells from the *Stevens* rained shrapnel onto the metal decks of the *Monitor*. Disaster seemed a distinct possibility. A well-placed Con-

Abraham Lincoln was neither shy of his generals nor of going into the field to meet with them. A few months after his Norfolk campaign, he would travel to Harpers Ferry, West Virginia, and to Maryland to have a showdown with stubborn Major General George McClellan, opposite (photographed October 3 or 4, 1862). Nor was Lincoln shy of gunfire: during Confederate Lieutenant General Jubal Early's 1864 raid on Washington, the president went to the scene to watch the fighting and narrowly missed injury. (Library of Congress)

federate shot or an off-tangent Federal shell near the president's tug would have brought tragedy to the Union.

Aboard the much-abused *Monitor*, noting that it was May 8, 1862, Acting Paymaster William Frederick Keeler documented what he saw in a letter to his wife; the keeper of the log of the *U.S.S. Dacotah* did likewise, as did some members of the *Susquehanna's* crew. They were unaware they were recording a first and collecting pieces of a picture puzzle that would remain precisely cut, but lie uncompleted for over a century. They were the witnesses; for the first time an American president was exposed to enemy fire.

Though history remembers that Lincoln often made front-line appearances, the bearded chief executive set two personal precedents that day: It was his first exposure to enemy fire, and his first opportunity to directly exercise his powers as commander-in-chief. The bombardment he was viewing was being carried out under his orders, as part of a much broader, ingenious plan.

A day earlier, Lincoln had reviewed cheering blue-clad troops at Camp Hamilton near Fort Monroe and had inspected the anchored Union fleet and naval armament of Hampton Roads in the James River. By the Constitution, investing him with commander-in-chief powers, he had subordinated his area military commanders. On his second day at the front, Lincoln ordered the bombardment of the Rebels' Sewell's Point batteries. He would personally capture Norfolk, and flush out and destroy the dread Confederate ironclad *Virginia*. He would clear the James River and secure Major General George B. McClellan's exposed left flank. His general's Peninsula Campaign could go forward.

From the tug's deck the president and his commander observed what the *Monitor's* incendiary shells could do at close range. The barracks and wooden buildings in the Sewell's Point works were blazing and the Rebels' poor fire was slackening. Then, in a few minutes, the Confederate guns turned silent.

An unexplained column of smoke rose above the pine trees beyond the Rebel position. Lookouts aboard the *Susquehanna* confirmed it; the *C.S.S. Virginia*, the ship old Yankee tars still called *Merrimac*, was leaving her Craney Island anchorage opposite Norfolk. The ironclad had put in almost daily appearances, steaming out from the secluded cover of the Sewell's Point area to remind others she was ready for a rematch with her smaller Federal adversary, *Monitor*. But today she was obviously interested in reconnoitering the Union-made commotion on the James.

With the appearance of the *Virginia*, the transports carrying Union regiments to storm the silent Sewell's Point batteries halted, awaiting further orders. The *Monitor* waited for her nemesis to enter the main ship channel. The *E.A. Stevens* remained stationary near Newport News on the north bank. The bombarding vessels hove-to. The ramming vessels moved aft of the *Monitor*, ready to run at the *Virginia* at the appropriate moment. Lincoln's tug proceeded to the rear of the line behind the flagship *Minnesota* to await the outcome.

The *Monitor*'s crew prepared specially designed hoses ready to repulse Rebel boarders with scalding water. Her commander, Lieutenant William N. Jeffers, reasoned that while the Rebels would be boiling on the outside, the *Monitor*'s well-placed incendiary shells would be "stewing" them on the inside.

A tense hour and a half passed. Flag Officer Louis M. Goldsborough, to whom Lincoln had delegated the command of the bombardment, gave a general signal from the *Minnesota*'s bridge. The wooden vessels were to resume their moorings for their protection. The huge *Vanderbilt*, with its specially equipped, serrated metal bow, turned about and headed for Fort Monroe. Even the *E.A. Stevens*, which was ordered to remain stationary with her fellow ironclad *Monitor*, turned about, heading for safer waters near Fort Monroe's big guns.

Major General John E. Wool, commandant of Fort Monroe and Camp Hamilton, was concerned with the threat of the *Virginia*, the safety of his troops, and the apparent stalemate to "the plan." He ordered the troop transports to return to the fort.

The *Monitor* and *Virginia* faced each other until dusk settled across the spring skies. But the *Virginia* had to concern herself with defending her port city, Norfolk. She fired an insulting blank shot portside and windward, turned about, and headed back to her moorings. Lincoln, viewing the exchange from the steam tug, returned, seething, to Fort Monroe to meet with his staff.

McClellan's Peninsula Campaign had gone too long and slow. The nation's foremost politician knew the mood of the Northern public. They wanted, nay, demanded a military victory. And it was not presumptuous to say Lincoln knew his staff, his cabinet, and his generals, with all their strengths, and sadly,

The U.S.S. Minnesota, at the center of this engraving, was the ship from which Flag Officer Louis M. Goldsborough commanded the bombardment. (Battles and Leaders of the Civil War)

all their weaknesses. Because he understood their failings, and because of his impatience, he had interrupted his inspection trip to southern Virginia and demanded to be carried into the fray. Understanding the situation no doubt as well as he, nonetheless, Lincoln's advisors and traveling companions, Secretary of the Treasury Salmon P. Chase and Secretary of War Edwin M. Stanton, had chosen to remain safely on the fortressed island of Rip Raps that day. But that evening, in sturdy Fort Monroe, they were more than willing to give their counsel.

With his companions, Stanton, Chase, and Brigadier General Egbert L. Viele, Lincoln sat down to decide what to do with Goldsborough's motionless armada and Wool's 10,000 untried troops. In the lamplight of Quarters No. 1 at Fort Monroe, the president ruled out sending Wool's forces either to Brigadier General Ambrose E. Burnside in the North Carolina sounds or to McClellan up Virginia's penin-

Brigadier General Egbert L. Viele. Following the success of his president's campaign, he became Norfolk's military governor. (Battles and Leaders of the Civil War)

sula. Doing either, the troops would avoid a confrontation with the *Virginia*. Instead, the troops would try for another landing, this time, well to the east of Norfolk and Sewell's Point, on a beach area near Willoughby Point and Ocean View, Virginia. By landing this far east, Lincoln reasoned, the *Virginia* would be less likely to menace any attempted Union disembarcations. To try this she would have to pass within point blank range of the lethal Sawyer gun on Rip Raps Island.

There was a dissenter. Colonel Thomas J. Cram of Wool's staff maintained the water was too shallow east of Sewell's Point for an amphibious landing. This point provoked already frustrated Secretary Chase to remonstrate that there were no depth markings on the naval charts to support Cram's contention. Chase offered to supervise soundings of the area himself the following morning. Lincoln ended the heated discussion by agreeing to Chase's offer. This decision ended the strategy session, and a disappointing day for the president.

Captain John Rodgers. While Lincoln was watching the fight at Sewell's Point, Rodgers was steaming up the James River aboard his experimental iron-plated Galena, on the president's orders, to reach McClellan's left. (National Archives)

Major General John E. Wool, commandant of Fort Monroe and Camp Hamilton, was concerned with the threat posed by the Confederate ironclad Virginia. (U.S. Army Military History Institute)

In retrospect, May 8 had not been a total loss either for Lincoln or for the Union. The president had sent Captain John Rodgers and his experimental, iron-plated *Galena* up the river that morning to open water communications between Fort Monroe and McClellan's left. The *Galena* was accompanied by the screw steamer *Aroostook* and the sidewheel steamer *Port Royal*. By evening, for Lincoln to give up would have meant abandoning his plan to secure the James River for McClellan's protection; it would also mean Rodgers would be left to his fate upriver.

The next morning, Secretary Chase, General Wool, Brigadier General Viele, and Colonel Cram conducted a successful depth sounding and reconnaissance of Ocean View beach across the James River. Civilians along the shore confirmed the intelligence reports of escaped slaves who had recently sailed across to Fort Monroe. The Confederates were abandoning Norfolk.

Since late April 1862, the Rebels had been making preparations to evacuate the town, if necessary. But Rodgers' movement up the James on May 8 changed a deliberate pace into wholesale panic. Captain John Taylor Wood of the *Virginia* recognized the impor-

The deck of the Galena, photographed June 1862. (U.S. Army Military History Institute)

tance of Lincoln's strategic dispatch of Rodger's flotilla upriver. "This movement is bad" Wood wrote his wife, "for it closed the river against us."

General Robert E. Lee knew McClellan's advance up the peninsula would not be the only factor necessitating Norfolk's evacuation. He telegraphed Norfolk's Major General Benjamin Huger that Union "possession of the James River would render the evacuation of Norfolk in time necessary."

Lincoln met Chase's returning contingent as it docked at Engineer's Wharf at Fort Monroe, then stepped aboard the tugboat, *Lioness*, and ordered everyone to head back across the James River to Ocean View. He had been checking naval charts with members of the 99th New York at the fort's mess hall and was persuaded by that regiment's captain, Richard Nixon, that there was a better landing spot a mile or so from the area Chase had found.

Within half an hour the *Miami* and *Lioness* were off shore from Ocean View. Captain Nixon and a detachment of the 99th New York manned a six-oared

boat and headed toward shore. The *Lioness*, with Lincoln aboard, followed close in her wake. The *Miami* remained well off shore.

Suddenly, Rebel cavalry galloped onto the beach. According to the 99th New York's Lieutenant Frederick A. Rowe, the Confederates began to fire at the landing party aboard the six-oared boat and at the *Lioness* some yards behind. Rowe, writing of the incident years later for a regimental publication, stated that as the bullets "whizzed" through the air, officers and men crowded around Lincoln to protect him, at the same time urging him to "seek a less exposed part of the boat." Rowe went on to state Lincoln was unconcerned about the danger of the rifle fire. But because of the forceful urging of the men of the 99th, he finally stepped behind the wheelhouse until the horsemen departed.

For possibly the second time in twenty-four hours and the second time in history, an American president, while in office, had been exposed to gunfire. A well-placed shot could have ended Lincoln's military campaign as well as his life.

From the *Miami*, Secretary Chase signaled the president, asking whether or not the *Miami* should open fire. Lincoln acknowledged the signal with a simple "No." Neither the *Miami's* log nor the letters of Secretary Chase made mention of any Rebel gunfire. The omission was likely due to the position of the *Miami*; at the time she was 600 or more yards from the *Lioness* and out of the sound range of any shots.

With the enemy gone, Lincoln used the six-oared boat to go ashore and inspect his suggested site for an amphibious assault. It was one closer to the fort, a few miles north of Chase's suggested site.

Lincoln wasted no time in organizing the final phase of his campaign. On the return trip to Fort Monroe, he verbally cataloged his list of orders. Wool was to brigade his men, load them onto all available transports, and head at once for Willoughby Point. Remembering the flat-bottomed canal boats tied up at the wharf, the president ordered Colonel Cram to tie them together in a giant train to facilitate disembarking the men, horses, and artillery from the transports to the beach. Lincoln may have been taking

advantage of precedent, a similar successful landing at Roanoke Island three months before.

Once ashore, Lincoln rode alone on horseback to Camp Hamilton to supervise Wool's preparations. But having ridden through camp all the way to the farthest outpost, he was suddenly placed under arrest for not giving the proper countersign. A few staff officers rode up to rescue Lincoln from the now red-faced arresting private. The punishment from the commander-in-chief was a verbal compliment to the still shaking soldier "for doing his duty."

The troop transports left Fort Monroe at midnight, May 9. At 4:00 a.m. the next day, Colonel Cram followed the president's verbal instructions given hours earlier. Taking the lead canal boat in a "crack the whip" fashion, he drove the train of boats at top speed toward the shore. The lead boat road a wave and coasted onto the beach. Within minutes, cheering troops hastened off steamers and transports and onto the canal boats, proceeding from boat to boat toward the enemy beach.

The participating regiments in Lincoln's "borrowed army" were the 20th New York, 16th Massachusetts, 1st Delaware, 10th New York, and part of

Fort Monroe's occupants felt so secure behind its walls that they turned its gun casemates over to domestic concerns. This somewhat less than martial spirit contributed to the lack of Federal success in that part of Virginia. (U.S. Army Military History Institute)

The physical position and altitude of gun emplacements along the James River often made them safe from navy gunfire. Naval cannon sometimes could not obtain enough elevation for effective shots. The gun emplacement shown here is a Union position. (U.S. Army Military History Institute)

the 1st New York Mounted Rifles. Arriving later that morning were the 99th New York, 20th Indiana, 58th Pennsylvania, 11th Pennsylvania Cavalry, and Battery D of the 4th U.S. Artillery.

By 8:00 that morning, the final regiments had landed, accompanied by President Lincoln, Secretaries Chase and Stanton, General Wool, and Brigadier General Viele. At Stanton's insistence, Chase and Viele obtained horses to supervise Wool's handling of the march on Norfolk. At that time, 78-year-old Wool was the oldest Union officer in active service. Many felt he was senile, but Lincoln chose to stick with this man of experience.

Back at the fort, Lincoln received the good news that the *Virginia* had not budged from its moorings and that Sewell's Point appeared abandoned. The Confederates had left their defenses. The Union landing to the southeast of the Point and the inland movement westward had exposed the weakly protected rear of the batteries, rendering their position untenable. Lincoln's ingenious move to embark troops to the east of the Point, as opposed to Wool's plan to storm it, had met decisive, overwhelming strategic success.

Across the river, Chase and Viele trotted on horseback past the advancing 99th New York, moving west-southwest on the road out of Ocean View. Heavy packs, blankets, heavy coats over the soldiers'

already bulky uniforms, and numerous felled pine trees across the roadways slowed the march considerably. Confusion was everywhere and with it, suspicion. Chase questioned staff officers regarding the identity of the brigade commander. Nobody seemed to know. It turned out Wool had not appointed a brigade commander, fearing Brigadier Generals Max Weber and J.K.F. Mansfield might be offended at having not been chosen.

Angrily, Chase upbraided Wool for not having chosen at least one as brigade commander. He labeled the two sensitive generals "cackling old hens." He then turned abruptly to Viele, ordering him to command one brigade and Weber to command the other. Wool was ordered to send Mansfield back to Fort Monroe for reinforcements.

A solid Confederate offensive at this point could have crushed Lincoln's Norfolk Campaign, killing or capturing a treasury secretary and four top generals. These possibilities heightened when the booming reports of enemy artillery ominously echoed from the west.

Unaware that Chase's troops were 300 to 400 yards away, and thinking the delay in the Union advance would give Wool's men more time to advance in force, the Rebels fired their field pieces and then retreated across the Tanner's Creek Indian Pole Bridge and set it ablaze. Within fifteen minutes, Chase, Viele, Wool, and the Union army arrived at the burning bridge and abandoned rifle pits. The city of Norfolk lay open and defenseless to their advancing force.

Without a Northern bullet expended that day, Norfolk had fallen. The first phase of Lincoln's plan was a resounding success. Norfolk Mayor W.W. Lamb led a group of solemn city fathers to the outskirts of the city to begin a long, laborious surrender ceremony. At the same time, this delay provided the rapidly retreating Confederates sufficient time for a complete, successful, destructive evacuation of the adjacent Portsmouth Naval Yard.

From the Fort Monroe ramparts, a brooding Lincoln watched menacing volumes of smoke covering the southwest horizon. It either meant the Confederates were burning stores during evacuation or the Union brigades were in battle. The president's uneasiness was made worse when he was notified that Mansfield had returned to the fort. He had expected Mansfield to be on the opposite bank in the campaign; he had assumed Wool had appointed Mansfield the main brigade commander. Lincoln's anger was directed at Wool's bureaucratic bungling of the troop brigading. He did not realize Mansfield had been ordered back by Chase.

The perturbed president ordered Mansfield and his aide, Colonel Joseph B. Carr, to meet him at Quarters No. 1. Lincoln questioned Colonel Carr first and asked him the whereabouts of his command.

"At Camp Hamilton, sir," replied the young, handsome colonel to the commander-in-chief.

"Why are you not on the other side at Norfolk?" questioned the president.

"I am awaiting orders" stated Carr, answering correctly, but nervously touching his styled mustache.

Lincoln then asked Mansfield why he was at the fort and not across the river in the march. Mansfield answered quickly, "I am ordered to the fort by General Wool."

Livid, Lincoln grabbed the lip of his stovepipe hat and slammed it to the floor. He exploded, "Send me someone who can write!" and got ready to dictate a new order.

Lincoln's baptism as a military commander at that moment was complete. He issued a directive to one of Wool's aides and sent all available troops across the James for the march on Norfolk.

The uncertainty of military campaigning continued to play havoc upon the president's nerves that evening. Reluctantly, he went to bed.

Toward midnight, an awakened president received news from returning Chase and Wool that Norfolk was in Union hands. Stanton, clad in his nightshirt, burst into Lincoln's room and heard Wool recite the good news. Stanton turned to the aged general and hugged him. An overjoyed Lincoln, in throes of rare laughter at the sight of Wool and Stanton, called out, "Look out Mars! If you don't, the General will throw you!"

During the morning hours of May 11 Josiah Tattnall, the *Virginia's* commander, was as confused as Lincoln was joyous. He had received conflicting orders: Keep the Federals from ascending the James River and defend Norfolk. He could not do both, and had failed to fulfill the first order when John Rodgers and his naval flotilla steamed past him two days before. Tattnall intended to remain at Norfolk as long as his port facilities were under Confederate army protection. But the abandonment of Sewell's Point and the news of Lincoln's "rapidly" advancing army, changed Tattnall's priorities.

Considering an escape up the James to Richmond, to lighten his vessel Tattnall unloaded heavy guns and supplies. Finally, between 1:00 and 2:00 in the morning, May 11, he received word from his pilots that the *Virginia* could not be sufficiently lightened. Desperate, frantic, he increased the amount of gunpowder on board to eighteen tons, landed the crew safely at Craney Island, and set the ironclad afire and adrift.

At 4:55 a.m. a blast rumbled up twenty miles of the peninsula. The *Virginia* had blown up. The Rebel terror was dead. Lincoln's grand plan had been fulfilled. The army and the command that he felt compelled to lead, even though he was not a trained military strategist, had triumphed at last. Trusting his feel for human behavior, Lincoln had overridden his generals and admirals and initiated his own successful strategy.

Lincoln himself regarded the capture of Norfolk and the destruction of the *Virginia* among the most important successes of the war to that point. His plan had been a simple one, too simple for some; but,

The C.S.S. Virginia's commanders, Confederate Admiral Franklin Buchanan and Captain Josiah Tattnall. It was Buchanan who took the Confederate ironclad to her first engagement. And it was Tattnall, seated at the right, who was forced to set her afire and send her to the bottom on May 11, 1862. (CWTI Collection)

18

Norfolk's navy yard, in ruins for the second time in little more than a year. The facility was first partially destroyed by order of its panicked Federal commander, Captain Charles S. McCauley, when he feared Virginians would seize it. Since its recapture by Lincoln's troops in 1862, it has remained in continuous use by the U.S. Navy. (Library of Congress)

unlike other Union commanders' schemes, this one had worked.

At 8:15 a.m., May 11, Lincoln arrived at Norfolk, choosing to stay aboard the *Baltimore*. Union regiments cheered him. Among them were sunburned members of the 10th New York National Zouaves who had shaved their heads, leaving emblems in hair in the shapes of stars, half moons, the number '10', or a few "N.Z.s."

The few white Southern women on the streets of Norfolk were dressed in mourning. Many blacks, fresh from Sunday worship services, lined the wharves, waving to the president.

The casual, entertaining observations were interrupted by putrid smoke from the still-smouldering Gosport Navy Yard. Blackened, broken hulls of steamers and unfinished gunboats lay in dry dock on their sides. Huge, burning piles of coal were scattered about the ruined vessels—Gosport was the graveyard of the Confederate navy.

Lincoln had seen enough. His main objective, the *Virginia*, lay behind him, buried in pieces, a few fathoms below. He ordered the *Baltimore* to weigh anchor and head for Fort Monroe, telling Chase and Stanton he needed to return to Washington, D.C. The civilian administration of the Civil War was as important as the fighting and maneuvering of the past few days.

The *Baltimore* had already rounded Sewell's Point toward Fort Monroe as Secretary Chase pleaded with Lincoln that they not leave. Chase spoke loudly, almost angrily, lobbying for a thrust up the James River to aid Captain Rodgers and the naval flotilla. Chase's conviction was that a small force of about 5,000 men embarked on transports and convoyed by gunboats, might take Richmond in advance of McClellan.

Lincoln declined the opportunity without giving any specific reasons. Chase was not easily discouraged; he brought it up repeatedly for the commander-in-chief to consider. But Lincoln chose not to interfere with further military endeavors for at least the next few months. McClellan had the York and the James rivers as his flanks and his lines of supply.

With Lincoln's departure, the army and navy's rivalry, temporarily subdued in deference to Lincoln's presence, was fanned to brighter flame. In the weeks following, McClellan would do little to dampen the feuding. His stubborn refusal to put aside past differences and openly cooperate with the navy on his left flank would help to seal the doom of his land plan to take Richmond. And McClellan's pride allowed Lincoln's Norfolk Campaign to be historically misconstrued, considered an afterthought to McClellan's military movements on the Peninsula. This quirk of circumstances, bound up with human emotion, obscured the significance of Lincoln's campaign for more than a century.

Though Lincoln was leaving the field of command, a part of his plan was still in progress; Rodgers was still upriver. Within a few hours, the *Monitor* and *E.A. Stevens* would join the *Galena*, the *Aroostook*, and the *Port Royal* in the approach to City Point, Virginia, silencing batteries en route and opening communication for the Peninsula Campaign.

Downriver, the *Baltimore* continued rounding Old Point Comfort northward into Chesapeake Bay. Lincoln sat in a deck chair, read his Bible, and set his sights on Washington.

"A few appropriate remarks" at Gettysburg

by Robert H. Fowler

Andrew G. Curtin, governor of Pennsylvania, visited Gettysburg immediately after Robert E. Lee had withdrawn his battered Confederate army from the vicinity. He found conditions chaotic. Practically every public building and many private homes had been turned into hospitals. The wreckage of war was strewn over several square miles.

The governor was most shocked at the way in which some 6,000 dead of both armies were buried in shallow trenches or, in some cases, not buried at all. Before returning to Harrisburg, he commissioned David Wills, a prominent, 32-year-old Gettysburg lawyer, to form a committee and buy land for the reburial of the Union dead. On July 24, just three weeks after the battle, Wills submitted a plan, which Curtin approved, for the loyal states to cooperate in the establishment of a fine cemetery. On August 14, Wills reported to the governor:

> The chief executive of 15 of the 17 states have already responded, pledging their states to unite in the movement...I have also at your request selected and purchased the grounds for this cemetery...The grounds embrace about 17 acres on Cemetery Hill, fronting on the Baltimore Turnpike and extending to the Taneytown Road....

Wills paid $2,475.87 for the land. He engaged William Saunders, a prominent landscape artist, to lay out the grounds. And he let a contract to F.W. Biesecker to remove the Union dead and rebury them, at $1.59 per body, in the new "national Soldiers' Cemetery."

With these important details settled, he turned to the dedication ceremony, originally set for October 23. Edward Everett was among the most popular speakers of that time. At 69, he had been president of Harvard University, both U.S. representative and senator from Massachusetts as well as governor of that state, ambassador to Great Britain, and unsuccessful candidate for the vice presidency of the United States. He was a natural choice to deliver the dedicatory oration.

Dr. Everett accepted the invitation on condition that the ceremony be postponed to November 19. He was committed for practically every day in October and he wanted plenty of time to prepare his address. So the ceremony was changed to November 19.

Printed invitations were sent to many public officials— congressmen, diplomats, state officials, and President Abraham Lincoln. No one really expected Lincoln to come. When he accepted, Wills and his committee had no alternative but to suggest that "after the Oration, you, as Chief Executive of the Nation, formally set apart these grounds to their sacred use by a few appropriate remarks." In a separate letter sent the same day, November 2, Wills invited Lincoln to "stop with me" while in Gettysburg.

Thaddeus Stevens, the Republican floor leader in the House of Representatives and a former Gettysburg resident, declined to attend. When he heard that Lincoln had accepted, he remarked that it was a case of "the dead going to bury the dead." He thought Lincoln would lose the presidential election the next year. Salmon P. Chase, Lincoln's Secretary of the Treasury, who hoped to succeed Lincoln as President, gave "imperative public duties" as his excuse. Secretary of War Edwin McM. Stanton likewise begged off attending.

Why did Lincoln accept? No one knows for certain, but these are several theories.

First, the cemetery was a pet project of Governor Curtin and here was a chance to please him without offending the opposing Republican faction in Pennsylvania.

Second, the previous year Lincoln had visited the Antietam battlefield in Maryland and a rumor had been spread that he had called on his crony, Ward Hill Lamon, to sing a bawdy song as he toured the scene. The report hurt Lincoln's feelings and, according to the theory, he wanted to demonstrate his respect for the Union dead.

And, he was eager for an opportunity to restate his faith in the rightness of the Union cause and to destroy any belief that he might give in to Copperhead pressure and make peace on the Confederacy's terms of absolute independence.

Despite Stevens' scoffing remarks or suspicions of his motives, there can be no doubt that Lincoln took seriously the little speech he was to deliver. His friends realized that he was concerned about speaking from the same platform as an orator of Dr. Everett's experience and polish. And his anxiety wasn't relieved when Everett sent him a newspaper proof of the main oration twelve days before the ceremony.

Dr. Everett wasn't the old windbag some twentieth-century accounts have made him appear. Even in manuscript his speech was a meaningful document. It presented, for the first time, a clear and accurate account of the "Battles of Gettysburg," based on reports of Union commanders. It marshaled a battery of both logical and emotional arguments against making peace with the Confederacy.

Lincoln would have fallen flat had he tried to emulate the master orator. Instead, as we know now, he fashioned a small gem to fit into Everett's large setting of golden oratory.

Just when, where, and how Lincoln wrote the Gettysburg address remains as debatable as why. It appears that he prepared part of it in Washington. One phrase, "of the people, by the people," etc., was reminiscent of an impromptu speech he made on the White House lawn just after the Gettysburg victory. Evidently, however, he did not complete his address until he reached Gettysburg.

As for reaching Gettysburg, Lincoln left the details to Secretary of War Stanton, who arranged for a special train to leave Washington early on Thursday, November 19, and arrive just in time for the ceremony. Lincoln overruled Stanton, saying that he didn't want "to run a gantlet," and ordered that the train leave at noon on the eighteenth.

Evidence of Lincoln's complete sincerity in wanting to speak at Gettysburg came just before departure time. His youngest son, Tad, became ill. The Lincolns were perhaps unduly anxious about him. Their son Willie had died the previous year. Still, Lincoln didn't back out. And he didn't let his concern becloud his sense of humor.

Original manuscript of the Gettysburg address. The first page of the manuscript was written in ink on a page of White House stationery and was carried by Lincoln in his pocket when he went to Gettysburg. The second part was written with a pencil on bluish-gray foolscap at Gettysburg in the house of David Wills.

Stanton sent Provost Marshall Gen. James B. Fry to be Lincoln's military escort, but when that officer arrived at the White House, the President wasn't ready. When Lincoln finally appeared, Fry urged him to hurry... which reminded the President of the story of a man about to be hanged. On his way to the gallows, the man observed people rushing to get a good view of the execution and shouted to them, "Boys, you needn't be in such a hurry; there won't be any fun till I get there."

At the Baltimore and Ohio station, Lincoln found that the rear third of the last car of the four-car train had been reserved for him. At Baltimore, the train was transferred to the Northern Central Railway. A baggage car was added to serve as a dining room for the President and his entourage, which included a number of Washington officials, diplomats, and others. Again at Hanover Junction, Pennsylvania, the car was shifted to the Hanover Junction and Gettysburg line. Along the way, people gathered to see the President. One little girl who brought him a bouquet got a presidential kiss and the compliment that she was "a sweet little rosebud herself."

The train arrived in Gettysburg about dusk and a carriage was waiting to take Lincoln to the home of David Wills, which faced "The Diamond," or public square. There he was given a bedroom on the second floor. Secretary of State William H. Seward was lodged next door at the home of Robert G. Harper, owner of *The Adams Sentinel.*

After eating supper and conversing with Wills and the other guests, Lincoln withdrew to his bedroom to work on his "little speech." It turned out this wasn't easy to do.

Gettysburg was in a gala mood, or at least the several thousands of visitors were. Bands played in the streets. Crowds tramped up and down, shouting and calling upon the various dignitaries to make speeches. One group halted below Lincoln's window and he stuck his head out to acknowledge their cries. They wanted a speech but he was too wrapped up in what he would say on the morrow to make one that night. So he made a few off-the-cuff remarks about how it was better to say nothing if you had nothing to say and the crowd went off grumbling next door, where Seward obliged them with a longer speech.

Lincoln worked on his speech for approximately an hour. About 10 p.m., he took the manuscript next door to show to Seward. He and his cabinet member talked for more than half an hour. By the time Lincoln was ready for bed, evidently he had his "few appropriate remarks" ready for delivery the next day. That was one worry off his mind. Another was concern for his son's health, and that was relieved by a telegram from Secretary of War Stanton saying, "On inquiry, Mrs. Lincoln informs me that your son is better this evening."

And so Abraham Lincoln turned in at the home of David Wills unaware that the words he would utter the next day would become immortal.

The next morning, after breakfast, Lincoln again retired to his room to go over his speech. Arrangements called for a procession to leave the square at 10 a.m. and for the ceremony to begin as soon as the dignitaries reached the cemetery. It was a mild autumn day.

Dressed in his familiar stovepipe hat, black suit, and white gloves, the President went out and found a horse saddled and waiting for him. It was a nice enough steed but of only average size according to most accounts.

But Lincoln, six feet four and wearing a high silk hat, made the horse look more like a pony. The spectacle made some onlookers titter as Lincoln mounted the horse and waited. Evidently parades in 1863 were like parades today — never on time. This one was an hour late in beginning. While he waited astride the horse, Lincoln chatted and shook hands with the people who crowded about.

At last the parade started. Out Baltimore Street it moved to the Emmitsburg Road (now Highway 15) and thence to the Taneytown Road up Cemetery Hill—a distance of about three-quarters of a mile. Minute guns posted along the way signaled the President's approach. From the spectators came cries of "Hurrah for Old Abe" and "We are coming, Father Abraham," all of which amused Lincoln.

The procession took 15 minutes. By this time, about 11:15 a.m., most of the estimated 15,000 spectators had already crowded about the speaker's platform, which stood in the center of the semicircle of grave plots.

Again Lincoln had to wait. Dr. Everett had wanted to make a last minute check of the battlefield terrain with Prof. Michael Jacobs of Pennsylvania College and it was nearly noon before he arrived and the ceremony could begin with a prayer by the Rev. Thomas H. Stockton, chaplain of the U.S. Senate, the text of which later filled a column of type in *The Adams Sentinel.* Then the band played Luther's "Old Hundredth" hymn and Benjamin B. French, custodian of public buildings in Washington, introduced Dr. Everett.

Apparently Dr. Everett used neither notes nor manu-

script during the next two hours. He harkened back first to Greek history and then to more recent European history. He recalled the events of July 1 to 4 at Gettysburg.

He ripped into the arguments for secession and absolute states' rights. He appealed to anti-Confederate sentiment in the South and ended his oration with praise for the dead of Gettysburg.

A hymn written by the same Benjamin French who had introduced Everett was then sung by the Baltimore Glee Club. Then Col. Ward Hill Lamon, marshal of the District of Columbia, parade marshal for the day, and a close friend of Abraham Lincoln, presented the President.

Memories of men are unreliable instruments. To this day—or especially in this day—it cannot be said for certain whether Lincoln read his speech verbatim, glanced occasionally at notes or whether he followed Everett's example and repeated it from memory.

We do not know whether his voice boomed out so that every one of the 15,000 heard him or whether they had to strain to hear. The Associated Press story noted applause several times and some present said later that the applause was frequent and thunderous. But others said the response was an awed hush. And still others said the speech made no impact at all.

There were about 270 words in the speech. It took Lincoln perhaps two minutes to say them.

A dirge was sung, the benediction pronounced, and history had been made without those present being aware of it. And that included Abraham Lincoln, who turned to his friend Lamon and commented that "the thing won't scour," meaning his speech had been a flop.

The procession is marching south on Baltimore Street and turning off on Emmitsburg Road, where today there is a traffic light. From this point it proceeded to the Taneytown Road and thence via the southern entrance to the cemetery. Note the spectators looking to the left: they were probably looking at the President who was mounted. (National Archives)

Dedication Ceremony—On the next two pages is reproduced a drawing by Joseph Becker, special artist of "Frank Leslie's," showing the exercises at the new National Soldiers' Cemetery at Gettysburg on November 19, 1863, when Abraham Lincoln delivered his immortal Gettysburg Address. Robert Taft, who made a special study of this drawing for "The Kansas Historical Quarterly" in 1954, concluded that the artist was actually present, and made his sketch from a point somewhere on East Cemetery Hill. Miss Josephine Cobb, specialist in iconography at the National Archives, notes, however, that the Becker drawing shows the flag at full mast. This indicates that Becker probably started his drawing on the 18th, since the flag was at half-mast on the 19th; likely he filled in the crowd on the 19th but failed to notice that the position of the flag had been changed.

Taft points out that South Mountain shows in the background, and lower is the wooded crest of Seminary Ridge. The arched brick structure was the Evergreen Cemetery gatehouse but today is a part of the National Cemetery. Modern visitors sometimes fail to realize that the Gettysburg Address was delivered where the Solders' National Monument stands—at the center of the concentric arcs of graves—and not farther south where there is a memorial bust of Lincoln.

Miss Cobb writes us that after Becker's drawing reached "Leslie's" many hours were still required to engrave it and many different engravers worked on the sky, trees, roads, and other features. The scene was then put together like blocks or pieces of a jigsaw puzzle. While studying patents of the Civil War period for photographic vans, Miss Cobb found a letter from Samuel Weaver, who with his brother owned one of these vans, which throws additional light on the gathering. Weaver states that there were upward of 40,000 persons from out of town present at the ceremony. This supports Becker's drawing, which shows a very large crowd. However, most published contemporary accounts estimate the crowd at 15,000-20,000.

UNION SOLD. GRAVES

GETTYS

DEDICA

MEADE'S HEADQUARTERS.

RO

PA.

REBEL GRAVES

CEREMONY

MOUNTAIN

UNION GRAVES.

Lincoln's speech was over but his visit wasn't. There were still hands to be shaken there on Cemetery Hill and later at a reception in Gettysburg.

Following the reception, Lincoln called for old John Burns, the civilian hero of Gettysburg, who had joined in the first day of battle and been wounded three times. "God bless you, old man," Lincoln said upon meeting the little shoemender and former constable. Then arm-in-arm the two men walked to the local Presbyterian Church to hear a patriotic address by Governor-elect Anderson of Ohio. Lincoln didn't have time to hear all of the speech. He left midway to catch his train back to Washington.

Disappointed with his little speech and already feeling the effect of an attack of varioloid (a mild form of small-pox) that was to put him to bed later, he boarded his train, stretched out on a seat, and asked for a wet towel to put across his eyes.

On the way to Gettysburg, Lincoln had met an old man whose son had been killed at Little Round Top the previous July. In talking to the man, Lincoln commented, "When I think of the sacrifice yet to be offered and the hearts and homes yet to be made desolate before this dreadful war is over, my heart is like lead within me and I feel at times like hiding in a deep darkness."

It was in this mood that he departed Gettysburg. Lincoln had no way of knowing that the combination of Grant and Sherman in time would bring the South to its knees. He had no way of knowing that the following November, he would receive in his re-election an over-whelming vote of confidence from the people.

And feeling as he did, he could not have dared to hope that appreciation of his "few appropriate remarks" would grow until thousands of school children would commit them to memory and they would become one of the classic liturgies of the democracy in which he had such faith.

Back in Washington the day after the dedication of the National Soldiers' Cemetery at Gettysburg, Edward Everett sent a note to Lincoln in which he said:

Permit me also to express my great admiration for the thoughts expressed by you, with such eloquent simplicity & appropri-ateness, at the consecration of the cemetery. I should be glad, if I could flatter myself that I came as near to the central idea of the occasion in two hours, as you did in two minutes.

Lincoln immediately replied, writing:

In our respective parts yesterday, you could not have been excused to make a short address, nor I a long one. I am pleased to know that in your judgment the little I did say was not entirely a failure. Of course I knew Mr. Everett would not fail; and yet while the whole discourse was eminently satis-factory, and will be of great value, there were passages in it which transcended my expectations. The point made against the theory of the general government being an agency, whose principles [sic] are the states, was new to me and, as I think, is one of the best arguments for national supremacy.

Below: Josephine Cobb has succeeded in identifying President Lincoln and several other notables on or near the platform, as this detail shows. Lincoln's face, in the circle, is partly obscured by what appears to be a woman's hat. It is thought that he has just stepped from the platform, which was three feet high, to shake hands with one of the spectators.

The crowded appearance of the platform is accounted for by the fact that it was small, and probably could not hold the 250 persons some-times said to have been on it. The main speaker, Edward Everett, cannot be identified among the persons on the platform. (National Archives)

The Man, the Myth
by Stephen B. Oates

In 1858, against a backdrop of heightening sectional tensions over slavery, Abraham Lincoln stood in the Great Hall of the Illinois House of Representatives, warning his countrymen that a house divided against itself could not stand. Across Illinois that year, in a series of forensic duels with Senator Stephen A. Douglas, this tall and melancholy man addressed himself boldly to the great and difficult problems of his day: to the haunting moral contradiction of slavery in a nation based on the Declaration of Independence. . . to the combustible issue of Negro social and political rights. . . to the meaning and historic mission of America's experiment in popular government. This same man went on to the presidency, charged with the awesome task of saving the Union—and its experiment in popular government—in the holocaust of civil war. In the end, after enduring four unendurable years, he himself became a casualty of that conflict, gunned down by actor John Wilkes Booth just when the war was won and popular government preserved for humankind the world over.

The man who died that dark and dismal day in April 1865 had flaws as well as strengths, made mistakes and suffered reversals just as surely as he enjoyed his remarkable achievements. But in the days that followed his assassination, the man himself was lost in an outpouring of flowery orations and tear-filled eulogies. As the seasons passed, Lincoln went on to legend and martyrdom, inflated by the myth-makers into a godly Emancipator who personified America's ideal Everyman.

As historian David Donald has noted, two schools of Lincoln myth-makers emerged after the Civil War. One school began on "Black Easter" 1865, when ministers across the Union portrayed Lincoln as an American Christ who died to expiate the sins of his guilty countrymen. A second mythical tradition, popularized by William Herndon, Lincoln's hyperbolic law partner, presented him as an Illinois Paul Bunyan, a mighty Western folk hero known as "Old Abe." And so the two mythical conceptions of Lincoln battled one another into the 20th Century. It remained for poet Carl Sandburg, in his lyrical epic of a biography, to blend the two conceptions and capture the Lincoln of that mythology more vividly and consistently than any other folk biographer. In Sandburg's telling, Lincoln's was "a mind, a spirit, a tongue, and a voice" for a pungent, sprawling American democracy caught in its greatest trial. In the "tornado years" of civil war, he was Father Abraham, a people's hero who patiently stuck to the cherished middle way, guiding the ship of state through to victory, only to be assassinated before he could bind up the nation's wounds with tender magnanimity. After Sandburg's volumes appeared, a procession of novels, plays, movies, children's books, school texts, and television shows purveyed the mythical Lincoln to a vast American public, until that Lincoln became for most Americans the real historical figure.

I have no quarrel with this Lincoln so long as we make a careful distinction between myth and history. A myth, after all, is not an untrue story to be avoided like some dread disease. On the contrary, myth carries a special truth of its own—a truth, however, that is different in meaning and purpose from historical truth. In the case of Lincoln, the myth is what Americans wish the man had been, not necessarily the way he was in real life. So the mythical Lincoln possesses what Americans have always considered their most noble traits—honesty, hard work, a capacity to forgive, a compassion for the underdog, a clear-sighted vision of what is right and what is wrong, a dedication to God and country, and an abiding concern for all. No one person has ever risen to such mythic proportions, to personify all that we have longed to be since 1776. No person can ever rise to such proportions. So we have invented a Lincoln who fulfills our deepest needs as a people. He is the Plain and Humble Man of the People who emerged from the toiling millions to guide us steadily through our greatest national ordeal. He is Father Abraham who in the stormy present still provides an example and shows us the way.

This Lincoln can have profound spiritual meaning for us. But so can the real Lincoln, the actual man of history.

What do we mean by the historical Lincoln? Do we mean some definitive portrait that will stand forever as the way he really was? No, we do not mean that at all. Historical biography, after all, is not an exact science. It is an interpretative art. In fact, the very materials we rely on to forge biography—letters, diaries, journals, interviews, recollections, and the like—were all recorded by people who filtered things through their own senses and sensibilities. Because biographical materials are themselves imprecise and interpretative, it is quite impossible for anyone to produce a definitive biography—a fixed and final portrait of Lincoln or any other historical figure.

In my own efforts to see Lincoln as he was, I have found a flawed, extraordinary, many-sided man. He was almost entirely self-educated, with a talent for expression that in another time and place might have led him into a distinguished literary career. He loved poetry, wrote verse himself, studied Shakespeare, Byron, and Oliver Wendell Holmes, and was attracted especially to writings with tragic and melancholy themes. He examined the way celebrated orators turned a phrase or employed a figure of speech, admiring great truths greatly told. Though never much at impromptu oratory, he could hold an audience of 15,000 spellbound when reading from a written speech, singing out in the shrill, high-pitched voice that became his trademark.

He was an intense, brooding man, plagued by chronic depression most of his life. "I am now the most miserable man living," he said on one occasion in 1841. "If what I feel were equally distributed to the whole human family, there would not be one cheerful face on the earth." He added: "To remain as I am is impossible; I must die or be better."

At the time he uttered this, Lincoln had fears of inadequacy as a man, doubting his ability to please or even care for a wife. In 1842 he confided in his closest friend, Joshua Speed, about his troubles; and they confessed mutual fears of premature death and of "nervous debility" with women. Speed went ahead and married anyway, then wrote Lincoln their anxieties were groundless. "I tell you, Speed, our forebodings for which you and I are rather peculiar, are all the worst sort of nonsense," Lincoln rejoiced. Encouraged by Speed's success, Lincoln finally wedded Mary Todd when he was thirty-three years old.

But before he met her, Lincoln's romantic life was a painful and lonely one, filled with ambivalent feelings about women and marriage. As for the storied early love for Ann Rutledge, there is no evidence whatever that Lincoln ever had a romantic attachment with her. There is no evidence that theirs was anything more than a platonic relationship. True, Lincoln was once engaged to Mary Owens, but his tortured letters to her reveal a confused young man so far as intimacy with a woman was concerned. It was with the encouragement of Speed and Mary Todd herself that Lincoln struggled with his self-doubts and overcame them enough to wed Mary. And she clearly helped him on this score, giving him the tender support and understanding he needed, for they developed a strong physical love for one another. Yet Mary, so maligned in Lincoln literature, has never received the credit she deserves for helping Lincoln resolve his fears of inadequacy with women.

Lincoln still remained moody and melancholy, given to long introspections about death and mortality. And death was a lifelong obsession with him. His poetry, speeches, and letters are studded with allusions to it. He spoke of the transitory nature of human life, spoke of how all people of this world are fated to die in the end—all are fated to die. He saw himself as only a passing moment in the river of time.

Preoccupied with death, he also feared insanity, afraid (as he phrased it) of "the pangs that kill the mind." In his late thirties, he wrote and rewrote a poem about a boyhood friend, one Matthew Gentry, who became deranged and was locked "in mental night," condemned to a living death, spinning out of control in some inner void. Lincoln retained a morbid fascination with Gentry's condition, writing about how Gentry was more an object of dread than death itself: "A human form with reason fled, while wretched life remains." Lincoln was fascinated with madness, troubled by it, afraid that what had happened to Matthew could also happen to him—his own reason destroyed, Lincoln spinning in mindless night without the power to know.

Lincoln, a teetotaler, said liquor left him "flabby and undone," blurring his mind and threatening his self-control. He dreaded and avoided anything threatening that. In one memorable speech, he heralded some great and distant day when all passions would be subdued, when reason would triumph and "mind, all conquering *mind*" would rule the earth.

One side of Lincoln was always supremely logical and analytical. He was intrigued with the clarity of mathematics; as an attorney he could command a mass of technical data. Yet he was also supersitious, believed in signs and visions, contending dreams were auguries of approaching triumph or calamity. Skeptical of organized religion, he never joined a church, but argued all human destinies were controlled by an omnipresent God.

It is true that Lincoln told folksy anecdotes to illustrate a point. But humor was also tremendous therapy for his depression—a device "to whistle down sadness," as a

The log cabin built in 1831 by Thomas and Abraham Lincoln on Goose Nest Prairie is a source of legend. (*Kean Archives*)

friend put it. Said Lincoln himself: "I tell you the truth when I say that a funny story, if it has the element of genuine wit, has the same effect on me that I suppose a good square drink of whiskey has on an old topper; it puts new life into me." Lincoln liked all manner of jokes, from puns and pungent rib-ticklers to bawdy tales that could make the priggish squirm. And when he lost his temper or was in the company of his male friends, he could utter "damn" and "hell" like the rest of us.

Contrary to legend, Lincoln was anything but a common man. One of the most ambitious human beings his friends had ever seen, he had an aspiration for high station in life that burned in him like a furnace. Instead of reading with an accomplished attorney, as was customary in these days, he taught himself the law entirely on his own. He was literally a self-made lawyer. Moreover, he entered the Illinois legislature at the age of twenty-five and became a leader of the state Whig party, a tireless party campaigner and regular candidate for public office.

By the 1850s, Lincoln was one of the most sought-after attorneys in Illinois, with a reputation as a lawyer's lawyer — a knowledgeable jurist who argued appeal cases for other attorneys. He did his most influential legal work, not in the circuit courts as mythology claims, but in the Supreme Court of Illinois, where he participated in 243 cases, winning most of them. He commanded the respect of his colleagues, all of whom called him "Mr. Lincoln," or just "Lincoln." He typically signed letters to his friends, "Yours as ever, A. Lincoln." Nobody called him Abe — at least not to his face. He loathed the nickname. It did not befit a respected professional who had struggled hard to overcome the limitations of his frontier background. Frankly, Lincoln enjoyed his status as a lawyer and politician — and he liked money, too, using it to measure his worth. By the 1850s, thanks to a combination of talent and sheer hard work, he amassed considerable wealth. He had an annual salary of $5,000 or more (the equivalent of many times that today) and large financial and real-estate investments.

Though a man of status and influence, he was as honest in real life as in the legend. Even his enemies admitted he was incorruptible. Moreover, he held broad humanitarian views, some of them in advance of his time. Though a teetotaler, he was extremely tolerant of alcoholics, regarding them not as criminals — as most temperance people did — but as unfortunates who deserved understanding. He noted some of the world's most gifted artists had succumbed to alcoholism, and believed them too sensitive to cope with their insights into the human condition. He believed women, like men, should vote so long as all paid taxes. And he had no ethnic prejudices. His law partner William Herndon, who raved against the Irish, reported that Lincoln was not at all bigoted against "the foreign element, tolerating — as I never could — even the Irish."

Politically, Lincoln was always a nationalist, an outlook that began when he was an Indiana farmboy tilling his father's mundane wheat field. While the plow horse was getting his breath at the end of a furrow, Lincoln would study Parson Weems' eulogistic biography of George Washington, daydream about the Republic, and reflect on Washington and Jefferson, great national statesmen who had shaped the course of history. By the time he became a politician, Lincoln idolized the Founding Fathers. He extolled them for beginning an experiment in popular government on these shores, to show a doubting Europe that people could govern themselves without hereditary monarchs and aristocracies. The foundation of the American experiment was the Declaration of Independence, which in Lincoln's view contained the highest political truths in history: that all men are created equal and are entitled to freedom and the pursuit of happiness. For Lincoln, this meant that men like him were not chained to the conditions of their births, that they could elevate their station in life and harvest the fruits of their own talents and industry. Thus he had a deep, personal reverence for the Declaration and insisted that all his political sentiment flowed from that document.

Lincoln during his brief career in the House of Representatives. Declining appointment to a vacant congressional seat in 1847, Lincoln won election to the office for the succeeding term. In Congress he opposed the Mexican War and had his honesty questioned by the New York Tribune, which claimed he padded his travel expense accounts. (Civil War Times Illustrated collection)

Lincoln went on to become the foremost American spokesman for the liberating impulses of his day. No American praised and defended the country's experiment in popular government, and the hope it held out to people the world over, more eloquently than he. In the 1850s his political goal was the national Senate, not the Presidency. In antebellum years it was the Senate that featured the great orators of the day—men like Daniel Webster, John C. Calhoun, and Henry Clay, Lincoln's political idol. The presidency, by contrast, was a mundane administrative job offering little to a man of Lincoln's oratorical abilities. Lincoln preferred the national Senate, because in that august body he could defend popular government, defend the containment of slavery, defend the rights of Negroes to enjoy the fruits of their toil, in speeches that would be widely read and preserved for posterity in the *Congressional Globe*.

By 1858, when he challenged Stephen A. Douglas for the Senate, Lincoln had become convinced that America and the world were caught in a profound historical crisis. In his view, an aggressive State Power was conspiring to nationalize human bondage, discredit and destroy the Declaration, and restore class, caste, and despotism. Should that happen, Lincoln feared, then all the great and good work since the Revolution would be obliterated. The world's best hope—America's experiment in popular government—would be expunged, and mankind would spin backwards into feudalism.

But in those same debates with Douglas, Lincoln expressed anti-Negro sentiments that merit careful discussion in the context of his time and place. He campaigned in a state and a region white supremacist to the core. And he was battling a man who persistently accused him of lusting for Negro equality and racial mongrelization. Lincoln did not want to discuss such matters. He complained bitterly racial equality and amalgamation were not the issue. The issue was whether slavery should expand and become permanent in the American house, or whether it should be contained in the South and left to perish there. But across Illinois, Douglas kept race-baiting Lincoln, warning white crowds his adversary was a war-mongering "black" Republican out to liberate the slaves so they could stampede into Northern neighborhoods, into Illinois neighborhoods, and work, vote, and marry with white people. These allegations forced Lincoln to take a stand; it was either that, or forget about becoming a United States senator. At Charleston, he conceded he was not and never had been in favor "of making voters or jurors of Negroes, nor of qualifying them to hold office, nor to intermarry with white people." There was, he said at Ottawa, "a physical difference" between the black and white races that would "probably" always prevent them from living together in perfect equality.

We shall probably never know whether Lincoln was voicing his own personal convictions in speeches like these. In the 1850s he had ambivalent feelings about black people when it came to what specific social and

Stephen Douglas, U.S. Senator from Illinois. A man of small physical stature paired with the towering Lincoln in the 1858 debates, his supporters dubbed him "The Little Giant."

political rights they ought to enjoy. But when compared to the white-supremacist, anti-Negro attitudes of Douglas and most other whites of that time, Lincoln comes off as an enlightened man in the matter of race relations. He consistently argued blacks were equal to Lincoln, Douglas, and "every living man" in their right to freedom, equality of opportunity, and the product of their own industry. Exasperated with Douglas and white Negrophobia in general, Lincoln begged American whites "to discard all this quibbling about this man and the other man—this race and that race and the other race as being inferior." He begged them to unite as one people and defend the ideals of the Declaration and its promise of liberty and opportunity for all.

Perhaps these remarks aggravated a lot of plain folks in Illinois, because they voted for Douglas and helped return Lincoln's arch-rival to the Senate. But you do not learn about this in the mythical recounting of Lincoln as a great people's hero. Nor do you learn that most Americans in 1860 thought him too radical and dangerous to occupy the White House.

Something emphatic must be said about Lincoln's opinion of slavery and the painful personal difficulty bondage in America caused him. He hated slavery. He said he hated it as much as any abolitionist. Yet Lincoln loved America and praised her example in the world with an impassioned sense of history. This left him trapped in an impossible psychological dilemma: he detested human bondage, yet worshipped a political system which protected that very institution with a web of national and state laws. Lincoln's dilemma—his hatred of slavery and his impotence to do anything about it where it already existed—must have fed his melancholy like wind on flames.

Lincoln toured the East prior to his inauguration. In Philadelphia on Washington's Birthday 1861, he raised an American flag in ceremonies near Independence Hall and was cheered by an enthusiastic crowd. With the outbreak of war his popularity, never universal, would diminish.

In the fires of civil war, Lincoln underwent seemingly endless crises that might have shattered a weaker president. A man who lacked administrative experience, suffered from chronic depression, who hated to fire inept subordinates and bungling generals (he had never liked personal confrontations), he was thrust into the center of a fratricidal conflict, a conflict that began as a 90-day war and swelled into a tornado of blood and wreckage with consequences beyond calculation for those swept up in it. Forced to make awesome decisions in a war that had no precedent in all American history, Lincoln pursued the conflict without constitutional or political guidelines to follow. At the same time, he had to live with the knowledge that he was the most unpopular president the Republic had known up to that time. His hate mail from the public was voluminous and grotesque. One such letter came to him in 1861: "You are nothing but a goddamn Black nigger."

Some people's president, this Lincoln of history. In the first two years of the war, Lincoln was a deeply troubled president, caught in a vortex of problems and pressures so great he did not think he could survive them. I have a recurring image of him standing as he often did at the White House windows, a haunted, harried man who did not know whether this war would ever end.

Yet Lincoln found the inner strength to surmount his multitude of woes—the strident criticism he got from all corners of the Union, the devastating loss of his cherished son Willie, the emotional breakdown of his wife, and above all the endless, endless war. As the war grew and changed, so Lincoln grew and changed. The cautious, diffident Lincoln of 1861 and 1862, developed into the tougher, more decisive, more innovative chief executive of 1863, 1864, and 1865. He learned from his mistakes. He learned to trust his own judgment and not surrender to malcontents and incompetents. He learned to dismiss the likes of Major Generals Don Carlos Buell and George B. McClellan. By the fall of 1863, White House Secretary John Hay was amazed at how masterfully the president was running the war. "I never knew with what tyrannous authority he rules the Cabinet, till now," Hay recorded in his diary. "The most important things he decides and there is no cavil...He will not be bullied—even by his friends."

Perhaps the hardest decision Lincoln had to make was that about slavery. At the outset of the war, he adopted a hands-off policy toward the peculiar institution, declaring his purpose was to save the Union and not to free the slaves. He feared emancipation would send loyal, slaveholding border states spiraling into the Confederacy, fretted that it would alienate Northern Democrats and smash his bipartisan war coalition. And he questioned the constitutional and legal grounds for wartime emancipation.

But the pressures of war caused Lincoln to abandon his hands-off policy and hurl his armies at slavery in the Rebel states, making emancipation a Union war objective. This creates one of the most difficult problems confronting those who try to interpret the Lincoln of history. Why, in little more than a year, did Lincoln change his mind about emancipation?

From the summer of 1861 on, several powerful Republicans from Capitol Hill—chief among them, Senators Charles Sumner of Massachusetts, Benjamin Wade of Ohio, and Zacharia Chandler of Michigan—sequestered themselves with Lincoln and implored him to free the slaves. Sumner, Lincoln's warm personal friend, was especially persistent. In war time, the senators argued, the national government could eradicate slavery by the war power; Lincoln should do it in his capacity as commander-in-chief. They explained that slavery was an enormous source of strength for the Confederacy, that bondsmen not only served as army workers, but provided a vast labor force for Rebel production. If Lincoln emancipated the slaves, it would cripple the Confederacy and hasten an end to the rebellion.

The senators pointed out their belief that slavery had caused the war, was the reason the Southern states had seceded, and was now the cornerstone of the Confederacy. It was preposterous, the senators contended, to fight a war without removing the thing that had brought it about. Should the South return to the Union with slavery intact, as Lincoln initially desired, Southerners would just start another war over slavery, whenever they thought the institution was threatened again. The current struggle would accomplish nothing. If Lincoln really wanted to save the Union, he must tear slavery out root and branch and obliterate the planter class, the group the senators believed had orchestrated secession and fomented war.

Sumner also insisted emancipation would keep mighty industrial England out of the conflict. England, proud of her antislavery heritage, would not interfere in a war for slave liberation. Emancipation would also clarify the status of slave refugees, who had liberated themselves in Dixie and flocked to Union lines by the thousands, often imperiling Union troop movements.

By 1862, Lincoln's armies suffered from manpower shortages on every front. As Sumner and others kept telling Lincoln, the slaves were an untapped reservoir of strength. "You need more men," Sumner declared, "not only at the North, but at the South. You need the slaves." If Lincoln freed them, he could recruit black men into his depleted armies.

Sumner reminded everyone, emancipation would break the chains of several million oppressed human beings and right America at last with her own ideals. Lincoln could no longer wait for the future to remove slavery. He must do it. The war, monstrous and terrible though it was, had given Lincoln the opportunity.

In summer 1862, as the war dragged on with no end in sight, Lincoln embraced all the arguments Sumner and his associates rehearsed for him. The conflict, Lincoln said, could not be won through forebearance toward

Above: *"President Lincoln, Writing The Proclamation of Freedom,"* while surrounded by influences and pressures good and bad. Below: *Lincoln traveled to New Orleans on a flatboat in 1831. It is reported that while there the sight of open slave trading disturbed him.*

Southern Rebels. The time had come to take a bold new path and strike at the very "heart of the rebellion." To hasten an end to the killing, to save the Union and its cherished system of popular government, and to rid the country of a cruel wrong, Lincoln finally issued the Emancipation Proclamation of January 1, 1863. In it, Lincoln declared war on slavery as an institution, commanding his armies to liberate all slaves—those of loyalists and Rebels alike. As Union forces slashed into Confederate territory, they would free all slaves in the areas and states they conquered.

Though often disparaged as a meaningless decree, Lincoln's proclamation was an unprecedented use of executive authority, which he justified as a wartime necessity to save the Union. For the first time in history, an American president had employed Federal military power to wipe out a state institution, free an enslaved race, and destroy a ruling class whose very existence depended on human bondage. The proclamation was the most revolutionary measure ever to come from an American president up to that time. It officially turned the war into what a more cautious Lincoln had warned against in 1861—a remorseless revolutionary struggle whose concussions are still being felt in our own time.

Emancipation ignited a powderbox of racial discontent across the North, exploding the mythical notion of "Old Abe" as a people's president, a folk hero who "knew his American people." Lincoln was far ahead of public opinion when he decided to issue an emancipation decree. This was proved by the massive racist backlash it caused among Union voters—including the common folk who feared it would lead to an exodus of Southern blacks into the North. Sullen, war-weary, the Union electorate dealt the Republican party a smashing political defeat in the by-elections following Lincoln's Preliminary Emancipation Proclamation of September 1862. To forestall more disasters, Lincoln and his party worked hard to sell Northern whites on the necessity for slave liberation, assuaging their racial anxieties. But emancipation remained the single most unpopular act of Lincoln's embattled administration.

Lincoln refused to retract a single word of his proclamation. Even in 1864, when so unpopular it seemed he would not be reelected unless he modified his slave policy, he refused to go backward. He had promised freedom to the slaves, he said. He meant to keep his word so long as he was in office.

What is more, emancipation did something for Lincoln personally that has never been stressed. In the process of liberating the slaves, Lincoln also freed himself from his old dilemma. In truth, emancipation brought the private and the public man together: now Lincoln the public statesman could obliterate a monstrous thing Lincoln the private citizen had always hated. The story of emancipation could well be called the liberation of Abraham Lincoln.

In history, Lincoln was hardly a moderate and gentle president, a folk hero who clung throughout war to some mythical middle course. Lincoln always felt closest to Sumner's wing of the party—the so-called Radical Republicans. He remarked that men like Sumner were the conscience of the Republican party, and he moved steadily toward Sumner's position as the war raged on. With no end in sight to the bloodshed, Lincoln embraced almost every harsh war measure the Radicals urged on him—not only emancipation, but confiscation, the use of Negro troops, the draft, and total warfare. As a consequence, conservative Republicans and dissident Democrats wailed in despair, complaining that Lincoln was a tool of the "howling and shrieking abolitionist faction," or that he himself was a howling and shrieking Abolitionist and a dictator to boot.

In Reconstruction, Lincoln did not play some forgiving middle role, while Sumner and his fellow "extremists" conspired to carve Dixie up in an ecstasy of revenge.

True, Lincoln and Sumner had substantial disagreements over Reconstruction, mainly over which branch of government—the President or Congress—should restore the Rebel states to the Union. But on a number of vital Reconstruction issues, Lincoln and Sumner actually stood together. Both agreed the South had to be remade. Both wanted to muzzle the rebellious Southern white majority, lest it overwhelm the Unionist majority there and return the old Southern ruling class to power—a class Lincoln had once castigated as slave-dealers in politics. Far from forgiving that class (as does the Lincoln mythology), the historical Lincoln agreed with Sumner it should be eradicated. The president's emancipation and Reconstruction policies were calculated to do just that.

At the same time, Lincoln was not far from Sumner's position on Negro suffrage. In 1864, Sumner demanded all Southern black men be enfranchised, while Lincoln endorsed limited Negro suffrage. By the last winter of the war, with emancipation a central war objective and thousands of blacks serving in his armed forces, Lincoln pri-

Noted for his humor, Lincoln's love of laughter was construed by detractors as insensitivity. This caustic cartoon shows his future Democratic adversary Major General George McClellan kneeling at right comforting his wounded, while Lincoln, with a cloak and Scots bonnet in hand, makes an inappropriate remark. The cloak and bonnet were rumored to be a disguise to escape assassination prior to inauguration.

vately acknowledged he wanted intelligent ex-slaves, and especially those who fought in his ranks, to have the ballot. But in his last speech on April 11, 1865, Lincoln went beyond this position and granted in public that the black man deserved the right to vote. And he meant the black man across the entire vanquished South. While he was not yet prepared to make Negro suffrage mandatory, it seems the president's direction was clear. It was toward full political rights for Southern blacks, not away from them. On the last day of Lincoln's life, Attorney General James Speed told Salmon Chase, a champion of full Negro suffrage (as Speed was), that the president "never seemed so near our views." Thus, in the matter of black political rights, Lincoln again showed his tremendous capacity for growth and change, proving the Lincoln of 1865 had come a long distance from the Lincoln of 1858.

By war's end, Lincoln seemed on the verge of a new Reconstruction program. A tough agenda, it would call for some form of Negro suffrage, more stringent voting qualifications for ex-Confederates (he had hinted at this in his 1864 Message to Congress), and, most likely, an army of occupation for the postwar South. At his last Cabinet meeting, Lincoln and his secretaries unanimously agreed such an army could well be necessary, not just to maintain order and stability in a war-torn region, but to safeguard Negro freedom and protect the unionist minority on whom Lincoln's entire Reconstruction program depended. In other words, the president was already considering in 1865 what Congress would later adopt in the days of "Radical Reconstruction." Perhaps a new and tougher program was what Lincoln had in mind in the closing line of his last speech: "It may be my duty to make some new announcement to the people of the South. I am considering, and shall not fail to act, when satisfied that action will be proper."

He never got the chance to make an announcement. But given his position on Reconstruction at war's end, it seems absurd to believe the president was ready to restore the defeated South with tender magnanimity. Lincoln would be magnanimous in that he would not resort to mass jailings and executions of the Southern insurrectionists. He bore them no malice, seeing the war as a divine punishment for the crime of slavery, a terrible retribution God visited on a guilty people, North and South alike. But there can be no doubt Lincoln desired to bring the South

into the mainstream of American republicanism, to install a free-labor system there for blacks as well as whites, to establish public schools for both races, to look after the welfare of freedmen, to grant them access to the ballot and the courts—to build a new South dedicated like Lincoln to the Declaration of Independence and the preservation of popular government for all generations to come.

In the end, Lincoln faced the conquered South as a toughened idealist, whose Reconstruction policies were bound to put him on a collision course with Unreconstructed Rebels. They would certainly oppose him as adamantly as they resisted Congress two years later. Lincoln stood for everything they had fought against for four long years. Under him they could look forward to an occupying army, black political rights, and disenfranchisement for almost the entire postwar and war-time Southern leadership—things they were bound to despise and resist. Even if Lincoln had lived, Reconstruction was going to be a painful ordeal for a war-scarred America. *He* knew that, and he said so several times before he died.

The historical Lincoln, as I have tried to approximate him, is remarkably different from the Lincoln of mythology—from the rumpled, simple, joke-cracking commoner transformed by the Civil War into an all-forgiving Father Abraham. A more realistic portrait, though, does not strip Lincoln of his extraordinary qualities. The historical Lincoln comes out more heroic than the mythical man, because we see him overcoming his deficiencies and self-doubts, often against tremendous odds. Lincoln's long struggle against adversity—inner adversity as well as the terrible difficulties of his apocalyptic era—is something anybody can identify with and learn from. We can learn from Lincoln's life that even those who rise to supreme heights have personal dilemmas—identity crises, ambivalences, hurts, setbacks, and even a loss of will—which they have to anguish over and work their way through. If the Lincoln of mythology reveals something about the spirited needs of our country, the Lincoln of history reveals a great deal about the suffering and triumph of the human spirit in its struggle with universal problems. As we cherish the myth, let us also celebrate the flawed, fatalistic, principled, and poetic figure of history who confronted the most troublesome issues of his time and made decisions and offered solutions for them, even if they were immensely unpopular. This Lincoln left behind for all of us, a caring and committed life.

A drawing of the Ford's Theater box where the life of Lincoln ended and the myth began. (Library of Congress)

Photographs of Lincoln: The Burden of Years

What did the strain of a divided nation do to Lincoln the man? These details of popular Lincoln portraits, arranged in chronological order, show the heavy passage of his last seven years. Photographs are from the Library of Congress unless otherwise credited.

April 25, 1858. *Lincoln posed for this sitting in Urbana, Illinois, in a coat borrowed from photographer Samuel G. Alschuler.*

February 27, 1860. *This was the first time Mathew Brady photographed Lincoln. (Lloyd Ostendorf Collection)*

June 3, 1860. *Alexander Hesler photographed Lincoln in Springfield, Illinois. Lincoln is believed to have said of the picture, "That looks better and expresses me better than any I have ever seen; if it pleases the people I am satisfied."*

February 1862. *An unknown photographer captured Lincoln in a reflective mood at Brady's Washington, D.C. gallery. The portrait was possibly taken soon after the death of Lincoln's son, Willie.*

August 9, 1863. *Lincoln posed for Alexander Gardner at the photographer's new gallery in Washington, D.C.*

November 8, 1863. *Lincoln sat for Gardner eleven days before the Gettysburg Address.*

Feburary-April 1865. *One of the last photographs of Lincoln by Alex-
ander Gardner, Washington, D.C. On April 14, 1865 John Wilkes
Booth shot Abraham Lincoln at Ford's Theatre in Washington, D.C.*
(Lloyd Ostendorf Collection)

JEFFERSON DAVIS

by Bell I. Wiley

APPRAISAL of Jefferson Davis as Confederate President requires consideration of the difficulties of his position. The new government lacked an adequate corps of experienced personnel: bureau chiefs, clerks, and other functionaries acquainted with each other and with their duties. Want of an organized and knowledgeable bureaucracy, such as that inherited by the Lincoln administration, increased the burdens and impaired the efficiency of the Confederacy's founding fathers.

The constitution drawn up at Montgomery defined the new government as the creation of "sovereign and independent" states. Davis subscribed to the principle of state sovereignty but he was far less provincial in his views than were many of his fellow Confederates, including Alexander Stephens, the Vice President, and most of the governors. As Chief Executive he was tremendously handicapped by the deep and pervasive attachment of Southerners to states rights.

Davis was also handicapped by the excessive individualism which characterized the South's ruling classes. On February 5, 1861, ex-Senator James H. Hammond of South Carolina wrote William Gilmore Simms: "Bigman-me-ism reigns supreme and every one thinks every other a jealous fool or an aspiring knave." The rampant individualism bemoaned by Hammond was a product of the plantation system. Each planter was in effect a petty sovereign and his exalted status tended to make him self-reliant, proud, resentful of opposition, and averse to teamwork.

DAVIS' difficulties were enormously increased by the war in which the Confederacy became involved two months after his inauguration. The new nation was greatly overmatched in virtually everything required to wage the sort of conflict that erupted at Fort Sumter. The twenty-three states adhering to the Union had a population of twenty-two million; the eleven states headed by Davis had only nine million, of whom more than one-third were slaves; the Negroes rendered considerable support to the Confederacy as farm laborers and defense workers, but in invaded areas most of them ran away, more than 100,000 donned the Union blue, and many thousands more served the North as military laborers, informers, or spies.

Even greater than the North's advantage in manpower was its superiority in factories, skilled artisans, experienced business leaders, liquid wealth, foreign credit, and developed national resources. It had 21,000 miles of railroads as against the Confederacy's 9,000 miles and its railroads were better connected and had far more ample rolling stock and repair facilities than those of the South. The Confederacy became so hard up for rails in the latter part of the war that it had to resort to the expedient of shifting track from one area to another to meet emergency situations. The South was at even greater disadvantage with respect to water transportation. Northerners owned most of the American merchant vessels which plied oceans and rivers in antebellum times, and when war came in 1861 they retained possession of nearly all these craft as well as the crews

The inauguration of Jefferson Davis as President of the Southern Confederacy at Montgomery, Alabama on the morning of February 18, 1861. (FL)

that operated them. The South's deficiencies in transportation were responsible for much of the hunger experienced by its soldiers and civilians.

THE Confederacy was also greatly handicapped by the inferiority of its Navy. When the Southern states seceded, the North retained possession of the Federal fleet and most of the shipyards. As the war progressed, it rapidly expanded its Navy, and thus was able to tighten the blockade and utilize sea lanes for establishing beachheads along the Southern coast. The North also built many shallow-draft gunboats to ply Southern rivers. These vessels, working in conjunction with land forces, enabled the Federals to utilize the Mississippi, Tennessee, and other rivers for invading the Southern heartland.

The Confederacy had other and less tangible shortcomings which added to the burdens of its Commander in Chief. The rate of illiteracy among Southerners was 20.3 percent in 1850, as against less than

10 percent in the Northwestern states, 3 percent in the Middle states and 0.42 percent in New England. Ignorance nurtured suspicion, gave credence to rumor, and worked against ready adjustment to new situations. The South's upper classes were generally literate but concern for slavery and devotion to agriculture had made them resistant to new ideas and new ways. A prominent South Carolinian, L. M. Keitt, revealed awareness of the South's crippling inflexibility when he wrote his wife in 1864: "Our people have not risen to the height of this present crisis. . . . They have cherished state pride and exclusiveness for 80 years, and no changes however great, no ruin however appalling could make them forget it for a moment. Our people will not move out of the old forms and routine."

THE man who took the helm of the Confederate Government in February 1861, was aware of the difficulties inherent in the position. Davis tried to forestall his election and when informed that the delegates at Montgomery had chosen him for the Presidency he was surprised and disappointed. Mrs. Davis, who was with him at their Mississippi plantation when he received notification of his election

Old print of General Zachary Taylor at the Battle of Buena Vista where the expert leadership of men like Jefferson Davis, Bragg, and Sherman saved the day for Taylor's army in a battle fought against superior numbers of Mexicans.

stated: "When reading the telegram he looked so grieved that I feared some evil had befallen our family. After a few minutes of painful silence he told me as a man might speak of a sentence of death." The President-elect thought it likely that the Confederacy would have to fight for its independence, and he would have much preferred military command to political leadership.

He appeared to be well qualified for the army position that he desired. His father, Samuel Davis, a son of a Welsh immigrant, was a Georgia captain in the Revolution. Jefferson Davis, tenth child of Samuel and Jane Davis, was born in Kentucky on June 3, 1808, more than a quarter of a century after his father returned to civilian life, but Samuel's Revolutionary experience was kept alive in family lore as the Davises moved about the country and finally settled on a small plantation near Woodville in southwestern Mississippi. Jefferson was proud of his father's role in the Revolution and his interest in military affairs must have been enhanced by a two-week sojourn at the Hermitage, home of Andrew Jackson, when Davis as a lad of 7 made the long journey from Mississippi to Kentucky to enter St. Thomas, a Catholic seminary near Bardstown.

After two years at St. Thomas, Jefferson went home to Mississippi in which state he attended Jefferson and Wilkinson academies. In this frontier country he heard much of the fighting between Indians and whites for control of the area. In 1821, at thirteen, he enrolled as a freshman at Transylvania, the oldest and best college west of the Appalachians. He entered actively into the social life of college and community and apparently profited from the excellent instruction that he received, especially in Latin and Greek.

DAVIS' military interests seem to have been latent during his sojourn at Transylvania, for it was his intention to pursue the study of law at the University of Virginia. But at the urging of his brother Joseph, his senior by twenty-four years, and a rapidly rising lawyer-planter in the fertile country below Vicksburg, he left Transylvania at the end of his junior year to accept appointment as a cadet at West Point.

Davis' record at West Point was far from brilliant and at graduation in 1828 he stood twenty-third in a class of thirty-four. His best grades were in rhetoric, moral philosophy, drawing, and French. In deportment his standing was consistently low and twice he narrowly escaped expulsion for involvement in drinking sprees. It is interesting to speculate on what changes might have been wrought in the career of Davis, and the Confederacy, if he had been dismissed from the Military Academy.

Throughout his career at West Point, Davis enjoyed the esteem of his fellow students and one of the greatest benefits of the four years' training was the acquaintance formed with future military leaders, North and South. Two of his closest friends among the cadets were Albert Sidney Johnston and Leonidas Polk.

FOLLOWING graduation from West Point, Davis spent nearly seven years as a lieutenant at army posts in the frontier country of Illinois and Wisconsin. Here his principal duty was to help maintain order and provide protection against the Indians. While serving under Colonel Zachary Taylor at Fort Crawford in 1833, he fell in love with the colonel's 19-year-old daughter, Knox. His affection was reciprocated but the colonel, for reasons that cannot be clearly determined, opposed the match. As is often the case, the romance thrived on parental opposition, and in June 1835, Davis resigned his commission and married the attractive young woman to whom he had been engaged for two years.

Davis and his bride went to "Hurricane," Joseph's plantation on the Mississippi below Vicksburg. There Jefferson began to clear the 1,800-acre tract of land assigned to him by Joseph, who after the death of Samuel Davis in 1824, became Jefferson's mentor in a relationship approximating that of father and son. In August 1835, both bride and groom were stricken with malaria, from which Knox shortly died.

DURING the next eight years, the sorrowing Davis lived the life of a recluse on his Mississippi plantation, "Brierfield." With the help of fifteen slaves, most of them purchased with money lent by Joseph, he built a dwelling and cleared additional land, most of which was devoted to the growth of cotton. His overseer was an able and trusted Negro, James Pemberton, inherited from Samuel Davis and intimately associated with his young master in the capacity of personal servant during seven years of army duty. Jefferson followed Joseph's example in instituting self-government on his plantation. Negroes charged with infractions of discipline were tried by their fellow slaves and sentences imposed by the jurors could be appealed to Davis, who on occasion remitted or lightened the penalty. Davis shared the prevailing Southern view that Negroes were innately inferior to whites, but slavery as administered by him represented the institution in its most humane form.

While running his plantation, Davis kept a close eye on political activities, through reading of the newspapers and the *Congressional Globe*. In November 1843 his fellow Democrats prevailed on him to become a candidate for the legislature. He had only a week to campaign and he lost to his Whig opponent. But the excellence of his speeches attracted favorable attention.

JOSEPH Davis was the moving spirit behind Jefferson's venture into politics; he also was the instigator of another and more momentous action designed to rescue the grieving young planter from his self-imposed seclusion. On Joseph's invitation, Varina Howell, 17-year-old daughter of Joseph's long-time friend, William B. Howell of Natchez, spent the Christmas holiday of 1843 at "Hurricane." Varina was a sprightly, intelligent girl and Jefferson quickly fell in love with her. Miss Howell, whose family were staunch Whigs, had some misgivings about the political affiliations of her suitor, but these were quickly dispelled by Jefferson's compelling attractions. The two were wedded on February 26, 1845. Despite the eighteen years difference in their ages, and notwithstanding recurrent tension between Varina and her brother-in-law Joseph, the marriage resulted in a mutual respect and devotion which deepened with the passing of time.

Shortly after the marriage, Davis was elected to Congress, but his first sojourn in Washington was of short duration. In June 1846, he resigned his seat to lead a small regiment of volunteers known as the "Mississippi Rifles" in the war against Mexico. Fighting under the command of his former father-in-law, Zachary Taylor, Davis won enthusiastic acclaim for his outstanding performance as a combat leader.

Jefferson Davis and his wife in 1849.

A WOUND received at Buena Vista put Davis on crutches for more than a year and marked the end of his active military service. But his experience in the Mexican War, brief and restricted though it was, in a sense was the most important episode in his life. Comradeship with Albert Sidney Johnston, Braxton Bragg, and other congenial associates was a welcome relief from the seclusion and loneliness of the plantation years. Successful command of troops in battle brought the greatest thrill that he ever experienced. The praise heaped upon him by soldiers and civilians warmed his heart and built up his confidence. Shortly after the wounded hero came home in June 1847, Mississippians sent him to Washington to represent them in the Senate. There he supported President James Polk in extending the western boundaries and strongly opposed Northern proposals to exclude slavery from the new Federal territories. He was one of the most eloquent and powerful opponents of the Compromise of 1850.

In 1851 he withdrew from the Senate to oppose Henry S. Foote, who was running for governor in Mississippi on a platform favoring the Compromise. He lost to Foote by a narrow margin, and he probably would have won if he had entered the race in its early stages. After two years at Brierfield, he re-entered public life as Secretary of War under Franklin Pierce. He felt at home in the War Department and effected much needed improvements in army organization, equipment, training, and morale. He used his political influence to help win acceptance of the Kansas-Nebraska Act and he was largely responsible for the Gadsden Purchase.

In 1857 the Mississippi Legislature sent Davis back to the U. S. Senate, where he remained until after his state seceded. During his last years in Washington, Davis followed the pattern of Calhoun in championing measures designed for the protection of states rights, slavery, and free trade. He believed that the measures for which he fought were essential to the security of his region and in accord with the principles on which the nation was founded. He supported his position with great earnestness and force, but he retained the respect and even the friendship of many Northerners who opposed his views.

DURING his career in the Senate, Davis kept in close touch with Army affairs by serving as chairman of the committee on military affairs. His first appointment after he left Washington in January 1861, was to a military position—that of commanding general of the state force in Mississippi. But he had hardly begun to function in the new job when the message from Montgomery summoned him to head the Confederate Government.

THE misgivings with which he accepted the responsibility thrust upon him were allayed to some extent by public response to his election. The Montgomery *Advertiser* described the President's long trip from Mississippi to Alabama as "one continuous ovation." At stations along the way, crowds of people shouted congratulations and praise. In response to their demonstrations, Davis made no less than twenty-five speeches, all of which were received with hearty hurrahs. From all parts of the Confederacy came enthusiastic congratulations.

When Davis arrived in Montgomery, he received a tremendous welcome during which the fiery and eloquent Alabama secessionist, William L. Yancey, told the jubilant throng: "How fortunate is our country. . . . She has found in the distinguished gentleman she has called to preside over her public affairs the statesman, the soldier, the patriot. . . . The man and the hour have met."

In his brief inaugural, on February 18, 1861, Davis declared that the Southern states in leaving the Union and forming a new compact were simply exercising the sovereign rights that had always been theirs. He expressed the hope that the Confederacy would be accorded a peaceful existence but added: "If this be denied to us . . . it will but remain for us with firm resolve to appeal to arms and invoke the blessing of Providence on a just cause."

THE outbreak of hostilities at Fort Sumter in April 1861, lifted Davis' popularity to even greater heights. This fact was vividly attested by the adulation heaped on him during the journey from Montgomery to the new capital in Virginia in May.

The recipient of these demonstrations possessed many admirable qualities. He was generous to the needy, loyal to his friends, and devoted to his family. His letters to his wife and children are marked by exceptional warmth and tenderness. One of the greatest sorrows of Davis' tragic life was the loss of all his four sons. Samuel Emerson, the first-born, died before his second birthday in 1854; Joseph Evan, born in 1859, was killed by a fall from the balcony of the Confederate White House in April 1864; William Howell, a smart and winsome child, succumbed to diphtheria at age 10 in 1872; Jefferson, Junior, born January 16, 1857, and a close companion of his father during the postwar years on the Gulf Coast, fell victim to yellow fever in 1878. The day after receiving news of William's passing Davis wrote his son-in-law: "I am crushed under such heavy and repeated blows. I presume not God to scorn, but the many and humble prayers offered before my boy was taken from me, are hushed in the despair of my bereavement." His two daughters, Mar-

garet and Varina Anne, both outlived their father and his relations with them were consistently close and affectionate.

When his high-spirited wife revealed traces of jealousy, as she occasionally did during absences of her spouse, he soothed her ruffled feelings with reassurances of devotion. On the thirty-second anniversary of their wedding he wrote: "My dear, Dearest Wife, Winnie, . . . The world goes wrong to me, men prove false, business affairs [worsen]. . . . Yet from all these clouds . . . I turn and am cheered by the memory of the day when a beautiful, gifted, accomplished girl gave me her soft hand and virgin heart, taking me for better or worse; and continues yet to say she has not regretted the compact then made."

UNFORTUNATELY for President Davis, few people outside his family were aware of the tenderness and warmth that lay deep in his nature. But almost all who observed him were greatly impressed by his appearance and demeanor. He could hardly be called handsome because of the hollowness of his cheeks and the sharpness of his features. But his military bearing, dignity, courtesy, poise, and self-assurance commanded attention and generated respect. An English officer, James Fremantle, after interviewing Davis in 1863, wrote: "He is nearly six feet high, but is extremely thin. . . . He wore a linen coat and gray trousers, and he looked what he evidently is, a well-bred gentleman. Nothing can exceed the charm of his manner, which is simple, easy, and most fascinating."

The attractive qualities noted by Fremantle were due in large part to the President's good education. This came not so much from schooling as from wide reading. During the years of seclusion, 1835-1843, he read extensively from Joseph's well-stocked library. He followed the course of current events by perusing a wide assortment of newspapers, including the *National Intelligencer* and the London *Times,* and for more serious study he turned to such works as the *Federalist, Elliot's Debates,* the treatises of John Locke, Adam Smith's *Wealth of Nations,* and the writings of Thomas Jefferson. Discussions with Joseph, a well-informed student of politics and government, helped Jefferson evaluate and absorb the material that he read. The study habits developed during this period of isolation were carried into public life and the

Attorney-General Ben'amin. Secretary Mallory. Secretary Memminger. Vice-President Stephens. Secretary Walker. President Davis.

learning thus acquired was abundantly reflected in Davis' writings and speeches.

Another asset which Davis took to the Confederate White House was integrity. Robert Barnwell Rhett, prominent secessionist of South Carolina, in letters written to his son early in the war, denounced Davis as a "dishonest man," "a liar," and "a great Rascal." In 1864 Alexander Stephens wrote his brother, Linton, that the President was "quite as much knave as fool." But these charges were made by men blinded by animosity. As President, Davis was not always as forthright as he might have been in dealing with difficult persons and situations, but he observed a strict code of conduct with respect to money, favors, and gifts.

DAVIS was as courageous as he was honest. His physical bravery was tested and proved in the Mexican War, and as President he repeatedly demonstrated his moral courage by unwavering support of unpopular individuals and measures.

Another point in Davis' favor was his rich experience in public affairs. Not only had he served in both houses of Congress and in the National Cabinet, but

The cabinet of the Confederate States at Montgomery, from a print in "Harper's Weekly" June 1, 1861.

Postmaster Reagan.   Secretary Toombs.

Black Hawk War. When he entered the White House he knew practically nothing of military science or personnel. Davis, on the other hand, possessed extensive knowledge of military organization, administration, and terminology. He knew many officers, high and low, and he had observed the performance of some of them in combat. Even though this knowledge did not always redound to the Confederacy's benefit, the fault lay not in the President's possession of it, but rather in the way it was applied.

Another of Davis' assets was his effectiveness as a public speaker. His addresses lack the music and the poetry of Lincoln's masterful pieces, but they are outstanding for clarity and logic. He was not given to soaring rhetoric, nor did he excel in the use of anecdote and wit. His prowess on the rostrum was due largely to the dignity of his bearing, the earnestness of his manner, the forcefulness of his personality, and the soft, but distinct quality of his voice. His political associates, many of them orators of outstanding renown, regarded "the gentleman from Mississippi" as one of the most accomplished speakers of his time.

ONE of Davis' most impressive attributes as President was profound dedication to the cause that he led. Many prominent Southerners, including Robert E. Lee, were troubled in conscience by slavery. Others, especially those of Whig background, never completely overcame the attachment to the Union that underlay their resistance to secession. But Davis never manifested any qualms about either slavery or secession. His support of state sovereignty and the Southern way of life was based on deep conviction. His belief in the justice of the Confederate cause deepened with the passing of time and caused him to urge continuation of the war after the surrender of the principal armies. There can be no doubt that Jefferson Davis gave to the Confederacy the very best leadership of which he was capable.

But he was a poor administrator. He failed to surround himself with capable assistants and entrust to them responsibilities commensurate with their positions. Benjamin was the only member of his Cabinet who could be rated as brilliant, and his usefulness was impaired by strong opposition in Congress, in the Army, and in journalistic circles. Davis' remissness in delegating authority was due largely to a compulsive desire to maintain close control over the executive departments. This was espe-

he had also held important committee assignments and played a leading role in shaping legislation. He had been a close friend and confidential adviser of President Pierce for many years and he had exerted a powerful influence in the Democratic party. In 1861 he was far more familiar with the workings of governmental machinery than was his opposite in Washington.

He also enjoyed an enormous advantage over Lincoln by virtue of his long and intimate association with the Army. The Union President's military experience was limited to token involvement in the cially true of the War Office. On August 23, 1863, Robert G. H. Kean, Chief of the Bureau of War, wrote in his diary: "Certainly the style of business with which his time is consumed is in our present circumstances almost a scandal—little trash which ought to be dispatched by clerks in the adjutant general's office. This absorption of the President's time in trifles (comparative) is due to two facts: 1st, his own desire to be personally conversant about everything. 2nd, the weakness of some of the men he has about him, who have accustomed him to have them run to him for instructions about every little matter. . . . Mr. Davis is a slow, very slow worker."

SIMILAR criticisms were made by Secretary of the Navy Stephen Mallory, who generally was well-disposed toward the President. On June 21, 1862, Mallory wrote in his journal: "The President does not consult his cabinet either as to plans or arrangements of campaigns, or the appointment of military men to office." In November 1862, following the resignation of Secretary of War George W. Randolph, Mallory commented: "The fact is that the President's familiarity with army matters induces his desire to mingle in them all & to control them: & this desire is augmented by the fear that details may be wrongly managed without his constant supervision." Shortly after the war Mallory wrote: "No labours of the War Office were too small for his attention. The amount of attention which he habitually bestowed upon details which are usually devolved upon subordinates surprised all who were familiar with his habits. . . . Letters from afflicted mothers, . . . complaints of friendless soldiers, . . . applications for pardons, . . . petitions from wives for the release of conscripted husbands, or from farmers for the restoration of impressed mules and horses, were in numerous instances read . . . and responded to by him. . . . A vast amount of such business which might well have been referred . . . to a Bureau officer . . . encumbered his table and occupied his time."

Davis also spent an inordinate amount of time writing letters justifying his military policies or replying to baseless criticism of executive acts. It is difficult to escape the conclusion that the President used involvement in trivia as an escape from the larger and more difficult problems associated with his position. Certainly, much of the time and energy expended on minutiae might more apppropriately have been devoted to such fundamental responsibilities as shaping strategy and recommending legislation for effective utilization of the country's resources. While the President focused on administrative details, the Confederacy drifted from crisis to crisis without benefit of comprehensive political guidance.

ANOTHER shortcoming of Davis was his lack of popular appeal. At no time in his life did he mingle freely with the masses under circumstances that might have enabled him to develop an appreciation of their aspirations and virtues. He never felt close

The Capitol in Richmond. From a war-time photo. (NA)

to them, nor they to him. The common soldiers of the Union Army regarded Lincoln as one of their kind, genuinely interested in their well-being and happiness. Hence, in their letters, they frequently referred to him as "Father Abraham," "Old Abe," or "Uncle Abe." Rarely are similar references to the Confederate President to be found in the letters of Johnny Rebs. In both Washington and Richmond, Davis shunned social gatherings and to many people of his own class he appeared excessively dignified and aloof. The friendly Mallory wrote of him in September 1865: "Few men could be more chillingly, freezingly cold."

Davis never succeeded in dramatizing the issues of the war or in arousing public enthusiasm for their support. Confederates liked to compare their struggle with the Colonial revolt against England. But their President was never able to infuse the Southern movement with the lofty purposes and timeless qualities that Jefferson and Paine breathed into the American Revolution.

DAVIS was conspicuously inept at getting along with people. Governor Thomas C. Reynolds of Missouri, one of Davis' staunch supporters, once confided to an acquaintance that the President was a person of "marked peculiarities," "stern and unbending" toward his enemies. And the patient and tolerant Seddon told a friend in 1864 that Davis was "the most difficult man to get along with" he had ever seen. The ever-generous and discreet Lee once remarked to General John B. Gordon: "You know that the President is very pertinacious in opinion and purpose." Lee and Davis never quarreled, but they came close to a break early in 1865. Disturbed by a rumor that Lee had ordered destruction of some tobacco stored in Richmond warehouses, the President telegraphed Lee to come to the capital for a conference. Lee replied that the military situation made it inadvisable for him to leave Petersburg, but that if Davis would send him the pertinent measures he would forward his views. Davis sent back a telegram stating: "Rest assured I will not ask your views in answer to measures. Your counsels are no longer wanted in this matter." On receipt of this brusque message, Lee, at considerable inconvenience, went to Richmond and soothed the President's ruffled temper.

DAVIS' strong devotion to his own ideas made him impatient of disagreement. Varina Howell, on first meeting Davis, was offended by his "way of taking for granted that everybody agrees with him" and in later life she wrote of her husband: "He sincerely thought all he said, and moreover could not understand any other man coming to a different conclusion after his premises were stated. It was his sincerity of opinion which sometimes gave him the manner

President and Mrs. Davis at a reception in Richmond during the war. Drawing by W. L. Sheppard. (Valentine Museum, Richmond, Va.)

to which his opponents objected as domineering."

What Mrs. Davis interpreted as exaggerated sincerity many others regarded as vanity, petulance, or stubbornness. W. B. Machen, Confederate Congressman from Kentucky, wrote in April 1863: "He is inveterately obstinate to a serious fault. It is impossible to correct that fault as it is bred in the bone." James H. Hammond, told a friend in April 1861: "He is the most irascible man I ever knew. . . . Quick-tempered, arbitrary, overbearing . . . he is as vain as a peacock." Another South Carolinian, William Porcher Miles, Chairman of the House Military Affairs Committee, wrote to General Beauregard on November 26, 1862: "He cannot brook opposition or criticism, and those who do not *bow down before him* have no chance of success with him."

This was harsh criticism, perhaps unduly so, but there can be no doubt that Davis found it almost impossible to like people who disagreed with him, and personal antagonisms, born of opposing opinions, often generated into bitter quarrels that weakened the Administration and hurt the Confederacy.

DAVIS was sadly deficient in tact. He seemed unable to concede a minor point in order to gain a major one. He never developed the art of soothing hurt feelings with oils of sympathy, flattery, cajolery, or humor. "Come and let us talk it over" were words rarely used by him in his dealings with offended Congressmen, cabinet members, or military leaders.

Admittedly many with whom the President quarreled were hypersensitive, difficult persons. But a wiser and a more magnanimous man than Davis would have prevented some of the strife which crippled Confederate leadership and would have saved for useful service capable officials who were estranged from the administrative team.

Governor Zebulon Vance of North Carolina did much to provoke the President by his repeated and ill-tempered charges that North Carolina did not receive her due share of recognition, and his excessive concern for states rights. But he was an honest, well-meaning, and patriotic public servant and the President made a serious mistake when, after an exchange of controversial letters, he wrote Vance on March 31, 1864: "I must beg that a correspondence so unprofitable in its character, and which was not initiated by me, may here end, and that your future communications may be restricted to such matters as may require official action."

Davis' deficiencies in dealing with individuals extended to his relations with his public. He did little to cultivate cordial relations with the press and he was bitterly opposed by some of the Confederacy's most prominent journalists, including E. A. Pollard and J. M. Daniel of the Richmond *Examiner,* and the Rhetts of the Charleston *Mercury.*

THE President's relations with Congress deteriorated from almost complete harmony in the beginning to open and widespread opposition in 1862, and the antipathy increased with the passing of time. Some of the friction between the Chief Executive and Congress was a normal concomitant of war. Even so, Davis himself was responsible for much of his difficulty with Congress. He did not actively cultivate the acquaintance of the legislators. His associations with them were restricted largely to formal conferences and these were not as frequent as they should have been.

Davis' failure to mingle more freely with government leaders and with the people at large was the more unfortunate in view of his potential charm in individual relationships and his exceptional ability as a public speaker. After Congressman Warren Akin called on the President early in 1865, he wrote his wife: "He was polite, attentive and . . . very cordial."

The speeches that Davis delivered on his trips through the country—he left the environs of Richmond only three times, and then mainly to check on military affairs—seem to have been of benefit both to him and to public morale. Davis and his wife attributed his reclusiveness to his poor health and absorption in matters of state. The truth of the matter seems to be that the President never realized the importance of cultivating good will and that he was unwilling to pay the price of becoming a popular leader.

ONE reason for the President's unpopularity was his persistent support of discredited officers such as Lucius B. Northrop, the Confederate Commissary General, and Generals Theophilus Holmes, John C. Pemberton, and Braxton Bragg. Northrop and Bragg were grossly incompetent and their long retention in high position, against an ever-increasing tide of public criticism, cannot be justified on any reasonable ground. Davis had formed an attachment for Northrop in prewar times and the key to his stubborn adherence to Bragg is to be found in a comment made to that general on August 5, 1862: "You have the misfortune of being regarded as my personal friend and one pursued therefore with malignant censure by men regardless of truth." When finally Bragg was relieved of army command at his own request after the catastrophe of November 25, 1863, at Missionary Ridge, Davis called him to Richmond as his principal military adviser. It is difficult to imagine a more tactless appointment, for it required a discredited and despised general to act as the President's go-between with Congress, cabinet members, governors, and field commanders.

Hardly less damaging to the President than his reluctance to dismiss unpopular "pets" was his questionable treatment of certain leaders who stood high in public esteem. One of these was General Beauregard, widely acclaimed as the hero of Sumter and First Manassas. Beauregard incurred Davis' disfavor in the autumn of 1861 by criticizing the President in an official report of Manassas published prematurely in the Richmond press. When Albert Sidney Johnston was killed at Shiloh, Beauregard succeeded to command of the Army of Tennessee. In June 1862, while the army was at Tupelo, the ailing Beauregard turned the command temporarily over to Bragg, the next ranking officer, and on his surgeon's certificate of disability went to Bladon Springs, Alabama, to recuperate. He did not obtain prior authority from the War Department, as he should have done, but on June 14 telegraphed Adjutant General Cooper of his intentions. On the same day Davis telegraphed Bragg to go to Jackson, Mississippi, to take charge temporarily of General Mans-

The White House of the Confederacy in Richmond. This was the residence of Jefferson Davis during the Civil War. The photograph was taken after the occupation of Richmond by Federal troops in 1865. This building is now the Confederate Museum. (The National Archives)

field Lovell's department; the order closed with the statement: "The necessity is urgent and absolute." When later Davis learned of Beauregard's unauthorized departure for Alabama, he was furious. On June 20 he transferred command of the army from Beauregard to Bragg.

There was a widespread feeling in Congress and throughout the country that Davis had taken unfair advantage of a minor mistake to remove from high command a brilliant general, against whom he bore a grudge. On September 13, 1862 Senators Thomas Semmes and Edward Sparrow of Louisiana presented to the President a paper signed by fifty-nine members from both houses of Congress protesting Beauregard's removal and petitioning his restoration to command of the Army of Tennessee. The President disregarded the arguments that Beauregard's absence was intended to be of short duration, that he could keep in close touch with his staff by telegraph, and if necessary could return to his headquarters in fifteen hours. Davis' standing with Congress and the country was also hurt by his long and bitter controversy with Joseph E. Johnston.

ANOTHER of Davis' shortcomings as Chief Executive was neglect of civil functions in favor of military matters. The preference for military connection that he expressed when he accepted the Presidency increased during his years in office. Mrs. Davis, in her memoir, quoted Davis as saying again and again during the dark days of 1863: "If I could take one wing and Lee the other, I think we could between us wrest a victory from those people." In a reference to the campaigns of 1864 she wrote: "After the army fell back to Petersburg, he looked forward personally to taking command in the West, and cooperating with General Lee in one great battle which he hoped to be decisive."

Davis' deep and abiding fondness for the Army and his dislike of political administration caused him to devote disproportionate attention to military affairs. His personal and official correspondence reveal a far greater concern about what went on in the Army than about the state of the country and the running of the Government. It is true that the two were inseparable and that in a nation at war, the commander in chief is responsible for the effectiveness of the armed services. But the Confederacy was relatively well off with respect to military command. Its dominant need was political guidance of a sort that would draw its discordant elements together and utilize to fullest advantage its limited manpower and material resources. Unfortunately for the South and for the President, Davis chose to concentrate his attention and energy in the area of lesser need. And as previously noted, much of the time that he gave to military matters was expended on routine details that should have been delegated to administrative assistants.

THROUGHOUT his career in the Confederate White House, Davis suffered from poor health. His wife stated that "he was a nervous dyspeptic by habit" and that "in the evening he was too exhausted to receive informal visitors." Her comments and those of others who were familiar with his life in Richmond, indicate that his most frequent complaints were neuralgia, eyestrain, headaches, indigestion, and insomnia. Any and all of these ailments could have been due in large measure to dislike of his job. Evidence supporting a relationship between his ills and the uncongeniality of his governmental duties is to be found in the fact that when he visited the Army, whether in Virginia or on long and tiring trips to the West, both his spirit and his health improved. His basic physical ruggedness is attested by his relatively good health after the war. Despite two years of imprisonment, economic adversity, and many other hardships, he lived to 81.

One of the greatest of all Davis' shortcomings as Chief Executive was his lack of capacity for growth. As previously noted, he brought to the Presidency assets which seemed to assure success. But, instead of focusing on major policies, confiding in and cultivating the support of his people, disregarding baseless criticism and admitting and profiting by mistakes, he fretted about his problems, fought back at his opponents, shrivelled in spirit, and declined in public esteem. Had the Confederacy enjoyed the peaceful existence which many of its leaders expected, Davis might well have been happy and successful as President. But he was too sensitive, reclusive, and rigid to cope with the formidable complications resulting from the war. He was a good man, possessed of exceptional ability. But he was unsuited for the role of leading the Southern revolution.

Could the Confederacy have achieved independence under other leadership? The only reasonable answer is "No." The North's advantages were too great to be offset by any rearrangement in the Confederate White House. But hindsight suggests at least one other Southerner who might have made a better President than Davis. He was Robert E. Lee. On March 1, 1862, William H. Trescot, a distinguished South Carolinian, wrote to a friend: "Lee . . . is the only man in the revolution whom I have met that at all rises to historical size." This discerning estimate, made while Lee was relatively obscure, was to be abundantly confirmed by subsequent events. Lee was not a politician, but he was remarkably intelligent and he grew rapidly as his responsibilities increased. His magnanimity, personal magnetism, and tact might have been a powerful force in combatting the South's excessive individualism and molding its dissident elements into something approaching a team. Certainly he displayed more of first-rate statesmanship than any other person who rose to high position in the CSA.

ULYSSES S. GRANT

Grant—Genius or Fortune's Child? by Wilbur S. Nye

The Singing Wire Conspiracy by Howard C. Westwood

Grant Remembers Appomattox by John Russell Young

H. A. Ogden: General Grant in the Wilderness.

Grant—Genius or Fortune's Child?

by Wilbur S. Nye

Many years ago the mother of one of my Army friends told me of her first encounter with Ulysses S. Grant. When a very small child she was taken for a visit in the White House during Grant's second term as president. He was away when she and her mother arrived, so they did not meet him for several days. Late one afternoon she was sliding backward down one of the long, curving banisters when at the bottom she bumped into Grant, who was passing through the dimly lighted hall.

"Boo!" said Grant, in an ill-considered attempt at informal humor. "I don't like little girls."

Grant didn't realize that the child was too young to appreciate his humor. She ran howling to her embarrassed mother, who was a member of the Dent tribe into which Grant had married. The girl nursed for the rest of her life the erroneous conviction that Grant disliked children. No doubt this illustrates how certain misconceptions of Grant's makeup have originated. A great deal has been told of Grant—some truth, much guff.

General Grant's numerous biographers conclude that he was an enigma. Actually he was no more a mystery than each human being must be to others. In many respects he was a common, ordinary fellow, a man of the soil; that is how he thought of himself. It is hard for the analysts to realize that a man can possess almost superhuman talents and at the same time have a fair measure of quite human foibles and weaknesses. How could a mean gnome like Richard Wagner compose music of such grandeur? How could Grant, one of the most successful military commanders of all time, be other than leonine, regal?

Unlike Robert E. Lee, Grant can never become an icon. His human failings have been too well publicized, and there has not been the same concerted effort to cast him in a heroic mold.

Prior to the Civil War, and even well into it, Grant had the reputation of being a man "who drinks." Compulsive drinkers in those days were not called alcoholics, and the evidence that Grant was one of these unfortunates is inconclusive. There are a few whispers suggesting it, such as the little-known fact that he once took the pledge and joined a Temperance Society, then fell—as alcoholics will—from grace. Also he is described as having a peculiar high-stepping walk strongly reminiscent of the "jake leg" gait of some alcoholics. However, the important thing to me is that Grant gradually tapered off in his drinking, and eventually became a moderate or only occasional drinker which, incidentally, is supposed to be an impossibility for the true addict—he must break off sharply and is never completely cured. The eventual outcome in Grant's case is an illuminating example of his tremendous will power. As an ordinary man he was a drinker. But in stopping the habit he was a giant.

Grant's reputation as a drinker harmed him in many instances. One of his bitterest experiences occurred early in 1862 after he had won renown by his victory at Fort Donelson. He received such a favorable press that his immediate superior, department commander Henry W. Halleck, churlishly abstained from congratulating him. Halleck, who disliked Grant and may have feared him as a rival, soon found a way to puncture Ulysses's rising balloon. He wrote to George B. McClellan, then General in Chief of the Army, complaining that Grant was sitting on his fundament, basking in the warmth of success and failing to reply to Halleck's daily demands for reports. This had been going on for a month, and Grant had even left his area, without authority, to visit Nashville. Halleck was, he said, fed up, and explained the dereliction of his subordinate by sending to Washington the following shaft of mendacious gossip:

> A rumor has reached me that...Grant has resumed his former bad habits....It will account for his neglect of my oft-repeated orders....

Two days later, with McClellan's approval, Halleck relieved Grant from command. Presently, perhaps fearing the action of an inspector general, he attempted to smooth over the affair by stating that he had learned that a disloyal telegraph operator at his headquarters was intercepting his messages to and from the front. Why, if he learned that dispatches were not coming in, did he allow the condition to persist for a month without looking into it and, if necessary, paying a surprise visit to the front? The whole business smells.

Other complaints about Grant's supposed elbow-hoisting reached Washington from time to time. It is a wonder he survived them. One of the most notorious seems to have done him more good than harm. According to a dispatch by Charles Halpine in the New York *Herald*, November 26, 1863, a number of clergymen waited upon the president to object to the retention in command of "our boys" of a whisky drinker. He was, they said, unsafe. Lincoln, the story ran, replied with the proverbial twinkle in his eye, "So General Grant drinks? Well, I wish some of you would tell me the brand of whisky he drinks. I would like to send a barrel of it to every one of my generals."

A fine story, which amused the nation and cast a glow around Old Abe and Grant. Unfortunately for the record, there was not a word of truth in it. Reporter Halpine invented the tale in its entirety, and Lincoln repeatedly denied that it had happened.

Another of Grant's supposed characteristics that has distressed his admirers was that he was a heartless butcher of men, the slaughter of Union soldiers in a fruitless charge at Cold Harbor being cited as a striking example. This accusation caused Grant as much anguish as anything that ever happened to him, for it was unjust. He realized after the battle that he had made a mistake, and he was far from insensitive to human suffering. Numerous episodes have been related to support this statement. But many students of the Civil War are convinced that Grant's campaign southward from the Rappahannock in 1864 was simply a straight-to-the-front slugging contest in which Grant disregarded losses in shoving General Robert E. Lee back toward Richmond. They forget that in each case, after failing to achieve a tactical victory, he resorted to maneuver, and continually outflanked the Army of Northern Virginia until finally he enclosed it in the ring around Richmond and Petersburg. Where Grant was chiefly at fault in this final campaign is in his full but tardy appreciation of the defensive capabilities of determined troops in well-built trenches with overhead cover. The armies in Georgia were learning it too, but Lee, the engineer, appreciated it earlier and more fully than Grant.

Grant was slovenly in his dress and military bearing. William E. Woodward, in his great biography *Meet General Grant*, attributes this to the hard physical labor Ulysses had to perform on the farm as a child. He thinks Grant's round shoulders and droopy appearance came from his being permanently tired.

This is an unfounded notion. Many West Point cadets come from the farm, yet they are unsurpassed in neatness of dress and in soldierly bearing. Grant was simply one of that type that occasionally survives the USMA demerit system and reverts to a sloppy and indifferent appearance as soon as he graduates. It does not seem to me that Grant was lazy, for he showed plenty of energy and drive during the Civil War, but in his *Memoirs* he claims that his besetting sin was laziness. Though his intellect was certainly average or better, his class standing at West Point was below the middle. Instead of studying, he spent most of his time reading romantic novels.

In his lack of neatness of dress and of military bearing Grant resembled an average American without military training rather than a professional soldier. Many of our countrymen, clodhoppers and city slickers alike, refuse to look proud when in uniform. They even accentuate a hangdog attitude because they fear people will think they are strutters if they stand straight and hold their heads up. Doubtless this is a vestige of our bourgeois or peasant background. In professional military circles, back into the dim past as well as forward to today, there has been a tendency to assume that a lack of military smartness in appearance is indicative of poor performance. The assumption is not always fully warranted. General Lee's ragged and unmilitary-looking soldiers were excellent fighters. Even as late as World War II, many of us who saw military history being made at close hand were compelled to admit that a Sad Sack, not admirable on the parade ground, who had to be hidden in the woods during the visit of an inspector general, often proved to be a brave, resourceful, and self-sacrificing battle soldier. Grant belonged to this category.

Though he was not a typical West Pointer in dress and bearing, Ulysses Grant was moderately handsome, as is seen from a photograph made when, as a young lieutenant, he had not yet acquired whiskers. He had regular features and clear blue eyes; his hair was light brown and his beard, when he grew one, was of the same shade until it became grizzled; it was normally cropped short. As a great general his eyes should have been either keen and piercing or imperious and flashing. But they were not. He normally wore a mild, reposeful expression or a slightly anxious one. Again this was not a mirror of the inner man. No general ever lived who had more determination, self-confidence without egotism, and sangfroid. He must have inherited his regular features and good looks from a grandparent, since his parents could have sat as models for Grant Wood in his famous painting of an austere rustic couple, "American Gothic." But he passed on to his descendants his pleasant appearance. His daughter Nellie was an authentic beauty. His grandson, U.S. Grant III, is handsome and distinguished looking.

Grant gave the impression of being slightly below medium height, as is attested by all but one or two of his biographers. Woodward says he was 5 feet 8 inches tall, which was two inches more than the average for that period. Up through the Civil War he also appeared thin, almost frail in physique, but in fact, although he did not have bulging muscles, he was agile, wiry, tough, and surprisingly strong. This was demonstrated in 1860 when he was employed in a store in Galena operated by his younger brothers. Though they regarded Ulysses with mild contempt, they sent him to Iowa to repossess some leather goods which a customer had refused to pay for. Grant, provided with a writ and accompanied by a sheriff, went to a stone building in which the miscreant had taken a defiant stand behind a locked door. He threatened to shoot if an effort was made to arrest him. The lawman would take no action but agreed to deputize Ulysses. The unarmed Grant thereupon kicked in the door and after a short, sharp scuffle subdued his burly opponent and forced him to box and ship the merchandise back to Galena.

Two other characteristics displayed by Grant in his early years should have given a hint—had they been noticed—that he might develop into a good military leader. One was the excellent grades he made at West Point in mathematics; it has long been known that immortals in the military realm, such as Napoleon and Robert E. Lee, were mathematically inclined, and outstandingly capable of the analytical straight-thinking that characterizes the mathematician. Also, for a long time there was the theory, perhaps overworked, that fearless horsemen made fine battle commanders. U.S. Grant was a superlatively good horseman. His record in high jumping stood unsurpassed at West Point for twenty-five years.

He loved horses. Almost the only thing that would rouse him to fury was the sight of a man abusing a horse. Further-

Grant's parents, Hannah Simpson Grant and Jesse Root Grant.

The house near Point Pleasant, Ohio, where Grant was born. From an engraving made about 1884.

more, though I do not think he was an out-and-out zoophile, he would not kill an animal or a bird. When he was with the 4th Infantry on the border after the Mexican War it was popular to hunt. But Grant would not, and he never even owned a shotgun. During the Civil War he habitually went about his duties unarmed.

Some observers thought Grant was an atheist or at least an agnostic, because he made no display of religion. Actually he was a Methodist, and had been raised in the strict atmosphere of that denomination. In his adult years he was not a regular church-goer until he became president, but he believed in God and the hereafter, as is shown by some of his last communications to his family.

One of Grant's biographers says he was no prude, but I think he was. He never exposed any part of his person. He always bathed in a closed tent, with all flaps tied. His associates stood out in front of their tents, naked as jaybirds, and had their orderlies douse them with buckets of water. Grant rarely used profanity, and even when he did it was of an innocuous variety. He abstained from obscenity, and did not contribute to the "parlor stories" usually swapped at the evening campfire, though he did not raise an objection to others doing so. He was not, as he is sometimes described, silent, taciturn, and morose. Though he kept his own counsel when mulling over military plans and was careful not to talk freely in the presence of newspaper correspondents, when in the circle of people whom he liked and trusted he could be quite a raconteur. Like many "old-timers" he liked best to tell stories of the Old Army. There is always an Old Army, with its "characters."

Loyalty was an important part of Grant's personal code — loyalty to those above him and to those junior to him. He was completely loyal to Halleck even when he was receiving cruel and unfair treatment from that stuffy intellectual snob. He supported subordinates whom he suspected of working to undercut him, so long as they appeared to be devoted to the common cause. He did not stand on his dignity or nurse a grudge when faced with obstreperous men like Brigadier General Ben Prentiss.

A short time after Grant had been made a brigadier he was replaced in command of a minor post by Prentiss, who had been promoted about the same time as Grant, and who Major General John C. Fremont thought was senior. Soon afterwards Fremont discovered his error and gave Grant command of a new expedition being organized to run down the troublesome Brigadier General Jeff Thompson and his will-of-the-wisp Rebel raiders. Several Federal columns, one of them under Prentiss, tried unsuccessfully to converge on Thompson. Contrary to his instructions Prentiss showed up near Cape Girardeau and encountered Grant.

Grant told him to go back where he belonged. Prentiss was not disposed to recognize Grant as his superior nor to obey his orders. Grant set him straight on this, but Prentiss took it in poor spirit. He flatly refused to comply, and when Grant stared him down he asked for a leave of absence to go back and complain to Fremont. This was refused. He then offered his resignation, likewise refused. Finally Prentiss put himself in arrest for insubordination, a novel antic, and went fuming off to St. Louis.

Grant was more tolerant than Prentiss deserved. "I regretted this incident very much," he wrote later. "He was a brave and earnest soldier. No man in the service was more sincere in his devotion to the cause for which we were battling; none more ready to make sacrifices or risk life in it." He made no effort to have Prentiss court-martialed or relieved from command.

Prentiss was less charitable. When he surrendered himself and twenty-two hundred men at Shiloh the following year he told William Candace Thompson and a group of other Confederates that "Grant at the outbreak of the battle was five miles down the river on a drunk at a private home."

This was untrue, and in any event it ill became Prentiss to make, to the enemy, such a remark about his commander.

Having considered some of the elements that made up Grant the man, we are now entitled to examine some of those that comprised Grant the superman.

Was U.S. Grant a genius, or was he simply fortunate?

The start of his Civil War career was due entirely to luck. He had been out of the service for seven years in 1861 and was unable to obtain an appointment commensurate with what he regarded as being his education and experience. Then, in June, the Governor of Illinois quite unexpectedly made him the colonel of a volunteer infantry regiment. It happened in this wise: Though still a civilian, Grant had offered to drill companies of recruits being assembled at Camp Yates, near the state capital. Some word of his good work reached the governor's office, but there was still no place for him other than a temporary job ruling administrative forms in the state adjutant general's office.

About that time a new regiment, the 21st Illinois, in an uproar over its worthless colonel, importuned the governor Richard Yates. "Whom do you suggest?"

"How about 'Captain' Grant?" someone asked. "He was a good drill instructor, and is a West Point man."

"U.S. Grant it shall be," said the governor, and signed the commission.

Grant's regiment had been on the verge of mutiny. He whipped it into shape in six weeks. This was not luck; it was ability, though hardly genius. It was not noticed then, and has not been commented upon in the intervening years. But in analyzing what he had done, based on the record, I was astonished. He is known to have put the unit halfway through the 1861 infantry training manual in a month and a half, without assistance except that he drilled the officers one day in what he required them to teach the men the next. The men became proficient in what today is called basic training —the school of the soldier, and the evolutions of the squad and company. This was then more important than simply being able to perform at ceremonies, for troops maneuvered and fought in close-order formations and any ineptness could lead to disaster in combat. They also learned the manual of arms, which involved twelve precise movements, and the more complicated loading and firing exercises which were thought necessary to enable the soldier to prepare and fire his piece in the excitement of battle. But above all, Grant produced a well-disciplined outfit with excellent morale. His methods were not mysterious. He simply awarded rigorous punishment to the ringleaders of the incipient uprising and gave the other regimental cutups so much work that they had no time for frolic. The men really appreciated this, for no soldier likes to belong to a poor outfit.

Doubtless the 21st Illinois would have benefited from more conditioning, but it was wartime. On July 3 Grant took the unit westward on a ninety-mile march that might have culminated, so far as he knew, in fighting. Confederates and partisans were active in eastern Missouri. There is nothing to show that Grant was hoping for a fight, but he must have been, at least subconsciously. As he developed during the war it became more and more clear that one of his most noteworthy qualities was his aggressive, combative spirit. This commended him strongly to Lincoln. On an occasion halfway through the war when Grant's growing fame had gone into temporary eclipse, one of the president's advisers, Alexander McClure, urged him to relieve Grant. "No," Lincoln replied firmly. "I cannot spare the man. He fights."

Grant's second advancement was also due purely to luck. On August 7, less than two months after he had been made colonel, he was promoted to brigadier general. It was a political appointment, though neither Grant himself nor any of his friends had exerted any influence to bring it about. At that time, when the Army was undergoing a rapid and substantial expansion, appointments to the rank of general officer were not being made on the basis of merit. They were political plums, distributed to states by quota. Four brigadier generalships having been allotted to Illinois, Elihu Washburne, a good Republican congressman from the district in which Galena was situated, was given the privilege of making one of the recommendations. Washburne knew of only one man in that area who had had prior military experience— Ulysses S. Grant, known locally as Captain Sam Grant. They had met once on the street but were not really acquainted. No one knows for sure why Washburne sent up Grant's name,

but he did; and Grant was made a general, to rank from May 17, which gave him considerable seniority.

This was the most important turning point in Grant's career. As he says, there were many officers who may have been as capable, but who never had the opportunity to display generalship. As a general he commanded large enough bodies of troops, almost from the outset, to have an influence on the course of the war in the West. In addition he was fortunate enough to have superiors, Fremont and later Halleck, who were desk men and left to subordinates the thrill of fighting. They didn't even visit him at the front, but left him mostly to his own resources, which was very fortunate indeed.

A general who is at or approaching the top will not last long unless he retains the confidence of the administration. It is helpful too if the American people think well of him. For this he needs a favorable press, and that is why every man wearing stars in our present age has a public relations officer who is dedicated to building and maintaining a favorable press for his client. Grant did not always have a favorable press, but he was persona grata in the White House at least in part because of his apparent lack of political ambition and his facility for turning a neat phrase and emitting catch phrases that appealed to the public. It is not a vast exaggeration to say that this talent contributed to his success in a measurable degree.

His pen flowed easily, producing a series of dispatches and proclamations couched in clear, simple English highly admirable in that age of involved sentences and purple passages. Lincoln admired his proclamations exceedingly, saying of one addressed to the citizens of Paducah: "The man who can write like that is fitted to command in the West." And soon the public at large began to know of a general who spoke such inspiring words as "unconditional surrender," "I propose to move immediately upon your works," and "I will fight it out on this line if it takes all summer."

Once when Grant by a spectacular military success had won nationwide acclaim, a newsman asked him what rewards he would like most. In the minds of political leaders at that time, notably Lincoln, was the fear that this military hero would run for the presidency in the 1864 campaign. But Grant replied to the reporter, "I wish they would build a sidewalk in Galena from the post office to the depot." The whole nation chuckled over this, and Lincoln and his coterie were vastly relieved. Grant was assured of continued and wholehearted governmental support. When Grant went home on a short leave and stepped from the train at Galena, he was greeted by a huge overhead banner that said, "General Grant, the sidewalk has been built."

Luck was not the only ingredient in Grant's astounding success. He had several dominant characteristics that were

The engraving at right, said to be based on a daguerrotype that was made in 1844, shows Lieutenant Grant at the left of his close friend Lieut. Alexander Hays. Hays was killed while serving under Grant in The Wilderness.

Below: Captain "Sam" Grant (left), from a daguerrotype he gave his wife to wear on a wristlet; and Brigadier General Grant (right), from an 1861 photograph sent to his father to show a dress uniform made in St. Louis. (Century Company)

The heavy losses of The Wilderness and Cold Harbor left their mark on Grant, as can be seen in this photo of him, with furrowed brow and eyes touched with pain, taken while he commanded the entire Union Army. (LC)

to contribute mightily. Among these were absolute courage and a granite-like determination. Even Confederate officers who conferred with him under flags of truce on several occasions commented on the latter quality. That Grant was outstandingly brave and resolute is undeniable; there has been too much documentation to entertain the least doubt. It is only worthwhile here to comment briefly on the origin of these aspects and how they were of value in his career.

His stubbornness and determination appeared so early that he must have been born with them, and they were manifest in a peculiar way when he was a boy. When he started on a trip or any like enterprise he would not turn back, no matter what obstacles were encountered. Horace Porter, who became one of his aides during the latter part of the Civil War, gives a later example:

> The General was a natural bushwhacker, in the sense of having an intuitive knowledge of the country. He was seldom known to make a mistake in taking a road, and when he did he had an aversion to turning back that amounted almost to a superstition. To reach the road he had missed he would undertake all sorts of cross-cuts, ford streams, and jump any number of fences, rather than retrace his steps to the fork at which he had made the wrong turn.

Similarly it is unnecessary to repeat the many examples of Grant's courage under fire that have been told by various observers. How he discovered this quality in himself is valuable to others who may encounter like situations and is obliquely revealing in that he did not seem to credit himself as being without fear. He tells it somewhat as follows.

In the summer of 1861 when he was still a colonel, he led his regiment south of the Salt River, in Missouri, against a force of Rebels under Colonel Thomas Harris. Grant says that as he approached the enemy camp his heart was getting higher and higher in his throat until it was choking him. Desperately he wished he were somewhere else but did not have the moral courage [so he says] to stop and consider what his next move should be. When at length his column reached the enemy campsite the Rebels had vanished.

"It occurred to me at once," said Grant, "that Harris had been as much afraid of me as I had been of him. This was a view I had never taken before; but it was one I never forgot afterwards. From that event to the close of the war I never experienced trepidation on confronting an enemy, though I always felt more or less anxiety. The lesson was valuable."

In humbly admitting that he always felt more or less anxiety in the face of danger, Grant does not seem to be entirely candid, although no one will ever know, of course, what his inner feelings actually were. Major General William T. Sherman gave an opinion on this:

> I'm a damn sight smarter than Grant...but I'll tell you where he beats me and where he beats the world. He don't give a damn for what the enemy does out of his sight but it scares me like hell.

Sherman expresses the generally accepted view of Grant's intrepid quality.

This valuable attribute was coupled with good luck. What good would it have done Grant (and the nation) to display an indifference to peril when bullets were flying nearby, if he had been clipped by one of them, as James B. McPherson was? Or Thomas J. Jackson, or J.E.B. Stuart?

On the other hand, consider how useful it was to Grant to be able to function calmly and efficiently in a tense situation. Ambrose E. Burnside was incapable of it, and so—more spectacularly—was Fighting Joe Hooker. In comparison with Grant they were very small men indeed.

The picture of Grant that has come down to us through the past hundred years is that he was a slow, deliberate butt-head who managed to bull his way through to victory because of overwhelming superiority in numbers and other resources. During the latter part of the war he did have those advantages. But this should not obscure his genuine skill as a strategist and tactician, and above all his preeminence in the field of logistics. Sir Frederick Maurice, J.C. Fuller, Kenneth Williams, W.E. Woodward, Bruce Catton, and other distinguished historians in recent years have done a good deal to correct the false image of Grant that has persisted since his detractors started yammering shortly after the Civil War. But they have not been entirely successful.

Consider again one of Grant's early achievements, one that points clearly to his less-known ability to operate rapidly. On August 8, 1861, he was passing through St. Louis with his regiment when he learned accidentally that he had been made a brigadier. He contacted department headquarters for instructions and was switched from his previous destination to Ironton, Missouri, believed to be threatened.

He and his men got off the train in Ironton that evening. By tattoo of the following day Grant had: (1) made up and sent to Fremont a consolidated roster of all troops on the post (something Fremont lacked); (2) inspected the garrison, finding all units except his own to be in a sorry condition; (3) reconnoitered the entire area and told the engineer where and how to build fortifications; (4) received reports from spies giving enemy strengths and dispositions; (5) taken action to make the command combat-ready; and (6) sent a full written report to Fremont.

I am open-mouthed over this celerity. In thirty-four years of military service I never saw anything like it. In eighteen hours after taking over a new command most senior officers would hardly complete reading the accumulation in their "in" baskets. In England, in 1944, while we were getting ready to invade Normandy, I received daily, by actual count, sixty-four thousand words of mimeographed tripe to read and initial. It wasn't that awful in Grant's day, but a detailed study of Army correspondence of the post-Civil War period indicates that it must have been pretty bad.

Within four days Grant made further rapid progress, including cramming some training down the throats of the disorganized troops (other than the 21st Illinois) that were infesting the post. He also organized a brigade supply train, using mules and wagons he impressed from local secessionists. Supply work was in his blood; he had been a regimental supply officer in his prewar service.

Now he gave a marked example of what he usually was thinking of. He had arrived in Ironton on August 8. On the twelfth he proposed marching south with his rag-tag brigade to attack Brigadier General William J. Hardee, a recognized Confederate hotshot who was supposed to have five thousand men. On the thirteenth he actually set forth on this expedition, when he was recalled by the erratic and ignorant Fremont, and replaced by Ben Prentiss, who did nothing. Maybe this was some more of Grant's luck. Hardee might have blighted his career.

The Vicksburg campaign illustrated on a grander scale Grant's ability to act rapidly when the situation permitted it. On May 1, 1863, while still completing the passage of his troops and supplies across the Mississippi near Bruinsburg, he lunged out of his bridgehead and defeated Lieutenant General John C. Pemberton's intercepting force near Port Gibson. Then he marched rapidly northeast in multiple columns and struck the gathering Confederates four heavy successive blows, first in one direction then another—all within six days. Thus he isolated Fortress Vicksburg, as was his intention, and its fall was assured.

Where did Grant learn such strategy and tactics? He says he never cracked a book on the subject and unlike many officers of that day, he was not an avid student of the Napoleonic campaigns. No one told him how to do these things; he made his own plans, and in this case was not guided by instructions from higher headquarters. His ability came from within. He must have had some qualities of genius. Francis V. Greene, an authority on this campaign, wrote: "We must go back to the campaigns of Napoleon to find equally brilliant results accomplished in the same space of time."

On the other hand, Grant's 1864 campaign that started on the Rappahannock has not been hailed as a manifestation of genius, especially in the realm of fast action. It gave him little or no chance to display the tactical speed and lightning thrusts of which he was capable. Essentially it was trench warfare interspersed with a series of turning movements. His rate of advance averaged little more than two miles per day which, in comparison with a similar type of warfare in 1915-18, is not too bad. He finally accomplished his mission, which was the capture of Lee's army, but neither luck nor genius seems to have been an ingredient of this success unless we include his numerical and material superiority. It was, however, a clear demonstration of his tenacity and determination.

It was also illustrative of another of Grant's chief characteristics: self-confidence. With one exception, Grant was always unswerving in his belief in himself. He was humble, in a sense, and not given to boasting. But somehow he never doubted that General U.S. Grant would win. In view of his unpromising background and record before the war, and his lack of outside help and influence, this confidence must have come from within. It must have been genius. For the nation it was the best of luck.

Danger and difficulty, any sort of crisis, did not appall or even disturb Grant. It simply stimulated him to a sharper, more decisive activity and confirmed his belief that all would be well. His calm imperturbability when the odor of impending disaster was rank in the air came from two unlike qualities, in addition to his belief in himself. One was an ability to arrive at a commonsense analysis of evidence missed by men who had eyes but could not see; and something akin to extrasensory perception, sometimes called intuition. An example of the first occurred at Fort Donelson in 1862. Grant arrived at the front late; he had been conferring with Flag Officer Andrew H. Foote, the commander of the naval contingent. The Rebels had just made a sortie, severely mauling John A. McClernand's division. Grant met an apprehensive group of officers and men at the front. The troops seemed ready to give way if the attack were renewed. Someone remarked that Confederates captured during the battle were carrying three days' rations in their knapsacks; this seemed to mean that they would stay in place for a protracted fight. Grant deduced the opposite. He said they were bent on getting away. He was proved right, and the measures he took, based on this conclusion, eventually won the battle.

Another case, occurring during the Battle of the Wilderness, illustrates the second kind of knowledge, that which comes from strange insight rather than external evidence. After a reverse to Federal troops near the Germanna Plank Road, a staff officer from the VI Corps fled to Grant's headquarters and gasped out that General John Sedgwick had been killed and VI Corps routed. "The elements of wholesale panic were present," writes Edward Steere (*The Wilderness Campaign*, Stackpole Co.). "One false step by the high command and Lee would have been given the victory he had despaired of winning. Grant calmly removed the cigar from his mouth and said, 'I don't believe it.'" Those around him were reassured. Panic was averted.

How did Grant know he was right? Did he have intuitive insight or ESP? Or was this simply a manifestation of steady self-confidence? To me, in either event, it was genius. No one gave Grant the answer. It came from within. President Lyndon B. Johnson once said that in his place of awesome responsibility the hardest thing is not in determining to do the right thing, but in determining what *is* the right thing.

In common with most men of true greatness, Grant had this faculty to an uncommon degree. Time after time, he chose the right military course and then followed it unswervingly.

Not all of General Grant's former war enemies were as generous to him in their opinions as he was magnanimous to them. But General James Longstreet, CSA, who had known Grant well before the war, eulogized him in later years: "Grant was a modest man, a simple man, a man believing in the honesty of his fellows, true to his friends, and of great personal honor.... His military genius was of the highest order. He was of the class and kind of Julius Caesar and Napoleon Bonaparte, superior to them in that his military achievements were actuated by the purest patriotism.... Personally, Grant was a warm-hearted, lovable friend, a magnanimous opponent. More than any man of the century he embodied in his character the genius of the American people."

In this picture, taken before the long and arduous Vicksburg Campaign, Grant is still thin, and his face has not yet become lined with care and responsibility. (NA)

Fort Monroe, with Hampton Roads anchorage indicated by small numeral 4. This odd perspective depiction of the area where the peace talks were held was lithographed by Virtue & Co. (LC)

The Singing Wire Conspiracy
by Howard C. Westwood

"Keep the champagne, but return the negro!"

Late on the afternoon of February 3, 1865, Secretary of State William H. Seward trumpeted that message across the choppy Virginia waters of Hampton Roads anchorage to three Confederate statesmen. They waved their handkerchiefs in thanks. Seward stood at the rail of the *River Queen,* the Confederates at the rail of the *Mary Martin,* two Hudson River boats that the Union armies had brought to serve them on the James River. A black man, in a row boat, was delivering a bottle of the choicest wine to the Confederates with Seward's compliments.

On the *River Queen* with Seward was his president, Abraham Lincoln. The two of them had just concluded four hours of talk in their ship's saloon with the now-departing Confederates, emissaries of Confederate President Jefferson Davis. These envoys were high ranking: Vice President Alexander Stephens, President *pro tem* of the Confederate Senate Senator Robert Hunter of Virginia, and Assistant Secretary of War John Campbell.

The five men had met with no one else present. No notes were taken. Their talk had been cordial, intimate, forthright. But they had talked peace and had gotten nowhere. There was an initial hurdle that could not be leaped, and Lincoln had constructed it. He would not consider a stop to the fighting unless the full authority of the United States was at once reestablished, and Rebel arms disbanded. The Confederates would entertain no such abject surrender, no matter how generous Lincoln's treatment of those erring sister states was if they returned to the family.

Assuming that Lincoln felt that a president of the United States could not enter into an agreement with "parties in arms against the government," Rebel Senator Hunter invoked history: Charles I in "repeated instances" had bargained with "people in arms against him." Lincoln quickly disposed of that precedent. He was not "posted in history," he said, but he did recollect that Charles I had "lost his head in the end."

This glib reply gave Jefferson Davis a propaganda weapon to briefly bolster sagging morale in the Confederate capital, Richmond. Eloquently, Davis was to proclaim the South must fight on with renewed determination for Lincoln had conclusively demonstrated his aim to stop at nothing short of the utter subjugation of the Southern people.

How did it happen that Lincoln, the consummate politician, handed such a verbal weapon to the Rebel chief? Responsibility for that diplomatic blunder was Union General-in-Chief Ulysses S. Grant's, and the story is involved.

The November 1864 reelection of Lincoln had dashed the South's hopes for a political revulsion in the North against prosecuting the war. Influential New York *Tribune* editor Horace Greeley speculated that this made the time propitious to have a try at peace talks. In December he wrote a timely letter to Lincoln's elderly adviser Francis P. Blair, Sr., on the subject of negotiations. It happened that at the time he received the editor's message the old gentleman had been contemplating a scheme to bring about reunion; Greeley's letter stirred him to action. He visited the president, and on December 28 obtained Lincoln's pass allowing him to cross the army's lines and "go south." He wanted to approach Jefferson Davis, his staunch friend of antebellum days, with a peace plan. But he was on his own; Lincoln would not listen to what he intended proposing.

It was not until January 12 that Blair finally was able to get through to Richmond and have a session with the Confederate president. There he proposed what he confessed were "perhaps merely the dreams of an old man"—that the North and South should enter into a "secret treaty" to cease their fighting and join in an expedition to Mexico to enforce the Monroe Doctrine by ousting the French government's puppet ruler Emperor Maximilian. This, he thought, might lead, somehow, to "the restoration of fraternal relations between the sections." After long talks Davis gave Blair a letter saying that if a Confederate commission would be received, he was ready to send one to "the United States Government" to confer "with a view to secure peace to the two countries." On January 14 Blair left to return to Washington.

The venerable adviser reported to the president with Davis's letter. Lincoln paid no attention to the preposterous idea of a joint expedition to Mexico, and it is apparent that he explained to Blair that he would not recognize Davis's phrase "two countries." There could be no "treaty." But Lincoln had been ready to talk peace all along. So on January 18 he gave Blair a letter informing him that he could tell Davis, as always, he was "ready to receive any agent" whom Davis might "informally send to me with the view of securing peace to the people of our one common country."

Blair went back to Richmond again to see Davis on January 22. He gave the Confederate president a copy of Lincoln's letter, urged that a way be found to respond, and on January 25 he returned through Union lines. After anxious consultation with his advisers, on January 28 Davis designated Alexander Stephens, Robert Hunter, and John Campbell as his emissaries and gave them credentials saying that in "conformity" with Lincoln's letter to Blair, they were to go to Washington "for an informal conference" on the issues of the war "and for the purpose of securing peace to the two countries."

There is little way of knowing how much Union Lieutenant General U.S. Grant understood of Blair's negotiations, but he must have known a good deal. Blair himself later said Grant knew what he intended proposing to Davis. And on at least two occasions during his North-South travels Blair had been at City Point, Virginia for long periods of time while Grant was there. The general-in-chief had also been personally involved in the arrangements for Blair's trips.

It is not surprising, then, that the old politician left an impression in Richmond that Grant understood what he was up to. On the afternoon of January 29, Davis's peace commissioners came to the front at Petersburg and sent word to the Union commander there that they wanted admission, en route to Washington, as peace envoys on a mission "in accordance with an understanding" with Grant.

Confederate envoy,
Vice President Alexander Stephens. (LC)

Confederate Senator
Robert Hunter of Virginia. (LC)

The general-in-chief was away on that day, occupied with arrangements for Major General John M. Schofield's move on Wilmington, North Carolina. Major General George Meade was absent too. Major General Edward Ord, the ranking commander present, was mystified; at 6:30 p.m. on the twenty-ninth he wired the Confederates' request to Union Secretary of War Edwin M. Stanton. That night Stanton telegraphed Ord that, pending further instructions, the Confederates were not to be allowed into the Union lines and that his department had no knowledge of any "understanding" with Grant. But the next morning at Lincoln's direction, Stanton wired Ord again to inform the Confederates that a messenger would be sent to them "at or near where they now are without unnecessary delay."

In the meantime, with no response to their overture, the Confederates had been getting nervous. The Southern officer who had orally delivered their request to pass the lines had been told by Union officers that Grant "was on a big drunk." Considering this, the Confederates decided they had better send a second message, this one in writing and directed to Grant himself. So, at about the time Stanton was telegraphing Ord on the morning of January 30 that a messenger would be coming, the Rebel emissaries were getting off a note across the lines addressed to Grant. The Confederates' dispatch said they wanted to go to Washington to confer with Lincoln to ascertain the terms on which the war "may be terminated, in pursuance of the course indicated by him in his letter to Mr. F.P. Blair of January 18, 1865, of which we presume you have a copy; and if not, we wish to see you in person, if convenient, and to confer with you upon the subject."

Grant got back to his headquarters at City Point early the next morning, January 31. On reading the Confederates' note to him he at once, without inquiry as to what may have happened in his absence, sent word to bring the Confederates to him. Then at 10:00 a.m. he wired directly to Lincoln the text of their note to him and said that he had sent for the envoys and expected them to reach his headquarters that evening. The general completed his message with the phrase "awaiting your instructions."

Grant had sent Colonel Orville E. Babcock of his staff to escort the Confederates. And he had done more. He had addressed them cordially, saying that he had telegraphed their note to Washington and had asked for instructions. "I have no doubt but that before you arrive at my headquarters an answer will be received directing me to comply with your request," he wrote.

Late that day Grant's attention was called to Stanton's previous day's instruction to Ord that the Confederates were to be met "at or near where they now are." At 7:30 that evening Grant wired Stanton that the Confederates had arrived at his headquarters on his invitation. He explained, "...Since their arrival I have been put in possession of the telegraphic correspondence which had been going on for two days previous. Had I known of this correspondence in time these gentlemen would not have been received within our lines."

By that time the general had a telegram from Lincoln replying to Grant's wire of that morning. It said that a messenger was on the way, that the "gentlemen" should be kept "in comfortable quarters," and that Grant should act on the message being brought, though it had "been made up . . . when the gentlemen were supposed to be beyond our lines."

On January 30 things had happened fast at the executive mansion after Lincoln got the word from Ord, via Stanton, that Confederate peace commissioners wanted to come to Washington. The chief telegrapher of the War Department, Major Thomas T. Eckert, enjoyed Lincoln's special confidence. Lincoln selected him as his messenger, giving him written instructions to see the Confederates and to deliver to them a letter predated February 1 that was drafted by Lincoln and signed by Eckert. It specified that they would be passed to Fort Monroe, Virginia, to meet with "some person or persons" for an informal conference, provided that in writing they agreed that the conference would be "on the basis of" Lincoln's January 18 letter to Blair, of which a copy was attached. Lincoln's instructions to Eckert concluded: if the Confederates proposed "other terms" they were not to be passed, "And this being your whole duty, return and report to me." The Confederates were to be passed only on their written agreement to confer "on the basis of . . . the view of securing peace to the people of our one common country." On the next day, January 31, Eckert departed and Lincoln dispatched Secretary of State Seward to Fort Monroe at Hampton Roads, to be the "person or persons" with whom the Confederates would confer if Eckert got the specified agreement from them.

Francis Preston Blair, Sr. (LC)

Eckert reached City Point the afternoon of February 1, and at 4:15 met with the Confederates. By that time they had been at City Point for nearly twenty-four hours, and been most royally treated. It was apparent that the rumor of the "big drunk" was, as Stephens was to put it later, "a canard of the Munchausen sort." Grant greeted them personally, apologetically explained that the delay had been caused by his absence, and told them that a messenger from Lincoln was on the way. He took them to comfortable quarters on the *Mary Martin*, docked nearby, and there presided at a banquet attended by about fifty of his principal officers, with Stephens sitting beside him. The talk was free and gay, with wine flowing—though Grant did not have a drop. After the feast Grant left, and Stephens, recently ill, went to his cabin. But Campbell and Hunter kept up spirited talk with their enemies until long after midnight. During all this talk some Federals assured the Confederates "that Mrs. Grant had expressed her opinion openly that her husband ought to send them on, and permit no vital difficulties to break up the interview."

The next morning, with the recently returned George Meade, Grant took the peace emissaries to meet his wife Julia and see his horses, and then offered to take his guests on a

Edward O.C. Ord.
(U.S. Army Military History Institute)

Secretary of War Edwin M. Stanton. (LC)

Major Thomas T. Eckert.
(Ostendorf Collection)

tour. But the cold weather made ailing Stephens demur, so back to the *Mary Martin* they went for more talk with the general. How much they adverted to their mission in all those conversations is not clear. But in a letter written to his wife that night Meade indicated that he, at least, talked with them extensively on the subject of peace. Grant's subordinate also wrote that he hoped Lincoln himself would see the Confederates, and it is a fair guess that he urged his commanding general to further their project.

While there is a conflict as to precisely how events unfolded from 4:15 p.m. on February 1 until late that night, one can construct a likely scenario.

Grant was talking with the Confederates when Eckert arrived. Eckert insisted on seeing them alone, to Grant's annoyance. He delivered his letter, drafted by Lincoln, that confined a permissible conference to one "on the basis of" Lincoln's "our one common country" letter to Blair of January 18. Eckert left them to consider their reply. They wrote a letter to Eckert, handed to him at 6:00 p.m. It quoted Davis's instructions of January 28, authorizing them to confer on "peace to the two countries." It went on to state that the "substantial object" of a conference would be to ascertain terms to end the war "honorably" and that though their instructions contemplated a conference with Lincoln in Washington they were ready to meet anyone anywhere as Lincoln might designate.

Eckert then met with the Confederates again, this time with Grant in attendance. Eckert told them that they had not met Lincoln's condition. Grant obviously was not happy with this position and started to speak, but the major interrupted him, insisting that under Lincoln's instructions Grant was "not permitted to say anything officially." Angry, Grant soon left. This second meeting ended shortly thereafter and Eckert left.

It appears that then Grant went back to see the Confederates. But this time Campbell was taken ill, so the general-in-chief talked only to Stephens and Hunter, suggesting that they modify their statement. After discussion, Stephens drafted a new letter, this one addressed to Grant. Hunter agreed with its content; Stephens took it to Campbell and he agreed with what it said. All three signed the letter. Bluntly it expressed their desire to go to Washington to confer with Lincoln informally "in reference to the matters mentioned" in Lincoln's January 18 letter to Blair, "without any personal compromise on any question in the letter." It closed with the statement that they had permission to do so from "the authorities in Richmond." Grant was pleased. "That will do," he said. He took the letter to Major Eckert at 8:00 p.m. But at 9:30 p.m. Eckert told the Confederates, much to Grant's chagrin, that "they could not proceed further unless they complied" with his Lincoln-drafted letter. Then, on leaving the Confederates—he was not to see them again—Eckert

Grant with his son Jesse and his wife. Julia Dent Grant wielded considerable influence on her husband's political decisions. (LC)

slipped. Though Lincoln had placed responsibility exclusively on him, he told them "to inform General Grant in case they concluded to accept the terms." The pressure of a lieutenant general on a major had had an effect.

A half-hour later, at 10:00 p.m., Eckert wired his report to Lincoln. It stated that the Confederates' reply to his Lincoln-drafted letter had not been satisfactory, quoted their 8:00 p.m. letter to Grant, said that at 9:30 p.m. he had notified them that they could not proceed unless they complied with the Lincoln-drafted letter, and noted that he thought they would not insist on going to Washington, but that Fort Monroe would be acceptable.

Earlier in the day Lincoln had wired Eckert, in care of Grant, that Seward would be at Fort Monroe and that he should call there for directions. So Eckert left for Monroe, arriving there at 9:00 the next morning, February 2. He apparently traveled on the steamer *Lady Long* which left City Point that night for Annapolis. And before his departure, Eckert tried wiring Stanton. The wording of his telegram, in a confused way, indicated that the Confederates' problem was that of agreeing to Lincoln's "our one common country" formula in the face of Davis's instructions. But Eckert's wire could not be sent. Allegedly the telegraph line was out of order, in spite of the fact that Eckert had been able to wire Lincoln shortly before, and in a few minutes Grant himself was sending a telegram to Stanton. It can only be supposed that Grant was seeing to it that Eckert played no further role.

Grant's wire to Stanton was written at 10:30 p.m. Received in Washington at 4:35 a.m., it stated he was convinced "upon conversation" with Stephens and Hunter that they sincerely desired "peace and union" and that he was sorry that Lincoln could not "have an interview" with them. He concluded that their letter to him—referring to their original note of January 30—"was all that the President's instructions contemplated to secure their safe conduct if they had used the same language to Major Eckert."

Grant did not stop with that. He went back for further talk with Stephens and Hunter. From that talk there evolved another letter, again drafted by Stephens but signed by all three. Dated February 2, it must have been written after midnight. This one was addressed to Major Eckert. The Confederates did not know that he was no longer at City Point. This letter said that they were "willing to proceed to Fortress Monroe and there to have an informal conference with any person or persons that President Lincoln may appoint on the basis of his letter to Francis P. Blair of the 18th of January ultimo, or upon any other terms or conditions that he may hereafter propose not inconsistent with the essential principles of self-government and popular rights, upon which our institutions are founded." The letter closed with a hedge. "We think it better to add that in accepting your passport we are not to be understood as committing ourselves to anything."

Grant indicated that he felt this letter would be satisfactory, and left, pretending he was going to check with Major Eckert. Soon he returned, saying Eckert was not satisfied, but he, Grant, had determined to send them on to Fort Monroe on his own responsibility. The peace envoys would leave the first thing in the morning.

Early on February 2 Grant wired Secretary Seward, who arrived at Fort Monroe the previous evening, that "The gentlemen here have accepted the proposed terms, and will leave for Fort Monroe at 9:30 a.m." The general sent a copy of that wire to War Secretary Stanton and it was received in Washington at 9:00 a.m. But Grant did not wire the text of the Confederates' last letter to Eckert (on the basis of which Grant had decided to pass them) to either Seward or Stanton.

Early that same morning, Lincoln received Eckert's last wire to him saying that the Confederates' position was not satisfactory. Considering giving up, Lincoln was about to recall Seward when he was shown the telegram from Grant to Stanton from the night before, the one saying that the Confederates sincerely desired "peace and union" and that he was sorry that Lincoln could not see them. At that Lincoln changed his mind; he decided to go himself to Fort Monroe and meet with Davis's emissaries.

At 9:00 a.m., before he saw Stanton's copy of Grant's wire to Seward, Lincoln telegraphed Grant to tell "the gentlemen" that he would "meet them personally at Fortress Monroe as soon as I can get there." At the same time Lincoln wired Seward that he was coming, induced by "a dispatch" from Grant.

Lincoln's telegram to Grant reached the lieutenant general just as the *Mary Martin* was getting up steam to pull away. The Confederates, on deck, saw Grant coming on a run. As Stephens was later to recount, Grant ran "with countenance beaming with joy. When he got within twenty or thirty paces he exclaimed, 'Gentlement, it is all right, I've got the authority.'" He climbed to the deck and read them Lincoln's wire. "The General . . . greatly elated," let Stephens take his black body servant with him as a goodwill gesture.

Grant's aide, Colonel Babcock, accompanied the Confederates to Fort Monroe, and at 4:30 that afternoon delivered to Major Eckert the letter the envoys had written to him the night before. The letter's existence came as a shock to the major, and when the president arrived late that evening, the letter surprised him as well. But the letter's presence, and whether or not Eckert liked what it had to say, were academic problems by then. The lieutenant general had seen to it that his president and the Confederate emissaries would talk face to face, and for good reasons.

On the night of February 1, while he tangled with the

president's single-minded major, events were taking place in Savannah, Georgia and along the Potomac River that were provoking Ulysses Grant to attempt his brash manipulation of men and letters. From Savannah Sherman had begun his march north for the conquest of the Carolinas and Major General Schofield was to transport his corps down the Potomac and on to North Carolina to link up with Sherman's troops. But the Potomac was iced over and Schofield's troop transports could not move; Grant feared that Sherman would be marching into the face of a desperate enemy without the possibility of getting reinforcements. Worse yet, for the past month he had received frequent reports that Richmond's evacuation was imminent. On February 7, when the Confederate peace commissioners were on their way home after the fruitless Hampton Roads conference with Lincoln, Grant admitted to Secretary of War Stanton, "I do not want to do anything to force the enemy from Richmond until Schofield has carried out his programme. He is to take Wilmington and then push out to Goldsborough, or as near it as he can

go, and build up the road after him. He will then be in a position to assist Sherman if Lee should leave Richmond with any considerable force, and the two together will be strong enough for all the enemy have to put against them."

It was no wonder that "the General was...greatly elated." If peace negotiations could be gotten under way, no matter how vain they might prove in the end, Jefferson Davis would never allow any move by General Robert E. Lee's Army of Northern Virginia that would leave the Confederate capital unprotected. To abandon Richmond in the face of a possible peace would weaken the Rebels' negotiating position.

Ulysses Grant confessed in his memoirs, "One of the most anxious periods of my experience during the rebellion was the last few weeks before Petersburg....I was afraid, every morning, that I would awake from my sleep to hear that Lee had gone....I knew he could move much more lightly and more rapidly than I...and the war might be prolonged another year." So, by his ruse, the Union's top general really had negotiated for peace.

The pier at City Point, Virginia, from which Confederate peace envoys departed for their meeting with Lincoln at Fort Monroe. Aside from being the site of Grant's unusual negotiations, this town northeast of Petersburg was the command center for Union supply and strategy in the final year of the war. (LC)

"The Surrender of General Lee to General Grant—From a Description by the Latter." (FL)

Grant Remembers Appomattox
by John Russell Young

"On the night before Lee's surrender," said General Grant, "I had a wretched headache—headaches to which I have been subject—nervous prostration, intense personal suffering. But, suffer or not, I had to keep moving. I saw clearly, especially after [Major General Philip H.] Sheridan had cut off the escape to Danville, that [General Robert E.] Lee must surrender or break and run into the mountains—break in all directions and leave us a dozen guerrilla bands to fight. The object of my campaign was not Richmond, not the defeat of Lee in actual fight, but to remove him and his army out of the contest, and, if possible, to have him use his influence in inducing the surrender of [General Joseph E.] Johnston and the other isolated armies. You see, the war was an enormous strain upon the country. Rich as we were, I do not now see how we could have endured it another year, even from a financial point of view. So with these views I wrote Lee, and opened the correspondence with which the world is familiar. Lee does not appear well in that correspondence, not nearly as well as he did in our subsequent interviews, where his whole bearing was that of a patriotic and gallant soldier, concerned alone for the welfare of his army and his State. I received word that Lee would meet me at a point within our lines near Sheridan's headquarters. I had to ride quite a distance through a muddy country. I remember now that I was concerned about my personal appearance. I had an old suit on, without my sword, and without any distinguishing mark of rank except the shoulder-straps of a lieutenant-general on a woolen blouse. I was splashed with mud in my long ride. I was afraid Lee might think I meant to show him studied discourtesy by so coming —at least I thought so. But I had no other clothes within reach, as Lee's letter found me away from my base of supplies. I kept on riding until I met Sheridan. The General, who was one of the heroes of the campaign, and whose pursuit of Lee was perfect in its generalship and energy, told me where to find Lee. I remember that Sheridan was impatient when I met him, anxious and suspicious about the whole business, feared there might be a plan to escape, that he had Lee at his feet, and wanted to end the business by going in and forcing an absolute surrender by capture. In fact, he had his troops ready for such an assault when Lee's white flag came within his lines. I went up to the house where Lee was waiting. I found him in a fine, new, splendid uniform, which only recalled my anxiety as to my own clothes while on my way to meet him. I expressed my regret that I was compelled to meet him in so unceremonious a manner, and he replied that the only suit he had available was one which had been sent him by some admirers in Baltimore, and which he then wore for the first time. We spoke of old friends in the army. I remembered having seen Lee in Mexico. He was so much higher in rank than myself at the time that I supposed he had no recollection of me. But he said he remembered me very well. We talked of old times and exchanged inquiries about friends. Lee then broached the subject of our meeting. I told him my terms, and Lee, listening attentively, asked me to write them down. I took out my 'manifold' order-book and pencil and wrote them down. General Lee put on his glasses and read them over. The conditions gave the officers their sidearms, private horses, and personal baggage. I said to Lee that I hoped and believed this would be the close of the war; that it was most important that the men should go home and go to work, and the Government would not throw any obstacles in the way. Lee answered that it would have a most happy effect, and accepted the terms. I handed over my penciled memorandum to an aid to put into ink, and we resumed our conversation about old times and old friends in the armies. Various officers came in—[James] Longstreet, John B. Gordon, [George E.] Pickett, from the South; Philip H. Sheridan, [Edward O.C.] Ord, and others from our side. Some were old friends—Longstreet and myself, for instance, and we had a general talk. Lee no doubt expected me to ask for his sword, but I did not want his sword. 'It would only,' said the General, smiling, 'have gone to the Patent Office to be worshiped by the Washington rebels.' There was a pause, when General Lee said that most of the animals in his cavalry and artillery were owned by the privates, and he would like to know, under the terms, whether they would be regarded as private property or the property of the Government. I said that under the terms of surrender they belonged to the Government. General Lee read over the letter and said that was so. I then said to the General that I believed and hoped this was the last battle of the war; that I saw the wisdom of these men getting home and to work as soon as possible, and that I would give orders to allow any soldier or officer claiming a horse or mule to take it. General Lee showed some emotion at this—a feeling which I also shared—and said it would have a most happy effect. The interview ended, I gave orders for rationing his troops."

The caption for this photograph of "Cincinnati," Grant's favorite mount, in Miller's Photographic History *states that it was taken at Cold Harbor in June 1864. However, the two stars of a major general on the saddle cloth indicate that it was made earlier, before Grant was promoted to lieutenant general.*

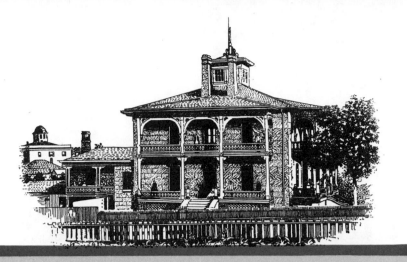

WILLIAM T. SHERMAN

The Failure by Albert Castel
The Subordinate by Albert Castel
The Conqueror by Albert Castel

THE LIFE OF A RISING SON

By Albert Castel

Part I: The Failure

Among Union generals, Sherman ranks second only to Grant. Most of his contemporaries so regarded him and few historians have challenged their judgment. Furthermore, everyone has always recognized that he possessed a brilliant if somewhat eccentric intellect, that he was a man of unique and fascinating personality, and that he embodied traits that made him "peculiarly American." However, from the outset of the Civil War down to the present there have been widely divergent opinions concerning his talents and methods as a military commander.

Some have portrayed him as a ruthless bully on horseback, violating the laws of war, terrifying "almost helpless" Southern civilians into submission; or as a bungler who never fought or won a full-scale battle and owed success to luck, skillful lieutenants and the mistakes of a weak enemy. Still others go to the opposite extreme, claiming that Sherman was one of the great captains of all time; the progenitor of modern warfare.

If one looks for the real Sherman in histories and biographies, he will find scores of bright books on the man, but none that provides a scholarly, thorough and systematic study of his campaigns and career. All one will find is unanimous, and sometimes violent, disagreement. But as Sherman once said about making war, so it can be said about writing history: it is not popularity seeking.

Sherman's military career began in 1836 at the age of 16 when his foster father, Senator Thomas Ewing, Sr., appointed him to West Point. There is no indication that Sherman (his first name was originally Tecumseh in honor of that famous warrior) desired such a career, and much evidence that he embarked on it simply out of

a sense of obligation to Ewing, who had taken him into his own home in Lancaster, Ohio, following the 1829 death of Sherman's father, a state judge. At the military academy he was a good student but a sloppy soldier: He accumulated so many demerits for discipline and infractions of the dress code that he finished sixth in a class of forty-three rather than fourth as entitled by his academic record. Nevertheless he became, and thereafter basically remained, a member of America's small, semi-isolated guild of professional soldiers, firmly convinced that only West Pointers were qualified for high command.

Graduation in 1840 was followed by army service which took him from New York to San Francisco and from Pittsburgh to New Orleans, but brought him no combat experience other than a few skirmishes with the Seminoles in Florida. During the Mexican War, when so many fellow West Pointers were winning fame and promotion on the battlefield, he spent most of his time on recruiting duty in Pennsylvania and occupation duty in California. By 1853 he was merely a captain in the Commissary Department, with no prospect of being anything else in the foreseeable future. Meanwhile he had acquired a wife—Ewing's pious daughter Ellen—and two children. This marriage strengthened his ties to the Ewing family and intensified the pressure on him to prove himself worthy of such an alliance. As it was, he

---

William Tecumseh Sherman, brilliant and eccentric exponent of modern "total" war.

could not support Ellen and the children in appropriate style on his army salary alone and was dependent to a degree on Ewing's financial assistance.

He asked his friend, Henry S. Turner, a former army officer who was then a partner in a St. Louis banking firm, for a job. Turner, who believed that Sherman was wasting his "intellectual energy" in the peacetime service, offered to appoint him manager of a branch bank in San Francisco. Sherman accepted, took a six-month leave, went to San Francisco, concluded he could make a fortune in banking and real estate, and so resigned his commission. For a while affairs went well and he built a fine house for his family. Then a business panic struck California. Sherman's bank survived but made little or no profit. The home office closed it—and then closed itself. As a consequence, in the summer of 1857 Sher-

The Sherman home in Lancaster, Ohio.

Senator Thomas Ewing, Sr. of Ohio, Sherman's foster father.

man found himself "used up financially." Without cause he blamed himself for this dismal outcome. "What I failed to do," he wrote his father-in-law, "and the bad debts that now stare me in the face, must stand forever as a monument to my want of . . . sagacity."

He paid most of his debts by selling all of his property, but was unable to secure a satisfactory business position and was unwilling to re-enter the army except at a higher rank than he left it. Late in 1858 he returned to Lancaster to take charge of Ewing's saltworks. Ellen was delighted to be back home. Sherman felt humiliated. As he frankly told Ewing, "I have been Captain so long that subordination will come a little hard. . . ." Deepening his sense of failure was the fact that his younger brother John was rising rapidly in politics, having just been elected to a second term in the Federal House of Representatives.

However, before he had to descend into the saltworks Ewing's oldest son, Thomas, Jr., asked Sherman to join his law firm in Leavenworth, Kansas Territory. Sherman at once hastened to "Bleeding Kansas," where he was admitted to the bar "on the ground of general intelligence and reputation." But clients were few, he lost his only case, and a corn speculation scheme, in which Ewing, Sr. and Ellen invested large sums at his urging, failed. In the summer of 1859 he again returned to Lancaster in defeat. "I look upon myself," he wrote Ellen before leaving Leavenworth, "as a dead cock in the pit. . . ."

Major General Don Carlos Buell.

But if unfortunate in business he was lucky in his friends. One of them, Major Don Carlos Buell, notified him that the position of superintendent of the newly established Louisiana Seminary of Learning and Military Academy (present-day Louisiana State University) was available. Sherman promptly applied, and thanks in part to the recommendations of P.G.T. Beauregard, Braxton Bragg, and Richard Taylor he received the appointment. During the ensuing months he proved to be a capable administrator and a popular teacher. However Ellen refused to join him in Louisiana and badgered him to return to Ohio. Her attitude annoyed Sherman, who believed that he had found his proper niche in life, at least for the time being. "As to my coming to Lancaster, and laying around doing nothing, I say without fear of being adjudged blasphemous I would rather be where your damn sinners [are]."

Ellen finally agreed to come to Louisiana where the house the academy had promised Sherman had been built. But scarcely had it been completed when early in 1861 Louisiana followed the rest of the Deep South out of the Union. Sherman, who had expected and dreaded this, immediately resigned as superintendent. Although he sympathized with the South and considered slavery the natural status for the Negro, he was passionately devoted to the Union and regarded secession as synonymous with revolution and anarchy.

So Ellen had her way after all and Sherman once more was, as he put it, a "vagabond." On returning

North he went to Washington where, accompanied by his brother, now a Republican senator, he offered his services to the recently inaugurated President Lincoln. However, Lincoln told him that military men were not needed—compromise would restore the Union peacefully. Such wishful thinking disgusted Sherman. A long, hard war, he predicted, would be needed to subdue the Southern rebellion.

He decided to bide his time until the government realized the seriousness of the crisis. Meanwhile, since he now had five children to support, he took a job from his old associate Turner as president of a streetcar company in St. Louis. He was in that city when the Confederates fired on Fort Sumter. Shortly thereafter the Lincoln Administration, which now needed military men very much, proposed making him a major general of volunteers, quartermaster general of the army, even assistant secretary of war. He rejected all of those posts. "The first movements of our Government will fail," he wrote brother John, "and the leaders will be cast aside. A second or third set will rise, and amongst them I may be, but at present I will not volunteer as a soldier or anything else."

Early in June, the War Department at his and John's behest offered him a commission as colonel in

John Sherman at the age of 33.

the Regular Army. This he accepted. In common with other West Pointers he distrusted volunteers—only trained and disciplined Regulars, he declared, could put down the Rebels, whom he described as being far more realistic and purposeful than the people of the North. He believed that the politicians would make scapegoats of those generals who, even through no fault of their own, failed. For politicians as a class he had utter contempt. Indeed, he despised democracy itself, equating it with mob rule, and he frankly avowed a preference for monarchy or dictatorship. Ideologically, Sherman "the American" had more in common with European aristocrats than he did with his countrymen.

Sherman reported to the army (to use the term loosely) to find that Brigadier General Irvin McDowell was assembling troops at Washington for the purpose (most Northerners were confident) of crushing the rebellion and winning the war. But instead of the regiment of Regulars he desired and expected, he was assigned command of a brigade of volunteers. He took a dim view of these raw troops, many of whom were ninety-day enlistees clamoring to go home. "With regulars," he wrote Ellen, "I would have no doubt, but these volunteers are subject to stampedes."

On July 21, at Bull Run, Sherman's fears came true. The Federal soldiers, after initially driving back the outflanked enemy, broke into a retreat that turned into a panic-stricken rout when they themselves were unexpectedly assailed on the flank. Sherman was disgusted not only with their conduct on the battlefield but also with the way they acted on the march to it. "No curse could be greater," he declared, "than invasion by a volunteer army. No Goths or Vandals ever had less respect for the lives and property of friends and foes. . . ."

Yet he himself performed well at Bull Run, especially in view of the fact that it was the first battle in which he had ever participated, much less commanded troops. Assigned the mission of pinning down the Confederates by feinting an attack on their front, he promptly and intelligently executed orders to make a real attack which contributed substantially to the early Northern success. Then, following the Union collapse, he kept his brigade in reasonably good order while it abandoned the battlefield. Finally, on reaching Washington, he took charge of rallying and reorganizing troops to defend the Capital in case the Rebels attempted to follow up their victory. In sum he displayed coolness, courage, initiative, and good judgment. The only serious weakness he revealed was in engaging his brigade regiment by regiment instead of as a whole. However, this was a fault common to all Northern commanders at Bull Run and probably inevitable given their inexperience in handling large bodies of troops. It speaks well

Pictorial Battles of the Civil War

Beginning of the action at Bull Run. Union battery engages a masked Confederate battery. Artist A.R. Waud represents himself sketching the scene from beside the rail fence. Engraving by Thomas Nast.

for Sherman that after the battle he obtained the latest manuals on tactics and used them to retrain himself so that he could better train his men.

Late in August the War Department promoted Sherman to brigadier general and ordered him to Kentucky. The promotion somewhat surprised him—he considered himself "disgraced" by his involvement in the Bull Run fiasco and told Ellen that "I suppose soon I can sneak into some quiet corner." On the other hand the transfer to Kentucky delighted him. For he believed, presciently as it turned out, that in the West the war would be won and the great military reputations made. However, for the time being, as he notified Lincoln, he preferred "to serve in a subordinate capacity, and in no event to be left in a superior command." He still feared that the unreliability of the volunteers and the unrealistic attitude of the government would inevitably result in disaster for Northern commanders. "Not till I see daylight ahead," he confided to Ellen, "do I want to lead."

Lincoln responded to Sherman's unique diffidence by posting him as second in command to Brigadier General Robert A. Anderson, who was in charge of the Department of the Cumberland and who had requested Sherman's services. Anderson, the "Hero of Fort Sumter," was endeavoring to organize Union forces in Kentucky,

his native state. But, as Sherman discovered on arriving at Louisville, he had succeeded in raising only a few troops and most of them were poorly armed and trained. Worse, after about a month Anderson fell ill and asked to be relieved. As a result Sherman was thrust into exactly the sort of position he had wanted to avoid—top command in a vital theater of war.

His reaction was one of semi-hysteria. He believed that General Albert Sidney Johnston's Confederate Army, which had moved up from Tennessee into Kentucky, possessed overwhelming numbers and intended to seize Louisville and invade Ohio and Indiana. Actually Johnston had fewer men than Sherman, and far from planning an offensive, he feared that Sherman would attack him! But Sherman, lacking an intelligence service and prey to an over-active imagination, had no doubt that he again faced defeat and disgrace. He bombarded the War Department with frantic pleas for large quantities of additional troops and equipment, warning that unless he got them "I will not be responsible for events...."

However, instead of reinforcements, Washington sent messages urging him to "liberate" East Tennessee, where most of the inhabitants remained loyal to the Union. This response persuaded him that he was being deliberately "sacrificed" by the politicians. "To advance," he wrote Ellen, "would be madness and to stand still folly. . . . The idea of going down in History with a fame such as threatens me nearly makes me crazy, indeed I may be so now."

Some people who observed him in his quarters on the ground floor of a Louisville hotel concluded that there could be no doubt about it—he was demented. Tall and thin, always looking like he needed a shave and his red hair never combed, he spent hours pacing back and forth, incessantly smoking cigars, head bent forward, hands behind his back, eyes darting about but seeing nothing. Other times he sprawled in a chair, thumbs in his vest, and spoke to whoever was present in a rapid, staccato fashion, jumping from subject to subject and expressing himself in language that was both vivid and vehement. When or if he ate and slept, no one could tell. He seemed to live on nervous energy and to be consumed by it at the same time.

On October 16 Secretary of War Simon Cameron arrived in Louisville on a tour of inspection. Sherman went to confer with him. In the room were several reporters—a breed Sherman deemed little better than spies. Cameron, lying on a bed with a whiskey bottle nearby, said, "Now General Sherman tell us your troubles." Sherman demanded that the reporters leave—they should not be present at such a discussion. But Cameron overruled him—"We are all friends, here." Sherman then proceeded to declare that he needed 60,000 men just to defend Kentucky, 200,000 to carry out an offensive. Astounded, Cameron quite correctly replied that such numbers simply were unavailable and that Sherman must be overestimating the Rebel strength. Later Sherman and his apologists claimed that in referring to 200,000 troops he had in mind a campaign to open up the entire Mississippi Valley, and that since it ultimately

Simon Cameron, Lincoln's first Secretary of War.

Harper's Weekly, May 3, 1862

This first portrait of Sherman by *Harper's* shows him full-bearded, *sans* mustache.

took that many (and more) he was not guilty of exaggeration but rather showed realistic foresight. However, the subject of Sherman's interview with Cameron was not long-range strategy but the immediate situation in Kentucky. Additionally, various documents, including some of Sherman's own dispatches, make it evident that he was thinking of the proposed invasion of East Tennessee and not of a march on New Orleans.

Cameron promised to order reinforcements to Kentucky—which he did. On the other hand, soon after leaving Louisville he told one of the reporters who had been present during his meeting with Sherman that the general was "unbalanced and that it would not be [wise] to leave him in command." This reporter in turn published a story, which was widely reprinted, deriding Sherman's "insane request" for 200,000 troops and implying that Sherman was mentally deranged. Worse, the official account of the Sherman-Cameron interview, which appeared early in November, spoke of Sherman's "gloomy . . . overestimate" of the enemy's strength. Angered and upset, Sherman on November 6 asked Major General George B. McClellan, the recently installed supreme commander of the Union Army, to replace him with someone of more "sanguine mind." McClellan, who had just received a report from one of his top aides stating that Sherman was not "sufficiently master of his judgment to warrant the intrusting to him of an important military command," promptly sent Sherman's old friend Don Carlos Buell, now a brigadier general, to take charge in Kentucky.

However the prospect of relief from the tribulations of command did not relieve Sherman's apprehensions. On November 11 he instructed his West Point classmate, Brigadier General George H. Thomas, commanding in eastern Kentucky, to make ready to retreat at once—Johnston was about to advance on Louisville with 45,000 men. Thomas answered that he would do so, although he doubted that the Confederates were that strong or intended to attack. In this he was absolutely right: Johnston had only 12,500 troops, many of them unarmed, whereas Union forces in Kentucky now numbered over 40,000. Sherman's belief, or rather delusion, that Johnston planned to strike at Louisville derived (as he himself admitted to Thomas) from the boasts of Confederate sympathizers in that city, not from reliable intelligence.

Sherman also remained despondent; in fact, he became more so. To brother John he declared, "If anybody can do better than I can for God's sake let him. I prefer to follow not to lead, as I confess I have not the confidence of a Leader in this war, and would be happy to slide into obscurity." And to Ellen he wrote, "I am almost crazy."

Alarmed by his condition, one of his staff officers urged Ellen to come to Louisville. She did so, bringing two of the children. At her behest John soon followed. Together they tried to restore Sherman's spirits and confidence but achieved little if any improvement. As John told his brother, "You have been so harassed with the magnitude of your labors and have allowed yourself so little rest . . . that your mind casts a sombre shadow upon everything."

CWTI Collection

Major General Henry Wager Halleck.

On November 15 Buell arrived and took command in Louisville. Six days later Sherman, predicting that "some terrible disaster is inevitable" in Kentucky, left for St. Louis. There he reported for duty to Major General Henry Wager Halleck, commander of the Department of Missouri. Halleck was a friend of Sherman's from California days and had a high opinion of his ability. He ignored the stories about Sherman's instability and sent him to inspect Union forces in central Missouri, with authority to take command of them if he saw fit.

Within a week Sherman was sending Halleck frantic dispatches to the effect that a huge Confederate Army was about to descend on Jefferson City and St. Louis. Unable to believe, but unwilling to reject these assertions out of hand, Halleck instructed Brigadier John Pope to check on them. Pope reported with complete accuracy that the enemy were too weak to pose a serious threat. At the same time new stories appeared in the papers depicting Sherman as going about with a "half-wild expression" and quoting him as having said that "the rebels could never be whipped."

Halleck immediately ordered Sherman back to St. Louis. To McClellan he wrote: "I am satisfied that General Sherman's physical and mental system is so completely broken by labor and care as to render him for the present entirely unfit for duty." Judging that Sherman needed rest, he gave him twenty-days' leave. Accompanied by Ellen, who had rushed to St. Louis on hearing that her husband once more was in trouble, Sherman returned to Lancaster.

Soon the Cincinnati *Commercial* published, under the headline, "General William T. Sherman Insane," an article which asserted that Sherman was "stark mad" while commanding in Kentucky, that in Missouri "the shocking fact that he was a madman was developed by orders that his subordinates knew to be preposterous and refused to obey," and that he had now been "relieved altogether from command." Numerous other newspapers reprinted the story.

Through his brother-in-law Phil Ewing, Sherman published a rebuttal to the *Commercial*'s article, which he charged had been written by a reporter whom he had arrested in Kentucky for defying military regulations. Nevertheless, he felt totally crushed. Again he had failed, again he had disgraced himself, again he had brought shame on his family. Efforts by Ellen, John and Thomas Ewing, Sr. to cheer him up proved unavailing, as did assurances from Halleck that he had not lost confidence in him. After returning to St. Louis, where Halleck assigned him to drilling recruits, he wrote John: "I am so sensible now of my disgrace from having exaggerated the force of our enemy in Kentucky that I do think I should have committed suicide were it not for my children. I do not think I can again be entrusted with a command. . . ."

Perhaps no general subsequently considered great performed more miserably when first given command responsibility than did Sherman in Kentucky and Missouri. There were three reasons why this was so. One is obvious and simple: inexperience. The Confederate general Richard S. Ewell remarked that as a result of his prewar military career he learned everything there was to know about commanding a troop of cavalry but forgot everything else. Sherman did not have the opportunity to learn even that much, and not until Bull Run did he as much as witness a battle. Hence he was right in not seeking a top command at the outset of the war, and it was unfortunate for him that he was thrust into one nevertheless.

The second reason likewise is quite apparent: Sherman lacked mental balance. Although it was made by a man who disliked him, there was considerable truth in the comment that Sherman's "brain is like a splendid piece

Mrs. Ellen Sherman.

of machinery with all of the screws a little loose.'' In Kentucky and Missouri those screws threatened to pop out altogether. Furthermore, he possessed too much imagination—a serious defect in a military man. Sherman once described himself as being "somewhat blind to what occurs near me," but as having a "clear perception of things and events remote." The trouble was that the "things and events" which he saw so clearly at a distance often were not actually there.

The third reason is more basic and also more complex. Sherman was gifted with an exceptional intelligence, enormous energy, and an impressive personality. Naturally he was aware of his superiority and just as naturally aspired to, even anticipated, a high degree of success in life. Further stimulating his ambition was a desire to prove himself worthy of the charity and support of his foster father and of the hopes and confidence of his wife and the rest of the Ewing-Sherman clan. But instead of rising spectacularly to the top, he spent his years from 20 to 40 bobbing up and down, going nowhere in particular. Meanwhile his younger brother John was achieving the distinction that the family had predicted for him. By 1861 Sherman was a classic example of a not uncommon type: a man who believes that because of his own qualities he deserves success but who, because of his past experience, doubts he ever will attain it; bad luck and the shortcomings of others will always deny it to him.

This seemingly paradoxical mixture of ambition and pessimism explains, even more than his realization that he lacked combat experience, why Sherman sought a subordinate post when the Civil War started. It also explains his conduct when placed in command in Kentucky and after being given a quasi-independent assignment in Missouri. By exaggerating the strength and aggressiveness of the enemy, by declaring his own forces hopelessly inadequate, and by denouncing the politicians in Washington for ignoring the dangers facing him, he prepared in advance alibis for the inevitable disaster to come. By constantly castigating himself and by expressing the wish to retire into some "quiet corner"—even commit suicide—he made it impossible for his family to reproach him for failing to succeed: Nothing they could say in criticism of him could match his own self-condemnation.

Sherman at the beginning of the Civil War possessed the physical courage and mental quickness to perform well in the heat of combat, as he demonstrated at Bull Run, but he lacked the strength of mind and character to exercise successfully a highly responsible independent command. What he needed was someone to guide and steady him, and to bear the burden of responsibility while he became better acquainted with war, developed the ability to view affairs more realistically, and—most important of all—learned to trust himself.

Early in 1862, while Sherman drilled troops in St. Louis, another native of Ohio was commanding them farther down the Mississippi River at Cairo, Illinois. He was slightly younger and much shorter than Sherman, but like him had graduated from West Point, resigned from the army, and experienced a rather dismal time of it as a civilian. In the summer of 1861, while commanding a regiment of volunteers in northeast Missouri, he had set out to attack a camp of Confederate guerrillas. It was the first time ever he had been in sole charge of a military operation and as he approached the camp, he later wrote, "my heart kept getting higher and higher until it felt to me as though it was in my throat." But on coming into sight of the camp he found that the Confederates had fled. "My heart resumed its place." Also, it occurred to him that the enemy had been as much afraid of him as he had been of the enemy. "This was a view of the question I had never taken before but it was one I never forgot afterwards. From that event to the close of the war, I never experienced trepidation upon confronting any enemy, though I always felt more or less anxiety. I never forgot that he had as much reason to fear my forces as I had his. The lesson was valuable."

The name of the man who learned this valuable lesson was Ulysses S. Grant. Sherman had known him slightly at West Point and had exchanged a few words with him in 1857 when he met him peddling firewood on the streets of St. Louis. Starting with 1862 a very special relationship would develop between these two men, one that was useful to Grant but absolutely essential to Sherman.

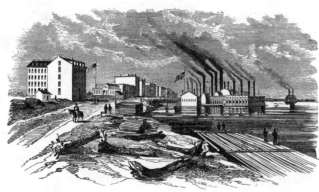

Lossing's Civil War in America

Waterfront at Cairo, Illinois.

PART II
The Subordinate
by Albert Castel

The most important decision Major General Henry Wager Halleck made during the Civil War came when, as commander of Union forces in Missouri and western Kentucky, he permitted Brigadier General U.S. Grant to attack and capture Forts Henry and Donelson in February 1862. This broke open the Confederates' front in the West and caused them to retreat from Kentucky and middle Tennessee. Following in their wake, the Federal Army of Major General Don Carlos Buell occupied Nashville on the Cumberland River and Grant moved south along the Tennessee River.

As this took place, Halleck made what possibly was his second most important decision: He gave Sherman, who had been relegated to drilling recruits in St. Louis after his failures in Kentucky and Missouri, another chance. According to Sherman's highly sympathetic biographer, Lloyd Lewis, he did so out of a self-interested desire to ingratiate himself with the politically influential Ewing-Sherman clan. Conceivably this was at least a minor consideration, but the weight of evidence and logic supports the conclusion that Halleck was motivated mainly by friendship and a belief that Sherman was capable of rendering, as he assured him, "important service" once his "nervous system so shattered by hard labor, anxiety & exposure" had been restored.

On February 13, after Grant launched his campaign against Forts Henry and Donelson, Halleck posted Sherman to Paducah, Kentucky, with instructions to forward troops and supplies to Grant. He performed this task with commendable efficiency. Also he gained Grant's attention and thanks by writing him notes of encouragement and offering to serve under him at the front despite being senior in rank.

CWTI Collection

William Tecumseh Sherman

Following the capture of the forts, Halleck placed Sherman in command of a newly organized division and assigned him to Grant, who, meanwhile, had been promoted to major general. Sherman loaded his troops (who regarded him with a certain apprehension because of the newspaper stories about his being crazy) aboard steamboats and proceeded up the Tennessee River with orders to cut the strategic Memphis & Charleston Railroad, which ran near the Tennessee-Mississippi line. Unable to do so because heavy rains had turned the roads into quagmires, he turned back and joined other Union forces which had disembarked at Pittsburg Landing. This area, he reported, would be the best place from which to attack the Confederates, who were concentrating at Corinth, Mississippi, some twenty miles to the southwest. Grant agreed, and during the latter part of March assembled 33,000 troops at Pittsburg Landing plus 5,000 more at Crump's Landing five miles to the north.

Halleck instructed Grant not to advance until reinforced by Buell's 40,000-man army which was moving overland from Nashville. While awaiting Buell, Grant decided to use this lull in operations to better train his own forces, most of whom were raw recruits. Accordingly he deployed the five divisions he had at Pittsburg Landing with an eye to convenience in drilling them rather than fighting a battle. For the same reason he dismissed as impractical and unnecessary the fortifying of their position. Sherman fully concurred. Like Grant, like nearly all professional military men at this stage of the war, he believed that intrenchments merely made soldiers timid. Furthermore, both he and Grant were confident that the Confederates, who by all accounts were badly demoralized by their recent setbacks, would not be so foolhardy as to leave their base to assault the Federal army at its base; this would have been contrary to the principles of sound strategy!

Both Grant and Sherman were mistaken—almost fatally so. Confederate commander General Albert Sidney Johnston was desperate to reverse the tide of war in the West and to redeem his own woefully impaired military reputation. Therefore he decided to destroy Grant before Buell arrived. On April 3 his army, 40,000 strong, marched northward from Corinth. Bad roads, ineptitude, and inexperience delayed its progress, but during the night of April 5 it reached the vicinity of Pittsburg Landing. The next morning it struck—and struck hard.

The British military historian B.H. Liddell Hart, who rarely finds fault with Grant and Sherman, states that they were victims of a "strategical" surprise but denies that they experienced a "tactical" surprise. Undoubtedly he is right about the first. When the Confederates attacked, Grant was, as he had been for most of the past several days, seven miles away at Savannah, Tennessee, on the east side of the Tennessee River, waiting for Buell. As always during his absences Sherman acted as his de facto deputy at Pittsburg Landing. On April 4 Rebel cavalry appeared near the Federal camp, and on the next day several clashes occurred between patrols from both armies. Furthermore, many Southern soldiers as they approached the Union lines fired their muskets in order to reload them with fresh charges.

General P.G.T. Beauregard, Johnston's second in command, was so convinced that the Yankees could not help being alerted that he proposed calling off the attack and returning to Corinth.

He need not have worried. Grant and Sherman no more anticipated a Confederate offensive than did American commanders the World War II Japanese air raid on Pearl Harbor. Sherman, who probably feared making the same mistake he had in Kentucky and Missouri of exaggerating the enemy threat, scoffed at reports of large Rebel forces being nearby and at those who delivered the reports. On the afternoon of April 5 he telegraphed Grant, "I do not apprehend anything like an attack upon our position." Grant in turn sent a dispatch to Halleck in St. Louis declaring, "I have scarcely the faintest idea of an attack (general one) being made upon us. . . ."

As for Liddell Hart's claim that there was no "tactical" surprise, he supports this (as did Grant and Sherman themselves) by pointing out that most of the Northern troops were able to form in line of battle before the Confederates charged. However, this is a pointless argument. No army as large and undisciplined as Johnston's could possibly have approached its objective without being detected. Indeed, on the morning of April 6 a Union patrol, sent out on the initiative of a Northern major, actually attacked the advancing Southerners before they made their assault. Furthermore, the Confederates were formed in such a fashion, the terrain of such a nature, and the Union camps so scattered that

A Federal battery on Sherman's front retreats under Confederate attack at the Battle of Shiloh. The artist shows tents of Federal camp in the background.

Major General Ulysses Simpson Grant, surprised at Shiloh.

ing and 20,000 more from Buell's army. In the morning Grant counterattacked and the Confederates, with Johnston dead and their strength reduced to no more than 20,000, began retreating back to Corinth.

Grant in his report on the battle singled out Sherman for "special mention" for having "displayed great judgment and skill in the management of his men." Halleck, on arriving at Pittsburg Landing to take personal charge of Grant's and Buell's armies, went further, informing the War Department that "It was the unanimous opinion here that Brig. Gen. W.T. Sherman saved the fortune of the day of the 6th and contributed largely to the glorious victory of the 7th." And Lloyd Lewis in his *Sherman, Fighting Prophet* contends that "So stoutly did Sherman hold the Union right that Johnston failed in his scheme for rolling up the Federal line like a sheet of paper," an opinion echoed by Liddell Hart who states Sherman's resistance on the right flank "formed an invaluable brake on the Confederate advance during its original impulse."

There can be no doubt that Sherman and his troops did preserve the Union right. However, this achievement needs to be placed in a more realistic perspective than it appears in the above quotations. First of all, Johnston did not plan to "roll up" Grant's line from the right. On the contrary he intended to deliver his main thrust against the Federal left with the object either of cutting off Grant from the Tennessee or else forcing him back to that river. That he first struck the Union center (Prentiss) and then the right (Sherman) was the product of circumstances rather than design.

only small portions of both armies were engaged at first, which meant that most of the Federal units had ample time in which to deploy. In brief, only if the Yankees had been deaf, blind and drunk could Johnston have achieved "tactical" surprise in the sense of catching them totally unprepared.

Sherman's division held the extreme Union right and was the second to be assailed, the first being Brigadier General Benjamin Prentiss' division, which was posted to the southwest of Sherman's in the direct line of the Confederate advance. Many of Sherman's inexperienced men fled from the shock of unexpected battle but most of them remained in their hastily formed lines. Sherman helped keep them there by his own calmness, even cheerfulness, under fire. In the words of a newspaper correspondent, his "usually hot nerves" seemed to be soothed by combat.

For several hours his division checked fierce Rebel charges, inflicting and suffering heavy losses in the process. Then, along with the rest of Grant's army, it fell back slowly until by late afternoon it was close to the Tennessee River. During the evening and night 5,000 reinforcements belatedly arrived from Crump's Land-

Later Major General Patrick Ronayne Cleburne lost half of his men in the first day's bitter fighting at Shiloh.

Secondly, Sherman's division enjoyed an extremely strong position even without fortifications. Its right was protected by Owl Creek, its front by Shiloh Creek. Furthermore, unlike Prentiss' division, it benefited from having Brigadier General John McClernand's division within close supporting distance. As a consequence it was nearly impregnable against frontal assault, as witness the fact that Brigadier General Patrick Cleburne's Confederate brigade which spearheaded that assault lost almost one-half its men. Not until Prentiss, who bore the brunt of Johnston's initial attack, retreated were the Rebels able to dislodge Sherman's and McClernand's intermingled forces by hitting their now exposed left flank.

Thirdly, and finally, after Sherman's withdrawal the Confederates made no further serious attacks on him; they lacked the strength and were concentrating on the Union left. This was fortunate for him, for as Liddell Hart points out, by then his division was "only a remnant" which "really formed an appendix to the line of McClernand's division." Most of its men were dead, wounded, or missing, with many of the latter being fugitives. It played only a minor role in the subsequent fighting on April 6, and contributed little to Grant's attack the following day.

To sum up, Sherman performed well in the Battle of Shiloh, but no better than several other division commanders, notably Prentiss, whose stubborn stand in the "Hornet's Nest" gave Grant the time he needed to form a defensive perimeter on the banks of the Tennessee from which he was able to fend off the last feeble Confederate assault and then launch his counterattack. Furthermore, his failure (of which Prentiss also was guilty) to heed the signs and reports of a major enemy offensive was a major reason why Johnston's desperate gamble came so close to success. To his credit, he made no claim to exceptional accomplishment at Shiloh. When, following the battle, he was promoted on Halleck's recommendation to major general, he informed his wife Ellen, "I received today the commission of Major General, but, I know not why, it gives me far less emotion than my old commission as 1st Lieutenant of Artillery. The latter, I knew, I merited; this I doubt. . . ."

Even so the promotion, the commendations from Halleck and Grant and the praise bestowed on him by a number of newspapers restored Sherman's reputation and bolstered his self-confidence. "I have worked hard to keep down," he wrote Ellen with obvious glee, "but somehow I am forced into prominence and might as well submit." To his father-in-law he declared proudly, "I know I can take what position I choose among my peers." Shiloh, for Sherman, was the turning point.

It also strengthened his ties to Grant. He realized that he shared with him much of the responsibility for the Confederates' near victory which, had it been fully achieved, would almost surely have ended both their mili-

Major General John Alexander McClernand.

tary careers in disgrace. When several newspapers denounced Grant as a bloody bungler for allowing himself to be surprised in an unfortified position, Sherman defended him in a public letter while privately vowing "to get even with the miserable class of corrupt editors." More important, on learning that Grant planned to leave the army out of resentment over being relegated by Halleck to the meaningless post of second in command, he persuaded him to reconsider and remain—which, in a sense, was possibly Sherman's greatest contribution to the Northern cause. Grant had good reasons in being grateful to Sherman, who for his part regarded Grant as a man in whom one could place "absolute faith."

However, he doubted that Grant possessed the intellect to be a great "strategist." Instead he considered "Old Brains" Halleck the North's only "Great Man thus far." He credited him with conceiving the plan by which the Confederate front in the West had been broken, was "astonished" by the "sagacity" he showed in his ponderous march on Corinth, and hailed his occupation of that town on May 30 as "a victory as brilliant and important as any recorded in history." When Halleck was summoned to Washington to serve as commander of all Union forces, he declared that there was no other general in the West who could replace him. Even allowing for Sherman's quite justified feeling of gratitude to Halleck for rescuing him from the military scrapheap, these extravagant words of praise for that timid general and his clumsy operations indicate that Sherman himself was still far from ready for high command.

Following the capture of Corinth the Union Army spread out to occupy western Tennessee and northern Mississippi. Sherman took command of the Memphis area. For the first time he had to deal with a large hostile population. At the beginning of the war he had spoken of reconciling Southerners to the Union. Now he believed that: it was impossible to "change the hearts of the people of the South," from which he drew the conclusion that if the Southerners "cannot be made to love us, they can be made to fear us" by making "war so terrible that they will realize the fact that, however brave and gallant and devoted to their country, still they are mortal. . . ."

In September, following a series of guerrilla attacks on unarmed Union supply ships along the Mississippi, Sherman had his soldiers burn the river village of Randolph, Tennessee, in retaliation and announced that henceforth ten families would be expelled from Mem-

phis every time a boat was fired on. He did not carry out the latter threat, but in October he sent troops over to Arkansas, where they destroyed a number of dwellings of persons suspected of aiding guerrillas. These measures, it should be noted, were no more harsh than those that other Northern commanders adopted in attempting to combat partisan warfare. Indeed they were mild in comparison with what his own brother-in-law, Brigadier General Thomas Ewing, Jr., did in Missouri in 1863. He depopulated four counties in an effort to suppress Quantrill's bushwhackers. The principal difference between Sherman and other Union officers who struggled against guerrillas lies not in practice but in the frankness and vehemence with which he justified reprisals against the civilians who in fact did aid the guerrillas. Moreover, he remained sufficiently objective to realize that the conduct of the Federal troops often was of such a nature as to arouse legitimate wrath among Southerners. In an order to his division he declared that "This demoralizing and disgraceful practice of pillage must cease, else the country will rise on us and justly shoot us down like dogs and wild beasts."

In December 1862 Grant made his first attempt to take Vicksburg, employing a plan worked out in collaboration with Sherman. Not only did the two friends hope to eliminate the last major Confederate stronghold on the Mississippi River, but they wanted to anticipate Major General John McClernand, a highly ambitious and influential Illinois politician to whom Lincoln had given command of an expedition against Vicksburg in return for raising troops in the Midwest. Both Sherman and Grant considered McClernand vain, incompetent, non-professional and a dangerous rival to their own military position and prospects.

Grant moved overland with 40,000 soldiers and threatened Lieutenant General John C. Pemberton's 24,000-man Confederate Army at Grenada, Mississippi, with the object of preventing Pemberton from reinforcing Vicksburg, which was held by a garrison of only 6,000. At the same time Sherman at Memphis hastily loaded 30,000 troops (most of whom had been recruited by McClernand) aboard transports and headed down the Mississippi, escorted by Rear Admiral David D. Porter's gunboat flotilla. On December 26 he landed just north of Vicksburg on the east bank of the Yazoo River. The next day he received word that McClernand was on his way to take command of the expedition. On the other hand there was no news from Grant and there were signs that Vicksburg was being reinforced. Fearful that delay would ruin any chance of victory he assaulted the Rebel defense line, which consisted of forts and trenches atop steep bluffs overlooking Chickasaw Bayou.

The attack was a total failure. Sherman lost 1,776 men, the Confederates only 187. Publicly Sherman took full responsibility for the defeat, privately he blamed poor leadership by Brigadier General George W. Mor-

Brigadier General Thomas Ewing, Jr., Sherman's brother-in-law.

Waterhouse's battery of Sherman's corps in position during the Siege of Vicksburg.

gan, whose division spearheaded the assault. Neither diagnosis, however, was correct. Unknown to Sherman, Grant had retreated northward from Grenada, thereby enabling Pemberton to reinforce Vicksburg so heavily with first-rate troops that it would have required a miracle for Sherman to break through the defenses on the Chickasaw Bluffs.

Grant's official reason for retreating was the destruction of his main supply base at Holly Springs, Mississippi, by Rebel cavalry on December 20. No doubt this was an important factor, but as Liddell Hart notes, Grant himself admitted that he could have lived off the countryside for another two months. Quite likely the news that McClernand was en route to Memphis had an even greater impact on Grant, for as soon as he received it he decided to go to Memphis and assume personal charge of the Vicksburg expedition. To be sure, he sent Sherman word of his withdrawal but this could not reach Sherman in time to prevent what was now a pointless assault on Chickasaw Bluffs. In effect Grant left Sherman in the lurch. But if Sherman resented Grant's conduct, he never mentioned it. In his memoirs he merely stated that "Grant sent me word" of his withdrawal but "it did not reach me in time."

On January 2 McClernand arrived on the Yazoo River and superseded Sherman, who was relegated to command of a corps. Realizing that it would be futile to renew the attempt to take Vicksburg, McClernand adopted a suggestion from Sherman and moved against the Confederate fort at Arkansas Post on the Arkansas River. A land assault directed by Sherman got nowhere but fire from Porter's gunboats scared some of the 5,000 defenders into making an unauthorized surrender, there-

by enabling the Federals to seize the fort on January 11. Amusingly, when Grant first heard of McClernand's expedition to Arkansas Post he denounced it as a "wild goose chase," but on learning that it had succeeded and that Sherman had originated it he promptly dubbed it a "very important" victory.

Brigadier General George W. Morgan, privately blamed by Sherman for the Union defeat at Chickasaw Bayou.

McClernand claimed and obtained credit for the conquest of Arkansas Post, whereas several newspapers condemned Sherman for the repulse at Chickasaw Bluffs. Once more his spirits drooped, again he talked of resigning. In particular he resented serving under McClernand: "Mr. Lincoln intended to insult me and the military profession by putting McClernand over me," he complained to brother Senator John Sherman. However, he felt better after Grant, with Halleck's backing and Lincoln's acquiescence, assumed command of all forces operating along the Mississippi. The result was that McClernand became, like himself, just a corps commander. Also his gratitude to Grant increased when Grant supported him in expelling a hostile reporter from his camp.

Brigadier General Stephen G. Burbridge plants the Stars and Stripes on the parapet of Fort Hindman during McClernand's capture of Arkansas Post, Jan. 11, 1863. Sketch by W.R. McComas.

The Soldier in Our Civil War

Late in April Grant began the brilliant campaign of maneuver, battle and siege which culminated on July 4 with the capture of Vicksburg and Pemberton's army. At the outset Sherman was pessimistic—he feared that Grant was taking excessive risks. But when it ended he frankly acknowledged to Grant that he had been right and Sherman wrong. In a moment of perceptive analysis of both himself and Grant he told a confidant, "I am a much brighter man than Grant; I can see things quicker than he can, and know more about books than he does, but I'll tell you where he beats me, and where he beats the world: he don't care a cent for what he can't see the enemy doing, but it scares me like hell!"

Despite his initial misgivings about Grant's strategy, Sherman executed his assignments in the Vicksburg operations with exemplary efficiency. First his corps, the XV, kept Pemberton off balance by bluffing another attack on Vicksburg from the north while Grant with his other two corps, McClernand's XIII and Major General James B. McPherson's XVII, swung across the Arkansas and the Mississippi Rivers south of the fortress city. Then he marched quickly to reinforce Grant, bringing badly needed supplies and transport. Next he participated in the sweep eastward to Jackson, Mississippi, where he destroyed that town's rail connections while Grant turned west, routed Pemberton at Champion Hill, and drove him back into Vicksburg. Up to this point

Sherman's corps had done little fighting but now it joined in Grant's two futile attempts to storm Vicksburg. In large part, during the second attempt it suffered severe casualties because a false report by McClernand, that he was on the verge of a breakthrough, caused him to prolong the assault. This incident and a brazen attempt by McClernand to grab the credit for defeating Pemberton provided Grant with a most welcome excuse for relieving that politician-general from command. For both him and Sherman this was a victory which in its way was as satisfying as the capture of Vicksburg.

As soon as Pemberton surrendered Grant sent Sherman with seven divisions to drive away the small Confederate Army that General Joseph E. Johnston had assembled east of Vicksburg. Johnston made a brief stand at Jackson, then retreated to Meridian, Mississippi. Sherman did not pursue. Instead he completed the job of destroying Jackson that he had started earlier. "Jackson will no longer be a point of danger," he informed Grant. "The inhabitants are subjugated. They cry aloud for mercy. The land is devastated for 30 miles around."

It is clear Sherman had a penchant for raids. Soon after Shiloh he had led a task force deep into Mississippi to burn a railroad bridge, and during the Yazoo River Expedition he had detached a division to wreck a railroad line in Arkansas (a pointless venture which conceivably cost him what chance he had of success at Chickasaw Bluffs by delaying his attack there). By the summer of 1863 he conceived of large-scale sweeps through the country as a good, perhaps the best, means

Hooker's troops storming Lookout Mountain, threatening Bragg's left. Sherman's attack was against the Confederate right on Missionary Ridge.

to break Confederate resistance by literally bringing home to Southerners the folly of their wickedness in trying to destroy the Union.

He evidently came to consider it futile to make a serious effort to prevent his troops from pillaging, vandalizing, and destroying private property—the sort of conduct which he had angrily denounced during the first year of the war. The Vicksburg campaign revealed to him the ease with which even a big army could live off the land—provided it kept moving.

Grant highly praised Sherman's performance in the Vicksburg operations and so did Sherman. To his brother John he wrote: "The share I have personally borne in all these events is one in which you may take pride for me. You know how I have avoided notoriety; and the press . . . may strip me of all popular applause, but not a soldier in the Army of the Tennessee but knows the part I have borne in this great drama. . . . In the events resulting thus, the guiding minds and hands were Grant's, Sherman's, and McPherson's. . . ." This was boasting —but it was true.

In October Grant became over-all commander in the West, with the special assignment of redeeming the situation at Chattanooga, where the Union Army of the Cumberland, after being defeated at Chickamauga, was hard-pressed by General Braxton Bragg's Confederates. As a consequence Sherman succeeded Grant as head of the Army of the Tennessee. He would have preferred, he told John, to have remained a corps commander, "But with Grant I will undertake anything within reason."

Grant transferred the Army of the Tennessee to the Chattanooga area. On November 24 he mounted an offensive designed to dislodge Bragg from Missionary Ridge, the heights overlooking Chattanooga from the east. A corps under Major General Joseph Hooker seized Lookout Mountain, thereby threatening Bragg's left flank; Major General George H. Thomas' Army of the Cumberland menaced the enemy's center; and Sherman, after crossing the Tennessee River in boats and over a rapidly laid pontoon bridge, moved against the Confederate right flank at the northern end of Missionary Ridge (in what Grant intended to be the main Union attack). On coming into sight of the Rebel position at 3:30 p.m. he discovered that the terrain over which he would have to advance to reach them was more difficult than Grant and he had thought. Instead of assaulting, he had his troops dig in. As a result Thomas remained motionless, his orders being not to attack until Sherman did.

Did Sherman blunder, as some critics subsequently charged, by "going to ground" instead of pushing forward? Probably he did. When he crossed the Tennessee the Confederates had only a thin screen of pickets cov-

ering their extreme right on Missionary Ridge. Bragg did not order his reserve, Major General Patrick Cleburne's division, to that point until 2 p.m.; not until late in the afternoon did two of Cleburne's brigades face Sherman, and not until after midnight did Cleburne (who had expected Bragg to withdraw from Missionary Ridge because of the loss of Lookout Mountain) begin fortifying the position. It is reasonable to believe that a strong, determined attack by Sherman once he got most of his approximately 25,000 troops on the east side of the Tennessee would have enabled him to seize the northern end of Missionary Ridge (which was held for its entire length by only 26,000 Confederate infantry) and outflank Bragg. By failing to assault, Sherman showed himself to be overly concerned by what might be on "the other side of the hill."

Grant ordered Sherman to attack at dawn on November 25. However he did not do so until midmorning. Later he claimed that he expected Bragg to attack him at daylight! If so, he was guilty either of timidity or wishful thinking—or both. In any event his troops gained nothing and lost heavily. They were up against some of the toughest fighters in the Confederate Army doggedly defending an almost impregnable position. The only

Library of Congress

and in danger of starving. Sherman drove away the Confederates and reached Knoxville—only to discover that Burnside had been in little danger and possessed ample food. Since his own men had suffered severely from cold, hunger, and fatigue in marching to Knoxville, understandably Sherman was disgusted.

In January he returned to Mississippi. Early the following month he set out for Vicksburg with 20,000 infantry. He again occupied what was left of Jackson, then pushed on to Meridian, where he spent five days destroying factories, military supplies, and railroad tracks. Then he marched back to Vicksburg, leaving in his wake, as he put it, "a swath of desolation fifty miles broad" and followed by "about ten miles of negroes."

The professed objective of the Meridian Expedition was to make it impossible for the Confederates to assemble sufficient force near the Mississippi to endanger Northern shipping on the river. However since the Confederates in this region soon had all they could handle attempting to turn back various Federal incursions, the Meridian Expedition in fact served no significant strategic purpose. But it did confirm for Sherman that a large, fast-moving army could support itself deep inside enemy territory. Also it marked a further application of his belief that it was necessary to strike at the Southern economy and people if the war was to be won.

In March Grant became commander of the entire Union Army with the rank of lieutenant general. In announcing his promotion to Sherman, he expressed thanks to Sherman and McPherson "as *the men* to whom, above all others, I feel indebted for whatever I have had of success." Sherman promptly replied, declaring that on the contrary it was he who was obligated to Grant: ". . . when you have completed your best preparations you go into battle without hesitation . . . no doubts, no reserve; and I tell you that it was this that made me act with confidence." Sherman then went on to urge Grant, who had gone to Washington, not to remain there and be ruined by intriguing politicians. Instead he should return to the West: "Here lies the seat of the coming empire; and from the West, when our task is done, we will make short work of Charleston and Richmond. . . ."

Grant, however, chose to establish his headquarters in the East, both to exercise with maximum efficiency his new responsibilities and to supervise personally operations in Virginia. Accordingly he named Sherman to succeed him as commander in the West. Ever since admirers of Thomas have maintained that he deserved that post. They point out that he had never failed but had always succeeded, that he had saved the day at Chicka-

thing that prevented Sherman's casualty list from being longer was that the nature of the ground made it impossible for him to deploy his entire force, with the result that he used only six out of sixteen available brigades. Apparently it never occurred to him to outflank the enemy position by sending some of the surplus brigades across Chickamauga Creek, which emptied into the Tennessee near the northern end of Missionary Ridge and over which his engineers had also thrown a pontoon bridge. But then Grant had instructed him to assault Bragg's right, not circle around it.

At 2 p.m. Grant, realizing that his planned strategy was not working and hoping to draw the Confederates away from Sherman's front, ordered Thomas to seize the first line of enemy trenches at the foot of the center of Missionary Ridge. Thomas' troops did so. Then, on their own spontaneous impulse, they charged onward. The poorly positioned, thinly spread, and already half-demoralized defenders fled in utter panic. Thus Grant won another great victory, but not the way he intended, and with Sherman, to whom he had assigned the star part, playing only a supporting role.

Immediately after the battle Grant sent Sherman and the Army of the Tennessee to relieve Major General Ambrose Burnside's forces at Knoxville where, reportedly, they were besieged by a superior Confederate Army mauga and won the day at Chattanooga. In contrast Sherman had panicked in Kentucky, broken down in Missouri, been surprised at Shiloh, and bloodily repulsed at Chickasaw Bluffs, Vicksburg, and Missionary Ridge.

Sherman himself said that Thomas was qualified for the Western command and declared that he would have been perfectly willing to have served under him. However, Grant's association with Thomas had been brief and formal, and for reasons that are somewhat obscure he disliked and distrusted him. On the other hand Grant and Sherman were the closest of friends, bound together by shared troubles, shared triumphs, and reciprocal gratitude. Grant's choice of Sherman was not only inevitable but probably for the best. Even if it be accepted that Thomas possessed greater military talent than Sherman, he would not have received from Grant the confidence and freedom of action that Sherman enjoyed and would have been hamstrung in the conduct of operations—as in the case of Nashville in December 1864 when Grant, totally without cause, nearly removed Thomas on the eve of the most complete battlefield victory of the war.

Sherman, who had failed miserably as an independent commander in 1861, received the second most important and responsible military assignment in the Federal service. He accepted it calmly. Behind him now were three years of war, two of them under the leadership and tutelage of Grant. He had learned much about his profession but above all had acquired confidence in himself. Shortly before becoming head of the Western armies he had declared that he had "done a full share in the real achievements of this war." He did not doubt that he would go on to even greater achievements. The upcoming campaigns of 1864, he wrote Ellen, would be decisive. "All that has gone before is mere skirmishing. The war now begins, and with heavy well-disciplined masses the issue must be settled in hard-fought battles.

Battles & Leaders of the Civil War

Major General George Henry Thomas. Sherman considered him best qualified for the Western command.

I think we can whip them in Alabama and it may be Georgia. . . ."

Sherman, the loyal subordinate, now was ready to become Sherman the conqueror.

VOLUNTEERS

As was mentioned in Part I of this Sherman biography, the general's dislike for volunteer troops at the outset of the war was founded on hard experience off the battlefield, as well as on it, as this brief contemporary news account attests. It is taken from the Harper's Weekly of June 15, 1861.

Cheers rose from the crowds as the dragoons went by; but before those cheers were done a vast rumbling was heard in the same direction which the dragoons had come from, and in the next instant [William T.] Sherman's famous battery, with six horses to each gun, were seen tearing around into the Avenue at fearful speed, the troopers and cannoneers screaming wildly, like so many madmen, as they went. Their rate of progress was so swift that in turning the Fourteenth Street corner the whirl of the gun-carriage spun off a left-hand wheel, and dashed the vehicle against an iron post, flinging the men off the caissons, and knocking down two of the horses. But the remaining horses were whipped on, dragging the fallen animals on their sides along the road, and the naked axle doing duty for the missing wheel. They passed shouting out of sight, and the accelerating huzzas of the equally crazy multitude went after them as long as their wheels and voices could be heard.

PART III
The Conqueror
by Albert Castel

On March 20, 1864, Lieutenant General U.S. Grant and Major General William T. Sherman met in a room at the Burnet House Hotel in Cincinnati to formulate the strategy by which they hoped to win the war. The plan that emerged was quite obvious and quite sound: While Grant hammered at General Robert E. Lee in Virginia, Sherman was to move into Georgia against the Confederacy's other main army, that of General Joseph E. Johnston. He was "to break it up, and to get into the interior of the enemy's country" as far as he could go, "inflicting all the damage" possible on the South's war resources. Both Grant and Sherman were to attack simultaneously and not cease attacking in order to prevent the Confederates from shifting troops from one front to the other.

To accomplish this task Sherman collected 100,000 men in the Chattanooga region of Tennessee, divided into Major General George H. Thomas' 60,000-man Army of the Cumberland, the 25,000 men of Major General James B. McPherson's Army of the Tennessee (soon increased to 34,000 by the addition of another corps), and Major General John M. Schofield's 15,000 troops called the Army of the Ohio. Nearly all of these troops and their officers were tough veterans thoroughly experienced in the latest techniques of combat. However, their discipline off the battlefield was poor and in the months ahead it would grow worse. The artillery numbered 254 pieces and was well-served. On the other hand, the cavalry, made up of 6,000 troopers organized into three divisions, was by Sherman's own admission inferior in "quantity and quality" to the enemy's. All in all, despite the deficiency in discipline and the weakness of the cavalry (for which he had little use in any case) Sherman rightly believed that he had "one of the best armies in the world."

His chief concern was the single railroad line connecting Chattanooga with Nashville and Louisville. It provided his forces with the bulk of their supplies. Should it falter in its operations or be cut by the Confederates the consequences could be disastrous. So prior to launching his offensive, he did everything possible to insure its efficient functioning and protect it against enemy cavalry raids. At the same time he made well-conceived arrangements to rebuild the railroad which ran through northern Georgia to Atlanta so that the Confederates would be unable to bring his army to a standstill by destroying it as they retreated. Thanks to this forethought and preparation, he was never seriously hampered by a shortage of food, forage, or material during the ensuing campaign. It was the greatest logistic achievement of the war, one which made possible the Union victory in Georgia and which far surpassed anything that any European army of the time was capable of doing.

On May 5, two days after Grant advanced against Lee, Sherman began his offensive. Johnston waited for him at Dalton, Georgia, with approximately 55,000 men; the vast majority were battle-hardened veterans. He hoped, apparently even expected, Sherman to attack him head-on and accordingly, constructed formidable fortifications. But Sherman had no intention of being so obliging. Instead, he sent Thomas and Schofield to demonstrate against Johnston's front while McPherson circled westward to his rear. He instructed McPherson to proceed through Snake Creek Gap (which Johnston had left unguarded because of his assumption that the Federals would strike directly at Dalton), tear up the railroad in the Resaca area, and then retire back into Snake Creek Gap. Johnston, his supply line broken,

Major General William Tecumseh Sherman, from a rare photograph after the war.

would then have to retreat, pursued by Thomas and Schofield; McPherson would assail his flank as he passed through Resaca. If all went as planned, Johnston's army would be smashed and not only Georgia but also the Carolinas would be open to conquest.

But all did not go as planned. McPherson successfully penetrated Snake Creek Gap on May 9 but then encountered difficult terrain and unexpected resistance of unknown strength. Instead of pushing forward in full strength, he merely skirmished, and only a handful of his troops reached the railroad and did no damage. At nightfall, fearing that Johnston might send a strong force to pounce on him from the north, he fell back to Snake Creek Gap. From there he reported his failure to cut the railroad to Sherman, adding that he could have done so had he possessed a division of good cavalry.

When Sherman learned that McPherson had passed through Snake Creek Gap he exclaimed, "I've got Joe Johnston dead!" But on receiving McPherson's report that the railroad had not been broken, he expressed anger and disappointment. Later he stated in his 1875 *Memoirs* that McPherson "could have placed his whole force astride the railroad above Resaca" and enabled the Union Army to trap and destroy Johnston. "McPherson," he continued, "seems to have been a little timid. Still, he was justified by his orders."

Sherman's criticism of McPherson is correct except for the last phrase. It should read "victimized by his orders." For Sherman did not tell McPherson to place "his whole force astride the railroad." He was merely to cut it, then fall back. Consequently McPherson conceived and conducted his operation as a raid rather than a move to block Johnston's line of retreat. To have done otherwise would have been for him to have shown great boldness and enterprise—far more, for example, than Sherman personally displayed at the Battle of Chattanooga, where his excess caution and rigid adherence to orders cost the Federals a chance to inflict an even worse defeat on the Confederates.

It was Thomas who suggested the Snake Creek maneuver to Sherman and had proposed making it with his Army of the Cumberland, indicating that he thought in terms of cutting Johnston's line of retreat as well as his line of supply. Sherman, however, preferred to use McPherson's smaller army and a lesser objective. By so doing he set the stage for the failure of the movement and consequently deserves, along with McPherson, to be criticized for being "a little timid."

After receiving McPherson's message that the railroad had not been broken, Sherman decided to send Thomas' army through Snake Creek Gap after all, leaving only Schofield and some cavalry in Johnston's front. Had he moved swiftly he still might have cut off Johnston. However, assuming that Johnston would "make no detachments" from his Dalton line, he did not hurry Thomas' march. As a result, when the combined forces of Thomas and McPherson emerged from Snake Creek Gap on the evening of May 13, they found Johnston's army with another corps and increased to about 70,000, strongly entrenched around Resaca.

With the frustration of his Snake Creek Gap plan Sherman lost what proved to be his best opportunity to accomplish his primary strategic mission—to "break up" Johnston's army. But although he paid lip service to it, in his own mind this was never his real objective. In letters written to his wife and brother prior to launching his invasion of Georgia he spoke constantly and solely of taking the great railroad and manufacturing center of Atlanta. Obviously he found this goal, which was in accordance with his secondary assignment "to get into the interior of the enemy's country," more congenial: It harmonized with his belief that the best way to win the war was to destroy the will and ability of the South to wage it.

During the next month Sherman and Johnston performed a sort of military waltz across the mountains and valleys of northern Georgia. Always both armies entrenched on coming into contact; rarely did either make a major attack; they skirmished almost constantly. Sooner or later Sherman, realizing that he could not break through the enemy's front, would take advantage of his superior numbers and his possession of the strategic initiative and slide one of his armies—usually McPherson's—around one of Johnston's flanks towards the railroad in his rear. Invariably Johnston would anticipate the move and retreat to the threatened point, where he would be found waiting and ready. Throughout all of this maneuvering Sherman, despite making some mistakes and missing some opportunities, displayed a skill which probably would have brought him a decisive victory over a less wary opponent. As it was he won the confidence and even the admiration of his soldiers, the majority of whom had seen enough war to appreciate good generalship. Soon not only the men of the Army of the Tennessee, his old command, but all of the Union troops were affectionately calling him "Uncle Billy."

By mid-June the Confederates had been maneuvered back almost to Marietta, less than 20 miles from Atlanta. But now they seemed determined to stay put. Anchoring their line on Kennesaw Mountain, a height which dominated the entire countryside, they fended off Sherman's attempts to get around them until his forces were stretched so thin that he feared to spread them farther. However, reasoning that Johnston's line must also be close to the breaking point, he decided to strike it head on at Kennesaw Mountain. If he could smash through there he could wreck the entire enemy army. And even if the attack failed, it would teach the Confederates and his own troops what he believed would be a salutary lesson: Not to expect him always to go around the flank.

On June 27 two divisions, one from the Army of

the Cumberland, the other from the Army of the Tennessee, marched up the slopes of Kennesaw Mountain. None of their officers and men believed that the assault could succeed. They were right. The Confederates, who had been hoping for just such a chance, mowed them down in heaps. Unable to advance and afraid to retreat, the survivors frantically dug in. When the fighting finally ended, 2,500 of some of the North's best soldiers lay dead or wounded. Two days later Sherman wrote his wife, "I begin to regard the death and mangling of a couple of thousand men as a small affair, a kind of morning dash. . . ."

Soon after the Kennesaw debacle McPherson and Schofield again began curling around the Confederate flanks; apparently such a maneuver was feasible after all. Johnston promptly withdrew to an already prepared stronghold on the north bank of the Chattahoochee

General Joseph Eggleston Johnston. His strategic withdrawal before Sherman earned him President Davis' displeasure.

River—the last natural barrier before Atlanta only five miles away. This move surprised Sherman, who expected the Confederates to make a stand on the south side of the river, but it did not baffle him. On July 8 he got Schofield's army across the Chattahoochee east of Johnston's position and forced him to fall back all the way to Atlanta.

This was too much for Confederate President Jefferson Davis. Convinced that Johnston had no intention of trying to hold Atlanta, on July 17 he replaced him with General John Bell Hood, who promised to make a fight for the city.

Hood kept his promise. On July 20 he struck Thomas at Peachtree Creek north of Atlanta. He rocked "The Rock of Chickamauga" but finally was driven back with heavy losses. Assuming that the Confederates had shot their bolt and now would evacuate Atlanta, Sherman then ordered his forces to sweep forward and occupy the city.

This time he was careless. On July 22, with two-thirds of his army, Hood pounced on the Army of the Tennessee east of Atlanta. The Confederates surprised both Sherman and McPherson, killed the latter, and savagely attacked in front, flank, and rear. Only luck and stalwart fighting saved the Army of the Tennessee from disaster. Sherman helped repulse the enemy assault by forming scores of cannons into a "monster battery" that cut bloody furrows through the Rebel ranks. However, he refused to call on Thomas and Schofield for reinforcements, explaining afterward in his *Memoirs* that "if any assistance were rendered by either of the other armies, the Army of the Tennessee would be jealous." A far better reason for allowing the Army of the Tennessee to slug it out alone would have been an attack on Atlanta by Thomas who, given the weakness of the defenders facing him, might well have taken the city or, at the very least, forced Hood to break off his assault on the Army of the Tennessee. But apparently it never occurred to Sherman to order such a move.

Both of Hood's grand sorties were defeated but they stopped the Federal drive on Atlanta from the north and east. Sherman responded by swinging the Army of the Tennessee, now under Major General Oliver O. Howard, around to the west side of Atlanta. This cut the sole remaining railroad connecting it with the rest of the South and compelled Hood to abandon the city. Again Hood counterattacked, this time at Ezra Church on July 28. Although the Army of the Tennessee slaughtered the Confederates it was unable to reach the railroad. Sherman then sent his cavalry southward against the tracks; not only did it fail to do any appreciable damage, but an entire brigade and its commander were captured. Cavalry, Sherman concluded disgustedly, "could not, or would not, make a sufficient lodgement on the railroad" to break it; so, early in August he tried once more with his infantry, only to be blocked at Utoy Creek southwest of Atlanta.

Northerners began to fear, Southerners began to

hope, that Sherman was as bogged down at Atlanta as Grant was at Richmond. However both Sherman and his men remained supremely confident of capturing Atlanta—it was merely a question of time. Meanwhile, after three months of almost constant marching and fighting, they needed an opportunity to get their second wind physically and psychologically. Therefore during the balance of August Sherman resorted to siege war, pounding Atlanta with large cannons. This bombardment made life miserable for the civilian population but did inconsequential military damage. The only positive function it served was to give the Northern troops

View from a Confederate fort on Peachtree Street, looking south toward the besieged city of Atlanta.

and people the feeling that at least something was being done against the defiant enemy inside the city.

By the end of August Sherman was ready to make another effort to slice Hood's railroad lifeline. He correctly perceived that previous attempts had failed because Hood had been able to anticipate them, they had been made too close to Atlanta, and they had been backed by inadequate strength. This time he avoided all of these mistakes. First, he pulled his army out of the trenches around Atlanta, causing Hood to jump to the conclusion that the cavalry raid he had launched earlier against Sherman's supply line had succeeded and that the Federals were retreating back towards Chattanooga. Next, after posting one corps to guard the rail bridge across the Chattahoochee, Sherman hurled the bulk of his army at Jonesboro, a village on the railroad twenty miles south of Atlanta.

Hood realized his mistake too late and reacted with too little. On September 1 Sherman's troops overwhelmed the Confederates defending Jonesboro. Hood had no choice except to evacuate Atlanta, which he did that night. The next day the Union corps which had been left at the Chattahoochee occupied the city. Sherman telegraphed Washington: "So Atlanta is ours and fairly won."

The strategy by which Sherman dislodged Hood from Atlanta was well-conceived and executed. But should he also have destroyed Hood's battered army? Some historians argue that he could have intercepted the Confederates when they pulled out of Atlanta, and that failing that he should have pursued them to Lovejoy's Station, to where they retreated after the Battle of Jonesboro.

Probably the first criticism is justified: Sherman was too cautious again. But the second one is dubious: In all likelihood the Confederates would have fallen back farther south if pressed by Sherman at Lovejoy's Station, and he could not have followed them without experiencing serious supply problems. Also, Sherman was not alone in being preoccupied with taking Atlanta—it was also the obsession of his troops, as their diaries and letters abundantly demonstrate. Once they held that objective in their grasp they were psychologically incapable of foregoing its immediate enjoyment. Even the normally stolid Thomas "snapped his fingers, whistled, and almost danced" when he learned that the Confederates had abandoned the city.

The "Calico House," Sherman's headquarters in Atlanta, was also a hospital for several months.

The capture of Atlanta was one of the decisive events of the Civil War. It strongly shook the South's ability and will to continue fighting, it revived the flagging determination of the North, and it assured—perhaps even made possible—Lincoln's re-election, which earlier had seemed doubtful even to Lincoln. It was Sherman's greatest military achievement, one for which he received and deserved most of the credit, and it fulfilled his forecast, made in 1861, that the first leaders in the war would fail and be cast aside, but that a "second or third set will rise, and amongst them I may be . . ."

Sherman spent the rest of September resting his army in Atlanta. In order to turn the city into a "pure Gibralter" he forced all civilians to leave it. The Confederates protested this act of "studied and ingenious cruelty." Sherman answered with one of the epigrammatic half-truths typical of him: "War is cruelty, and you cannot refine it. . . ."

Early in October the indefatigable Hood swung into northern Georgia with the purpose of drawing Sherman out of Atlanta by threatening his supply line, then drawing him out of Georgia by invading Tennessee. Leaving

Confederate fort that became Federal Fort No. 7 at Atlanta. This view looks north toward the Chattanooga Railroad past guns of Battery M, 5th US Artillery. General Sherman leans on the parapet in the right background.

a corps to hold Atlanta, Sherman with the bulk of his army pursued Hood all the way to Dalton, then westward across the Alabama line, but was unable to catch him. By the middle of the month he found himself in a strategic dilemma, the consequence of his failure to destroy the Johnston-Hood forces. On the one hand, it obviously was futile to chase Hood who, as Sherman put it, "can turn and twist like a fox." On the other hand should he move into Tennessee to defend it against Hood this would make the capture of Atlanta seem a barren victory and have a depressing effect on Northern morale on the eve of the presidential election.

Sherman's solution, which he proposed to Grant, was to leave Hood to Thomas, who he had sent to take command in Tennessee, and return to Atlanta from where he would march to Savannah and "make Georgia howl." This plan was motivated by Sherman's penchant for raiding and his desire to terrorize the Southern people into submission. Nevertheless it was his best alternative under the circumstances. Not only did it rescue him from the military impasse created by Hood's northern movement but it also—and this was the advantage he emphasized—made it possible, once he secured a new base of operations at Savannah, to carry the war into the Carolinas and threaten Lee's rear in Virginia.

Reluctantly Grant agreed to Sherman's proposal. On November 2, after obtaining assurances that Thomas

Sherman and his generals in the Atlanta Campaign. Left to right: Howard, Logan, Hazen, Sherman, Davis, Slocum, and Mower. McPherson, not shown, was killed at Atlanta.

would have ample strength to defeat a Confederate invasion of Tennessee, he gave Sherman permission to make the march. Two weeks later Sherman with 62,000 of his best troops set out from the burning city of Atlanta.

He instructed his men to "forage liberally on the country." This they did—and looted and destroyed. In front of them there were only a few brigades of cavalry and the old men and young boys of the Georgia militia. Behind them they left a trail of devastation sixty miles wide. Accompanying them were hordes of Negroes rejoicing in their liberation from slavery. Their presence annoyed Sherman, who considered the Emancipation Proclamation a mistake. Most of his soldiers felt the same way. Once they deliberately left hundreds of Negroes stranded on the other side of a river.

In mid-December Sherman's legions reached the outskirts of Savannah. Possibly, had he moved in the right way and with sufficient speed, he might have bagged the city's 10,000-man garrison. But he was more concerned with establishing contact with the Northern navy than with the garrison commander's resolve not to be trapped. So the Confederates, after a brief show of resistance, had no difficulty getting away. On December 21 the Union troops entered the city and Sherman telegraphed Lincoln: "I beg to present to you as a Christmas gift the city of Savannah."

Harper's Pictorial History of the Great Rebellion

The XIV and XX Corps start the March to the Sea, leaving Atlanta behind them in flame.

The North acclaimed Sherman. He now surpassed Grant's popularity, who seemed to be going nowhere in Virginia while Sherman romped through Georgia. Afterward the public regarded "The March to the Sea" as his greatest accomplishment. No doubt it was highly dramatic. No doubt too it was a glorious adventure for the soldiers who made it. But what were its actual results?

It destroyed, according to Sherman's own estimate, $100,000,000 of property, but he admitted, only $20,000,000 of that amount "inured to our advantage," the remainder was "simple waste and destruction." It left thousands of civilians hungry but had little or no impact on the supply situation of Lee's and Hood's armies. Also, the miles of tracks that Sherman's soldiers tore up did not seriously handicap Confederate military operations; not until his forces reached Branchville, South Carolina, in February was the South's east-west rail system totally cut. And although the march had a depressing effect on many Southerners, especially Georgians, it also infuriated many of them and so strengthened, rather than weakened, their will to fight on. There is also no hard evidence that the march, or its eventual continuation into the Carolinas, was the main cause of the high desertion rate from Lee's army during the 1864-65 winter, as some historians have asserted. The most important and common motives were hunger, privation, and the increasingly obvious hopelessness of the Confederate cause.

The March to the Sea probably did not shorten the war. On the contrary, by making it with an unnecessarily large force of 62,000 (50,000 would have been more than ample) Sherman risked prolonging the war—

even giving the Confederacy a new lease on life. Despite the fact that Hood was moving northward and was 300 miles from Atlanta by mid-November, Sherman predicted that he would follow him to Savannah! Subsequently he left Thomas with less than 60,000 widely scattered and mostly inexperienced troops to oppose Hood's more than 50,000 veterans. To be sure Thomas himself expressed confidence that he could handle Hood and of course he did so, destroying his army at Nashville on December 15-16. However only a chain of bad mistakes and ill luck prevented Hood from defeating or cutting through the Union forces in Tennessee before Thomas united them. Had this happened—and it came very close—the March to the Sea would stand as a classic example of military folly.

Early in December, when he learned that Sherman was nearing Savannah, Grant proposed that Sherman not even bother to seize that city but instead load most of his army on ships to be transported to Virginia, where it would join the Union forces around Richmond to overwhelm Lee. Without hesitation Sherman agreed to do this, observing that he could reach Virginia much sooner by sea than by land. However, the destruction of Hood's army at Nashville caused Grant to change his mind about bringing Sherman to the Richmond front at once. Instead he in effect left it up to Sherman's preference. Sherman promptly chose to march northward through the Carolinas—which is what he had hoped to do all along. By so doing, he wrote Grant, "we can punish South Carolina as she deserves." Also, he asserted that by smashing Lee's supply system and making his ultimate defeat inevitable, such a campaign would be "as much a direct attack upon Lee's army as though we were operating within the sound of his artillery." Finally he stated: "I attach more importance to these deep inci-

sions into the enemy's country, because this war differs from European wars in this particular: we are not only fighting hostile armies, but a hostile people, and must make old and young, rich and poor, feel the hard hand of war. . . ."

At the end of January 1865 Sherman crossed into South Carolina. His troops devastated the countryside with literal vengeance, for like most Northerners, they considered South Carolina the birthplace of the rebellion. However, the most famous episode of their march through the state, the "Burning of Columbia" on the night of February 17, occurred primarily because Southern cavalry, before evacuating the town, set fire to cotton bales piled in the main street. Of course, had not the enemy unwittingly spared him the bother, Sherman would have burned at least the government buildings and military installations of Columbia anyway—in fact he announced his intention to do so back in December.

In South Carolina, as during the March to the Sea, Sherman encountered no opposition worthy of the name. But after entering North Carolina he found himself confronted by a significant enemy force under his old adversary Johnston. Near Bentonville on March 19 Johnston, manifesting uncharacteristic and unexpected aggressiveness, ambushed Sherman's left wing. Only errors by Johnston and his key subordinates saved it from a severe mauling. Then, two days later, an equally uncharacteristic lack of caution by Johnston gave Sherman an excellent chance to cut his line of communications. However Sherman was so intent on reaching Goldsboro, where reinforcements—brought to North Carolina by sea—were awaiting him, that he allowed Johnston to escape.

Sherman's army, now 85,000 strong, halted at Goldsboro to rest and refit. While it did, Sherman, at a conference with Grant in Virginia, proposed joining his forces with the 120,000 Union troops already outside of Richmond to overwhelm Lee's 55,000 scarecrows. Grant, however, did not want the long-frustrated Army of the Potomac (and perhaps himself) to have to share with Sherman's Westerners the honor of defeating Lee. He instructed Sherman to move against Johnston in order to prevent or at least delay a link-up between him and Lee. Sherman promised to start his operation on April 10.

But he was not needed. At the beginning of April Grant forced Lee out of Petersburg and Richmond and on April 9 accepted his surrender at Appomattox. Johnston, seeing no point in persisting in a lost war, came to terms with Sherman on April 26 at a farmhouse near Raleigh. Sherman, who in 1862 had vowed to "make war terrible" for the South and who had done so, now sought to make peace as easy as could be. In the process he trespassed onto political matters. Andrew Johnson, now President, had no choice except to repudiate Sherman's pact. Sherman, half-expecting this, was not offended. But he was incensed by the way Secretary of War Edwin M. Stanton and Major General Henry W. Halleck, who now was chief of staff of the army, handled the affair: They implied that he was betraying the Union and seeking to make himself military dictator. In retaliation he snubbed Stanton at the grand review of his army in Washington and broke with Halleck, the man who had given him his chance to rise to the top by picking him up after he fell in Missouri in 1861.

"Santa Claus Sherman putting Savannah into Uncle Sam's stocking." A cartoon from *Frank Leslie's Illustrated Newspaper*.

So, on this sour note, Sherman's Civil War career ended. In the years that followed he engaged in warfare and peace negotiations with the Indians of the Western Plains; he rejected an offer from President Johnson, who hoped to exploit his popularity for political purposes, to appoint him Secretary of War; he became Grant's successor as commanding general of the army, a post he held from 1869 to 1883; he rejected the possible Republican nomination for President in 1884 when he announced: "If nominated, I will not accept. If elected, I will not serve." Yet it was all anti-climactic. Although he lived until 1891, what he did between 1861 and 1865 determined his place in history and his status as a military leader. But how should he be rated?

Sherman was too cautious when conducting a battle. As a consequence he tended to hold back both in the employment and deployment of his forces. This in turn either cost him defeats, as at Missionary Ridge, or else lost him the full fruits of victory, as at Jonesboro. To a degree this cautiousness in combat reflected his personality—he simply lacked the "killer instinct." But it was mainly the result of his awareness that as commander of the stronger army he was bound to win so long as he avoided unnecessary risks and major mistakes. Even Napoleon's daring declined as the number of his troops rose.

Sherman tended to assume that the enemy would act or react in a certain way and therefore overlooked other possibilities. This is why he overestimated the danger from the Confederates in Kentucky and Missouri, underestimated it at Shiloh, moved with insufficient force and speed at Snake Creek Gap, walked blithely into a near-disastrous trap at Atlanta, and discounted Hood's tenacity and ingenuity. He was being facetious, yet he revealed something of his character as a general when he complained in October 1864 that Hood "is eccentric and I cannot guess his movements as I could those of Johnston, who was a sensible man and only did sensible things."

Sherman was guilty of making the same dubious assumption that many other war leaders before and since have made: That the enemy could be terrorized into submission by devastating his farms and towns. Rarely is this the case, certainly it was not true of the South in the Civil War. Although the havoc wreaked by Sherman's hordes contributed to Confederate defeat,

Celebrities in the stand at the Grand Review of the Armies. Sherman is fourth from the right in the front row.

this contribution was so indirect and ambiguous that it did not justify militarily, much less morally, the human misery that accompanied and followed it. This is particularly true of what Sherman himself considered to be his greatest accomplishment—the march through the Carolinas. Had his army proceeded, as at first planned, from Savannah to Richmond by sea, the war almost certainly would have been ended at least a month, probably two months, sooner. But Grant is more to blame for this not occurring than is Sherman.

But Sherman had no superior, perhaps no equal, among Civil War commanders when it came to supplying and operating large armies over vast distances. His campaign through Georgia and the Carolinas was a masterpiece of logistical planning and execution. By the same token, anyone studying his military correspondence will be impressed, even awed, by the virtuosity in dealing with multitudes of administrative details, for he was his own operations, personnel, and intelligence officer. The highly able British general of World Wars I and II, Archibald Wavell, wrote at the end of his career: "The more I see of war, the more I realize how it all depends on administration and transportation. . . ." Judged by this criterion, Sherman stands high as a commander.

Although nervous in deportment and emotional in temperament, in emergencies Sherman was calm and quick-thinking, as he revealed at Shiloh and above all on July 22, 1864, at Atlanta. He was able to do what every good commander does—react effectively to the unexpected and potentially disastrous. Equally important, he possessed that hardness of mind and spirit which is essential to a successful general. He could order men into battle without qualm: "The very object of war is to

produce results by death and slaughter," he wrote his wife after Shiloh.

After taking command in the West in 1864 Sherman dominated, by the force of his intellect and personality, the generals who served under him. The sole exception was Thomas, with whom his relationship was both unique and complex. He also secured the confidence and even the admiration of the rank and file, who on seeing him ride by would say, "There goes the old man. All's right." As a result the veteran—but heterogeneous—forces that assembled around Chattanooga in the spring of 1864 became a fighting machine matched in effectiveness only by Lee's army at its peak.

To a list of Sherman's merits his biographer and admirer, the British military historian Liddell Hart, has added the highest of all—genius. According to Hart, Sherman deserves this designation because he cleverly employed the "indirect approach" both in tactics and strategy; he constantly placed his opponents on the "horns of the dilemma" by marching in widely dispersed columns, preventing—as in Georgia and the Carolinas —a concentration of force against him; he ushered in the age of modern warfare by making the enemy's home-front as important an objective as his battlefront and he carried out *blitzkrieg* penetrations deep into his rear.

What Liddell Hart claims has the ring of truth, but maybe Sherman was not so much a military genius as he was a man who could attack a knotty problem with a practical solution. As an old quartermaster he knew the needs of a large body of troops; how else could his army have moved rapidly and still have lived off the land without fanning out? Also, giving up the chase after Hood to head for Savannah, and efforts at flanking the

Postwar portrait of Sherman in full general's regalia.

formidable Rebel defenses thrown up in his army's path make someone like "Uncle Billy" seem to be a person possessed of common-sense rather than superior military intellect. His men's long and often unopposed hikes through the South destroyed no enemy army, the object of a *blitzkrieg*, and would hardly seem to place him in the military *avant-garde*. And the tactic of allowing troops to bully and rob non-combatants is no more modern than Attila or Genghis Khan.

There is a major reason why one hesitates to place Sherman among the Great Captains. Apart from his brief and unhappy experience in Kentucky in 1861, he did not hold a top command until the last year of the war. By then the Confederacy was half-defeated, its troops declining in numbers and quality, many of its best generals dead or crippled, its morale shaken, and its economy staggering. Consequently, in the Atlanta Campaign Sherman faced an enemy army decidedly inferior to his own and commanded first by Johnston who rarely attacked when he could find an excuse to retreat, and next by Hood, who rarely retreated when he could find an excuse to attack. And during the march through Georgia and the Carolinas he was unopposed and never in serious danger. In short, his military skill and character remained untested in the sense of having to cope with an opponent of comparable strength and talent.

But there can be no reasonable doubt that Sherman was an exceptional man who developed into an excellent general. During the final year of the war he accomplished much—maybe even made Northern victory possible. Few other Union generals would have done as well; only Grant might have done better. So Sherman ranks, as he always has, right behind his friend and mentor, Grant. He would not object.

Major General William Tecumseh Sherman outside Atlanta. (National Archives)

ROBERT E. LEE

by Mark Grimsley

The pages of history are spattered with the names of famous people: movers and shakers, artisans of human progress and human destruction. For the most part, their fame was not inevitable. It came as the result of being at the right place at the right time, and—if they are remembered favorably—equipped with the right abilities.

Great as he is now considered, Robert E. Lee, like so many of his generation, would have remained unknown but for the advent of civil war in America. Until 1861 he was merely a colonel in the diminutive U.S. Army, noteworthy only to his family and the handful of others who knew him well. Without the war, he may have wound up simply a name on army retirement lists. Or he may have quit the service to pursue his pipe dream of becoming a farmer. Instead, in spring 1861 he suddenly found himself serving as a full general in the fledgling Confederate States Army. And fourteen months after the war's outbreak, a combination of luck and talent placed him in command of the South's principal fighting force. After that, the military genius that had always lain dormant inside him began to show. There was a string of victories . . . battles called The Seven Days, Second Manassas, Fredericksburg, Chancellorsville. Within weeks of assuming high command, his masterful audacity, combativeness, and determination catapulted his name into lasting renown. And as an admiring world came to recognize him as one of the great captains of history, it began to examine Lee's personal character, discovering there a simple nobility, a nobility promptly lionized into something superhuman. At length, when the doomed Confederacy finally went down to defeat, and the gauzy fantasies of Southern chivalry and romance disappeared beneath the heel of grimy, industrialized modernity, Lee became the symbol of all good that men saw in a vanished way of life. He became a paladin, a legend, what biographer Thomas Connelly has called "The Marble Man."

"Nothing," wrote 20th-century novelist John Updike, "sinks quicker in history than people's actual motives, unless it be their sexual charm." In the case of Robert Edward Lee the basic truth of this assertion is vastly multiplied. The inner workings of Lee's mind have all but disappeared in the depths of national mythology, and the idea that he could possibly have possessed "sexual charm" now borders on blasphemy. The real Lee has largely been erased, transformed into a perfection that has reflected what others have needed to see.

Lee's earliest biographers were ex-Confederates, men who viewed Lee as the Christlike embodiment of their "Lost Cause," and who worked with fierce zeal to discredit anyone who portrayed him differently. His most famous biographer, Pulitzer Prize winner

Douglas Southall Freeman, set forth in his four-volume work *R.E. Lee* a near-perfect man who affirmed his own conceptions about Virginia's superior culture. Only a recent study (1977) by renowned Civil War historian Thomas Connelly has cast Lee in substantially different terms. Connelly has debunked interpretations of a flawless Lee and instead set forth

The "master general," Robert E. Lee, who became commander in chief of all Confederate troops. (National Archives)

a picture of an individual plagued by melancholia, a bad marriage, and a sense of personal failure. Such an interpretation attempts to depict a human being, not a titan. But an accurate portrayal of Lee is now unlikely. The man and myth are inseparable.

Lee grew up primarily in Alexandria, Virginia, the son of Revolutionary War hero Henry "Light Horse Harry" Lee. A brilliant but erratic man, Henry Lee never fulfilled the promise of his early military career. A mania for land speculation wrecked his finances, reputation, and self-respect; in 1813 he went into self-imposed exile and spent the remainder of his life in the West Indies. Robert, born January 19, 1807, was barely six when Henry Lee left home. He was raised by his mother, Ann Carter Lee, who took him and the rest of her impoverished brood on frequent extended visits to powerful relatives, especially the wealthy Carter clan. As a boy Lee attended a school maintained by the Carters exclusively for their own prolific offspring. Later he went to Alexandria Academy. A teacher recalled him as studious, courteous, and unobtrusive. "His specialty," the man wrote, "was *finishing up*. He imparted a finish and a neatness, as he proceeded, to everything he undertook."

Two personalities dominated Lee's youth. The first, George Washington, died before Lee's birth but still served him as a hero and role model. Lee's father had known the first U.S. President personally and in tribute to him coined the famous epigram "First in war, first in peace, and first in the hearts of his countrymen." His son venerated the august Washington, and in later years many would mark the resemblance between the two. But if Washington provided the role model, Ann Carter Lee provided the day-by-day guidance that created in Robert Lee a spirit of gentleness, thrift, and self-control. Her death in 1829 was a blow he never forgot. Forty years later he gazed into the room where she had died and sadly remembered her passing. "It seems now but yesterday," he said.

Armed with a testimonial letter signed by five senators and three representatives—evidence of his powerful family connections—Lee entered the United States Military Academy at West Point, New York, in 1825. He survived the four-year curriculum without accruing a single demerit, attained the coveted cadet rank of adjutant, and graduated second in his class. Success usually brings with it the jealousy of others, but not in Lee's case. "I doubt if he ever excited envy in any man," wrote a fellow cadet. "All his accomplishments and alluring virtues appeared natural to him, and he was free from the anxiety, distrust, and awkwardness that attend a sense of inferiority."

Despite success at West Point, little suggests Lee was a born soldier. He embarked upon a military career chiefly because it offered a secure future and a free education. In old age he came to regret the decision to become a soldier, believing it the greatest mistake of his life.

Lee's gleaming West Point record enabled him to enter the Corps of Engineers, an elite arm that attracted the army's brightest officers. And he loved the corps; its tasks appealed to his sense of order and creativity. But even so, his duties were frequently grueling and unglamorous. Lee's first assignment took him to marshy Cockspur Island, Georgia, where he worked, often in hip-deep water, to prepare the foundation for a heavy coastal fort. Two years later he helped to complete another coastal strongpoint at Fort Monroe, Virginia.

In summer 1829, Lee began courting a twenty-one-year-old debutante named Mary Anne Randolph Custis, a distant relative he had known since childhood. Her father, George Washington Parke Custis, was the adopted son of General George Washington and owner of Arlington, a palatial Virginia estate overlooking the nation's capital. Lee became a frequent visitor to Arlington during his furloughs from Cockspur Island. Mr. Custis found the young lieutenant's interest in his daughter disquieting: he had nothing against Lee personally, but he had not given Mary a luxurious childhood only to have her taste poverty as the wife of a penniless subaltern. Both Mrs. Custis and Mary, however, were united in their regard for the earnest young suitor, and on June 30, 1831, Mary Custis became Mrs. R.E. Lee.

Robert and Mary made an odd match. When he was punctual, she was tardy. Where he thrived on order and industry, she dallied and kept a slovenly household. Careless of her appearance, on one occasion she found her hair in such a mess that she simply took a pair of scissors to it. She had a strong will; unfortunately she used it more frequently to undermine her husband than to support him.

The marriage may or may not have been an unhappy one for Robert Lee. The question is too exacting for biographers to explore definitively. Lee biographer Douglas S. Freeman believed it a satisfactory union. Historian Thomas Connelly, on the other hand, maintains that its barrenness led Lee to seek emotional outlet in platonic relationships with other women. He flirted with Harriet Talcott, the gorgeous wife of a brother officer, in a joking-but-serious way. And his correspondence with one of Mary's cousins, Martha "Markie" Williams, continued until his death. Examining the letters, Connelly concludes: "However harmless, it seems evident that Markie Williams was the object of Lee's love."

Happy or not, the marriage produced a brood of lively and attractive children: Custis (born in 1832), Mary (1835), Fitzhugh (1837), Annie (1839), Agnes

Above: Lieutenant of Engineers Robert E. Lee and his bride, Mary Anne Randolph Custis, painted in 1838. (Both: Washington/Custis/Lee Collection, Washington and Lee University)

(1841), Robert, Jr. (1843), and Mildred (1846). A conscientious father, the unavoidable but lengthy absences caused by army service sometimes grieved Lee. He was mortified when, after one such absence, he failed to recognize his youngest son.* Nevertheless, the children idolized him and he would tell them stories in exchange for having his hands and feet tickled, a simple pleasure he particularly enjoyed. All of his sons entered Confederate service during the Civil War; two became generals. None of his daughters ever married because they could never find anyone who met, in their eyes, the standard of their father. Years after his death, Lee's daughter Mildred wrote, "To me he seems a Hero—and all other men small in comparison."

Never in radiant health, the stress of bearing seven children in fourteen years eventually reduced Mary to an invalid. In 1835 Lee returned from a survey of the Ohio-Michigan boundary to find that she had contracted a severe pelvic infection. The illness left her somewhat lame and gave Lee a scare. To remain close

*Sadly, this would not be the only time Lee did not recognize his youngest son. On August 30, 1862, at Second Manassas, then Confederate General Robert E. Lee stopped beside an artillery unit, the Rockbridge Battery. There he "was told one of the cannoneers wanted to speak with him . . . 'Well my man, what can I do for you?' he said pulling down his binoculars. 'Why general, don't you know me?' Under the grime covering him, Lee did not see at first it was his youngest son, Robert E. Lee, Jr."

Lee and his son W.H. Fitzhugh Lee, photographed before the Mexican War. Young Lee rose to major general in the Confederate army. He was called "Rooney," to avoid confusing him with his cousin Fitzhugh Lee. (Virginia Historical Society.)

to her he spent several tours of duty at the engineering office in Washington, D.C., balancing the virtues of a solid home life against the frustrations of government bureaucracy. Eventually, however, the frustrations won out, and he requested a transfer to Saint Louis, Missouri. There he spent thirty months battling financial, legal, and engineering obstacles in a successful bid to prevent silt from blocking the St. Louis dockside. For this he was promoted to captain.

The outbreak of war with Mexico in 1846 found Lee stationed at New York Harbor. Although ostensibly a war of self-defense, the real American objective in this conflict quickly became the conquest of all Mexican territory between Texas and the Pacific Ocean. Lee deplored the expansionist nature of the conflict, but as a professional soldier wanted desperately to participate. After several months of anxious waiting, he received orders to report to Brigadier General John Wool at San Antonio de Bexar, Texas.

By the time Lee arrived in Texas, however, the war's territorial objectives had largely been won. The new task became to make the Mexicans quit the war, and as the months went by it became obvious that this could not be done in northern Mexico. The U.S. Army's general-in-chief, Lieutenant General Winfield Scott, believed that only the capture of the enemy capital itself, Mexico City, promised a decisive victory. He began to assemble an army for this task at Brazos, Texas. Lee, after conducting numerous but unavailing reconnaissances for Brigadier General John Wool in northern Mexico, received orders to report to Brazos as a member of Scott's personal staff. This proved a fortunate assignment.

Storming ashore at Veracruz, Mexico, in March 1847, Scott's army began a campaign to the Mexican capital. It required five months and was fought with marginal resources. On several occasions during the campaign Lee served invaluably by locating key flanking routes that enabled the Americans to outmaneuver and defeat a more numerous enemy. He possessed an uncanny eye for terrain and exhibited surprising determination for a man generally considered gentle and restrained. Before the Battle of Contreras, for example, through thunderstorms he several times scrambled miles over the broken rocks and boulders of a lava field to deliver some vital information to General Scott and lead other officers to advantageous positions. His "grit" astounded Scott. This same terrain had been considered impassable by the enemy. Scott called Lee's exploit the greatest feat of physical and moral courage he had ever known. And at a victory celebration upon the fall of Mexico City, he toasted the captain as the man "without whose help we would not be here."

Lee emerged from the war with a brevet colonelcy and a reputation as a brilliant staff officer. Scott marked him for high command and thought the cost would be cheap if the United States could absolutely insure Lee's life even at the cost of 5 million dollars a year. Lee, he proclaimed, "was the very best soldier I ever saw in the field."

Following the war, Robert Lee returned to the familiar routine of constructing coastal defenses and in 1852 received a plum assignment: superintendent of West Point. Only the ninth man to have held this position, he oversaw the extension of the academy's course of study from four to five years, encouraged the study of strategy, and improved cadet discipline by weeding out the lazy and incompetent. Perhaps the most famous cadet to get the boot from Lee was First Classman James McNeill Whistler, whose haphazard academic work was crowned by complete failure in chemistry. "Had silicon been a gas," he jested in later life, "I would have been a major general." Whistler settled instead for becoming a world-famous artist, and to the end of his days staunchly admired the superintendent who had dismissed him.

The slowness of promotion in the Corps of Engineers led Lee in 1855 to accept a position as lieutenant-colonel of the newly formed 2d Cavalry Regiment, and for the next several years he spent most of his active service in the wilds of central and western Texas. From bleak frontier outposts Lee dealt with Indians, Mexican bandits, and the pain of separation from his family. A steady stream of letters flowed from his pen to Mary and the children. "You will have to send me a kitten in your next letter," he wrote Mildred. "The Indians have none, as there are so many wolves prowling around that they frighten away all the mice. My rattlesnake, my only pet, is dead. He grew sick and would not eat his frogs, etc., and died one night."

In October 1857 Lee's father-in-law passed away and Lee, then age fifty, seems at that point to have begun reconsidering his life. To Colonel Albert Sidney Johnston, his commanding officer, he wrote, "I can see that I have at last to decide the question, which I have staved off for 20 years, whether I am to continue in the Army all my life, or to leave it now. My preferences which have clung to me from boyhood impel me to adopt the former course, but yet I feel that a man's family has its claims too." Lee's second thoughts were common in a profession that offered little but drabness and routine. Promotion came tardily or not at all, leading many officers to resign in pursuit of more lucrative civilian careers.

Lee eventually decided to stay on, but it took him thirty years of service to reach the permanent rank of colonel, and in 1860 his income amounted to a paltry $4,060. During that same year Ohio resident George McClellan, a much younger officer who had resigned to become a railroad executive (and who would later become a Union major general), made over $10,000.

Upon the death of his father-in-law, Lee went back to Arlington to serve as executor of the Custis estate. Unfortunately Custis had left a poorly written will, debts totalling $10,000, little operating cash, and lands that betrayed years of neglect and mismanagement. Nursing the estate back to health became Lee's second career. Forced to ask the War Department for several leaves of absence, he spent the next two years at Arlington.

During this period changes occurred that would make all the difference in Lee's life and in the life of his country. The war with Mexico, while it brought vast new territories into the United States, had by that very fact accelerated the arguments and tensions over sectionalism and slavery. An apolitical man who detested controversy, Lee tried to ignore these new eruptions. But if he was not interested in events, events were interested in him. The volatile issues of the 1850s eventually forced him to make the most difficult and lasting decision of his life.

Had he been astute he may have seen the decision coming as early as October 1859, when abolitionist John Brown and some followers raided Harpers Ferry, Virginia, and attempted to seize the Federal arsenal there. The War Department summoned Lee to quell the insurrection. With four companies of local militia and a handful of U.S. Marines, Lee surrounded the engine house in which these 19th-century terrorists had barricaded themselves and sent in army Lieutenant James Ewell Brown "Jeb" Stuart with a message for them to surrender. Brown attempted to negotiate. Stuart replied that it was impossible. When Brown persisted, Stuart stepped back from the door, raised his hat, and a party of marines successfully stormed the engine house.

With Brown's men either dead or in custody, Lee handed Brown over to Virginia authorities and returned to Arlington. Strangely, he never took the raid very seriously. He regarded Brown as a lunatic and dismissed his followers as mere rioters. But the rest of the nation found in Harpers Ferry the storm center of a bitter and violent conflict. The forces that had clashed there were the ones that would plunge the nation into civil war within eighteen months.

The crisis culminated while Lee was in the Department of Texas, after settling the Custis estate. Shortly after Abraham Lincoln's election to the U.S. Presidency in 1860, Lee wrote one of his sons, "The Southern states seem to be in a convulsion," and in January 1861 he denounced the secessionist fever that was sweeping the Deep South. "Secession is nothing but revolution," he wrote. "The framers of our Constitution never exhausted so much labor, wisdom and forbearance in its formation, and surrounded it with so many guards and securities, if it was intended to be broken by every member of the Confederacy at will . . . Still," he concluded sadly, "a Union that can only be maintained by swords and bayonets, and in which strife and civil war are to take the place of brotherly love and kindness, has no charm for me. . . ."

The forces of the colonel's heritage began to pull him. To his political conviction that a citizen's first loyalty belonged to his state were added the more visceral bonds of family. Lees, Carters, Randolphs, Fitzhughs, the greatest families of Virginia, numbered him among their scions. These dynasties had created the state, drawn forth its wealth, and governed it. In a sense they were Virginia, even as he was part of them. Compelled by this deeply personal loyalty, Lee automatically tied his fate to that of his state.

Others felt differently. Although a Virginian himself, Winfield Scott remained firmly for the Union, and in early 1861 he summoned Lee to Washington to persuade his favorite protégé to stand for the Union, too. En route, Lee discovered that the military Department of Texas had surrendered to the secessionists. "Has it come so soon as this?" Lee gasped when he heard the news, and tears welled in his eyes. When he met with Scott, however, he apparently gave no assurances that he would stay with the Union if Virginia seceded.

Perhaps as an incentive to remain loyal to the Federal Government, Lee was given command of the 1st Cavalry Regiment in mid-March. But he had no time to enjoy his new assignment. On April 12 Confederate batteries in South Carolina's Charleston Harbor fired upon Union-held Fort Sumter. Three days later President Abraham Lincoln issued a call for 75,000 volunteers. On April 17 a letter arrived at Arlington from General Scott, asking Lee to call on him the following day. So did a message conveyed in a note from one of Lee's cousins. It said that Francis P. Blair, Sr., a former editor of the Congressional *Globe* and a friend of the new administration, wanted to see Lee as well.

Visiting Blair first, Lee learned that Secretary of War Simon Cameron wanted him to take command of the forces needed to put down the rebellion. As candidly and courteously as he could, Lee outlined his own position. Although opposed to secession and deprecating war, he could take no part in an invasion of the Southern states. Afterward, he went to Scott's office and told him what had happened. The old general received the news with sad resignation. "Lee," Scott rumbled, "you have made the greatest mistake of your life; but I feared it would be so."

Lee returned to Arlington and there considered Scott's parting suggestion; if he could not serve the Federal Government wholeheartedly he ought to resign his commission. He was still pondering this when Virginia made the matter academic. On April 19, while on business in Alexandria, Lee learned that the state had seceded. To a local druggist he murmured, "I must say that I am one of those dull creatures that cannot see the good of secession." Shortly after midnight, on the morning of April 20, he resigned his commission. To General Scott he penned a regretful note that included the line, "Save in defense of my native State, I never desire again to draw my sword." In a letter to his sister Ann, a unionist, he stressed his decision was more personal than political: "With all my devotion to the Union and the feeling of loyalty and duty of an American citizen, I have not been able to make up my mind to raise my hand against my relatives, my children, my home . . . I know you will blame me; but you must think as kindly of me as you can, and believe that I have endeavored to do what I thought right."

On the evening of April 20 a letter arrived from Judge John Robertson of Richmond, Virginia, requesting that Lee see him. Some weeks previously the Confederate Secretary of War had offered Lee a brigadier general's commission; Robertson's message could only mean a renewal of the offer or something similar. Lee agreed to meet the judge in Alexandria the following day. Robertson was delayed and missed the appointment, but later invited Lee in the name of Virginia's Governor John Letcher to visit Letcher in Richmond. On April 22 Lee departed, never again to see Arlington until long after the war's end. The course he had chosen would bring him no pleasure and little satisfaction, but he never doubted the correctness of his decision. "I did only what my duty demanded," he would affirm long afterward. "I could have taken no other course without dishonor. And if it were all to be done over again, I should act in precisely the same manner."

"Granny" Lee

The job Governor Letcher had in mind for Robert E. Lee involved nothing less than command of all Virginia's military and naval forces. Commissioned a brigadier general on May 14, at the time Lee took the assignment those forces did not amount to much; Virginia's army consisted of poorly trained

and ill-equipped militia, and its navy numbered only a few requisitioned merchant vessels. Thousands of Virginians, however, thronged to the colors, and since Union forces were quite as ill-prepared as the Southerners, Lee had sufficient time to organize them. By June 8, 1861, when Virginia formally placed its forces under Confederate control, Lee had supervised the deployment of over 40,000 men. He received a full general's commission on June 14.

Lee's first assignment did not culminate in actual field command, although his dispositions heavily influenced the early stages of the war. Instead, he entered a period of doldrums during which his responsibilities were vague and comparatively minor. Meanwhile, other Confederate officers forged impressive battlefield reputations by besting a large amateur enemy army in First Manassas. Finally, at the end of July, Confederate President Jefferson Davis sent Lee to western Virginia to coordinate Rebel forces in that region. This began Lee's first and most dismal campaign.

Confederate fortunes in the western Virginia mountains had already waned. The region's population voiced unionist sentiment, and invading Federal troops had already inflicted two sharp defeats on Confederate forces. Lee, faced with the challenge of repairing these disasters, proved unequal to it. And though perhaps no man could have retrieved the Confederate situation in western Virginia, Lee's efforts did not simply fail, they failed miserably. The primary reason was his complete inability to persuade the local Confederate generals to work in harness. Each of the three regional commanders operated independently, each cordially despised the others, and each responded grudgingly to Lee's attempts to make them cooperate. The general found their behavior baffling. A courteous, self-effacing, and disciplined man himself, he never knew what to make of arrogant Brigadier General John B. Floyd, irascible Brigadier General Henry Wise, or the incredibly disputatious Brigadier General William W. Loring. He tried diplomacy. He should have tried cracking heads, but that was a quality of leadership Lee never possessed. For better or worse, he simply could not bear down on a man.

In addition to command difficulties, Lee also faced the ravages of torrential rains that washed out roads, hampered supply operations, and assisted in the spread of a measles and fever epidemic that prostrated half his force. Still, from the major Confederate position at Valley Mountain, Lee daily inspected the Union lines on Cheat and Rich mountains and waited for an opening to strike. Early in September news came that the Cheat Mountain position could be turned. Lee ordered the movement, but entrusted

118

it to a novice colonel whose only qualification was that he had discovered the flanking route. The battle plan called for the turning movement to be followed by a four-brigade frontal assault. The date of the attack was set for September 12. Unfortunately, heavy rains intervened, the flanking column bogged down, and as Lee impatiently rode from unit to unit, waiting for the novice colonel to get into position, he narrowly avoided capture by Union cavalry. The anticipated battle degenerated into scattered skirmishes, and one of Lee's friends, staff officer Colonel John Washington, was killed. His loss added grief to a thoroughly disappointing day for Lee.

Virginia newspapers, which until then had lionized him, took to calling him "Granny" Lee. Richmond newspaper editor E.A. Pollard soon produced a review of *The First Year Of The War* that included a damning assessment of the failed Cheat Mountain campaign. "The most remarkable circumstance of this campaign," Pollard commented acidly, "was that it was conducted by a general who had never fought a battle, who had a pious horror of guerrillas and whose extreme tenderness of blood induced him to depend exclusively upon the resources of strategy to essay the achievement of victory without loss of life."

Confederate President Jefferson Davis, however, continued to have confidence in Lee, and in November dispatched him to command a military department composed of the coastlines of South Carolina, Georgia, and eastern Florida. Lee regarded his new assignment gloomily. "Another forlorn hope expedition. Worse than western Virginia," he confided to his daughter Mildred. Even before his arrival in the department, a Federal fleet managed to force open South Carolina's Port Royal Sound on November 7. After four or five hours' sustained bombardment, the Confederate garrisons of the earthen forts defending the sound withdrew, Union troops landed to secure the area, and Port Royal became a coaling station for Federal blockade ships.

Lee's south Atlantic coast command impressed upon him the Confederacy's basic strategic problem. Politically, its aims were defensive, but it had too many exposed points to protect and not enough troops to do the job. In the face of superior Union seapower and, therefore, superior mobility, Lee could not possibly cover more than 300 miles of coastline with the 20,000 troops at his disposal. Despite extensive fortification and judicious deployment, a purely defensive military posture could attain only precarious results: if it was true of the Carolina coast, it was true of all the Confederacy. The general began to perceive that if the South was to succeed it must concentrate its forces and attack.

When he returned to Richmond in March 1862, Lee began to put this conception of the offense to work. His new assignment charged him with the conduct of Confederate military operations under the "direction" of President Davis. This made him Davis' military adviser, little more. Even so, the post gave Lee significant opportunities to influence strategy, especially in the East.

The Virginia front at that time appeared unpromising. Near Centreville some 40,000 Confederates commanded by General Joseph E. Johnston faced nearly three times that number of Federals. In the Shenandoah Valley a small force operated under Confederate Major General Thomas J. "Stonewall" Jackson. The Confederates seemed to face daunting odds, but Johnston took comfort in the extreme caution of his adversary, Major General George McClellan, late of the Illinois Central and Ohio & Mississippi Railroads. McClellan kept his burgeoning Army of the Potomac harmlessly behind extensive Washington, D.C. fortifications. When spring arrived, however, Johnston fell back to a more protected position behind the Rappahannock River. There he waited for McClellan to act.

Jackson decided not to wait, and on March 23, 1862, he attacked a superior Union detachment in a sharp battle at Kernstown in the Shenandoah Valley. Tactically, his gamble failed, but strategically, it paid dividends—surprised Federals suspended their own offensive plans in Virginia. Meanwhile, McClellan, using the North's seapower advantage, slipped down the Chesapeake Bay and landed his army at Union-held Fort Monroe on the tip of Virginia's Peninsula. On April 4 the Confederate commander in the region, Major General John B. Magruder, excitedly reported that vastly superior forces were assailing his positions near Yorktown. Lee told him to hold fast and began channelling reinforcements from Johnston's army to his aid. By mid-April most of that army, including Johnston himself, had filed into the Yorktown trenches. Fortunately for the Southerners, McClellan, outnumbering the Confederates 100,000 to 53,000, elected to conduct a siege; this gave Lee and the high command time to ponder the best strategy to defeat the Federals.

The Confederates would be faced with a total of four major threats, of which McClellan was merely the largest. In the Shenandoah Valley a Union corps under command of Major General Nathaniel Banks menaced important Confederate supply sources; a second corps commanded by Union Major General Irvin McDowell could march south from its camps in northern Virginia; Federals in western Virginia, now under command of Major General John C. Frémont,

also seemed active; and McClellan, of course, marching north on the Peninsula, threatened Richmond
itself. In every instance the Federals far outnumbered
the Rebel forces opposing them. A passive defense
could never hope to resist so many pressures.

Lee believed the only viable solution was to com-
bine against one of the threats, eliminate it, and thus
dislocate the remaining Union forces. On April 21 he
wrote Jackson suggesting a preferred course of action
in which Jackson would be reinforced by a second
division led by Major General Richard S. Ewell. He
would then hurl both divisions against Banks' isolated Union corps. Jackson, however, replied that
even with Ewell's help, he would still need 5,000 more
troops to attack with any chance of success. When
Lee could not furnish the extra 5,000, Jackson proposed a modified plan. Instead of striking Banks, he
would unite with 2,800 troops under Confederate
Major General Edward "Allegheny Ed" Johnson and
hit Frémont's advance guard. Then, using both Ewell
and Johnson, he would attack Banks. Lee approved
the plan May 1, and Jackson began his preparations.

This episode provides the first concrete example of
a trait that became the hallmark of Lee's generalship.
Time and again, he would seize the initiative and
parry enemy thrusts by hitting them hard. His offensive-defensive brand of warfare stressed surprise, mobility, and power. And as events would show, in
Jackson he had found a man whose practice of war
matched his own.

Lee and Jackson, in many ways, presented a study
in contrasts. Lee came from Virginia's "Tidewater"
aristocracy, Jackson from a hard-scrabble mountain
background that barely prepared him for the academic pressures of West Point. Where Lee finished
near the top of his class, Jackson had to struggle even
to keep up. Where Lee possessed great charm and
social ability, Jackson had a reputation for gawkiness.
Lee was moral and religious in a conventional way,
Jackson had the sort of passionate Christian commit-
ment that usually made Lee uncomfortable. But they
had three things in common: solid accomplishments
in the Mexican War, close personal ties to Virginia,
and a thoroughgoing preference for the offensive.

Confederate General Joseph E. Johnston, then
commander of the principal Rebel army in Virginia,
on the other hand, had a penchant for the defensive.
This officer, a veteran of the antebellum U.S. Army,
had helped secure Confederate victory at First Manassas and enjoyed the confidence of many professional soldiers. On May 1 he notified Richmond authorities that the Yorktown position was untenable,
that he intended to withdraw, and that all possible

reinforcements should be concentrated near the Confederate capital. Two nights later his army left Yorktown.

The retreat had severe strategic costs. It opened the
York and James rivers to Federal gunboats, and
caused the loss of Norfolk and its navy yard and the
destruction of the daunting Confederate ironclad
warship *Virginia*.

As fears of the loss of Richmond increased, the
Confederate Government began packing its records
for shipment to the Deep South. Anxious Cabinet
officials, wondering when and if they should order
the evacuation of the Confederate capital, asked Lee
where the next defense line might be placed. Dutifully, Lee replied that the Staunton River, 100 miles
south, might suit the purpose. Then his composure
cracked. "Richmond must not be given up," he said,
tears welling in his eyes; "it shall not be given up!" His
intensity astounded those who thought Lee possessed
boundless sangfroid. "I have seen him on many occasions," one of them later wrote, "when the very fate
of the Confederacy hung in the balance; but I never
saw him show equally deep emotion."

Fortunately, Southern defenses began to stiffen. In
the Shenandoah Valley, Jackson succeeded in defeating Frémont's advance guard and began turning to
engage Banks. On May 15 several artillery batteries at
Drewry's Bluff, below Richmond, rebuffed the
Federal navy's lunge up the James River. Hopes rose,
as Southerners learned that Union seapower was not
invincible. On its own, the Union navy had captured
New Orleans, Louisiana, the month before. But it
looked unlikely that it could repeat this performance
at Richmond. The Union looked instead to Mc-
Clellan to seize the Confederate capital. McClellan's
army, however, its nose bloodied in a severe rear
guard action at Williamsburg on May 4–5, was approaching Richmond gingerly.

Despite such encouraging successes Johnston had
nothing positive to report. Instead he began pouting,
saying that Lee had been directing the movements of
Jackson and Ewell, troops that were still nominally
under his own personal command. His complaint
merits a bit of exploration. As military adviser to
Davis, Lee possessed a certain authority to direct the
movements of troops, and Davis quietly saw to it that
he began to handle the movements of Jackson and
Ewell. He did this primarily because, for many personal and political reasons, he heartily detested
Johnston. Lee, for his part, appreciated Johnston's
sensitivity. But he could hardly second-guess President Davis' command arrangement, and he felt he
knew best how to utilize Jackson and Ewell.

Johnston next huffily requested to be relieved of

responsibility for the forces in question. Lee smoothed his feathers with a tactfully-written letter, saying, in effect, both he and Johnston would continue to exercise dual authority over Jackson and Ewell. Unfortunately, this arrangement did not work well. They sometimes issued contradictory instructions, and on at least one occasion, this messy command structure nearly scuttled the hoped-for attack on Banks. In mid-May Jackson sent Lee an urgent telegram to the effect that he wanted to do as Lee wished and strike Banks, "but under instructions just received from General Johnston I do not feel at liberty to make an attack. Please answer by telegraph at once."

What happened next is uncertain. Lee may have prevailed upon Johnston to countermand his previous instruction, or he may have gone to Davis and laid the case before him. It is even possible that he ordered Jackson to advance on his own authority. In any event, at dawn on May 21 Jackson set out to join Ewell for an attack on Banks. For five days neither Lee nor anyone else heard from him. Then came word that he had defeated Banks in three separate engagements, sent the Federals in headlong retreat across the Potomac and thrown Washington into momentary panic. The Lincoln Administration, fearful for the safety of its capital, permanently suspended its plans for McDowell's corps to join McClellan. Three of the four Union threats had been blunted or neutralized, thanks in no small part to Lee's suggestion that Jackson take the offensive, and to his unswerving support for the subsequent attacks on Frémont and Banks. There remained only the problem of McClellan's encroaching army, then within seven miles of Richmond.

Hoping to defeat McClellan while the rain-swollen Chickahominy River separated the two halves of his Union army, on May 31 Johnston unleashed his forces in a major, but poorly managed attack at Seven Pines. Lee and Davis knew such an attack was imminent, but Johnston did not bother to inform them of the assault before it was made. The chief executive and his military adviser were much perplexed, as they rode toward the sound of the guns during the afternoon. Upon reaching the battlefield, they found it a confused mess where chaos reigned. Lee, merely an observer since he was squarely on Johnston's turf, could not act. But Davis made a hurried reconnaissance and began giving orders for troop movements. Soon afterward, they heard rumors that Johnston had been shot, and moments later a litter came by bearing the general, conscious but in pain from two wounds. Setting aside personal differences, Davis knelt by Johnston and spoke to him reassuringly. Afterward he lingered to hear reports of the debacle,

then turned to Lee and informed him that he should take charge of the army.

For the first time in his thirty-six years as a soldier, Lee would have full command of an army in the field. His first act as commanding general was to give his new army the name it would possess from then on: The Army of Northern Virginia.

Reversing the Tide

When he assumed his new post, neither the army nor his countrymen regarded Lee highly. People still remembered the Cheat Mountain fiasco. "Evacuating Lee, who has never yet risked a single battle with the invader, is commanding general," sniped the Richmond *Examiner*. But a scattered few felt differently, among them Lee's predecessor. Told by a friend that his wounding was a calamity for the South, Joseph Johnston replied, "No, sir. The shot that struck me down is the very best that has been fired for the Southern cause yet. For I possess in no degree the confidence of our government, and now they have in my place one who does possess it, and who can accomplish what I never could have done—the concentration of our armies for the defense of the capital of the Confederacy." Another man with confidence in Lee was Colonel Joseph Ives, an officer who had served with Lee in the Carolinas. When a colleague suggested that Lee may lack the audacity to defend Richmond with proper vigor, Ives set him straight. "Alexander," he said, "if there is one man in either army, Confederate or Federal, head and shoulders above every other in *audacity*, it is General Lee. His name might be audacity. He will take more desperate chances, and take them quicker than any other general in this country, North or South; and you will live to see it, too."

Events proved Ives correct. But General Robert E. Lee possessed many other qualities besides audacity, among them sound administrative ability and reassuring "horse sense." Habitually gracious in all dealings with subordinates, Lee could also show great determination. When one of his generals whined about how McClellan's long-range guns would make defeat mathematically certain, Lee simply told him to stop it. "[I]f you go to ciphering we are whipped before-hand," he said. Instead, he preferred to concentrate on such positive measures as the construction of extensive field fortifications and the reorganization of his field artillery to increase its efficiency. He also renewed meditations on the virtues of the offensive-defensive strategy. Jackson, for example, was wreaking havoc in the Shenandoah Valley and insisting that with 40,000 troops he could invade the North. Lee felt such an invasion must await the relief of Richmond but viewed the idea with interest. "I think if it was possible to reinforce Jackson strongly, it would change the character of the war," he wrote Davis. He did reinforce Jackson in hopes that Stonewall might crush the remaining Federals in the valley. But when no Union forces offered themselves for immediate crushing, he changed plans, instructed Jackson to leave his weaker units in position and bring the remainder to Richmond. All possible Confederate forces must be concentrated to defend the capital.

In Lee's mind such a defense could not be passive; a passive defense would allow McClellan the maximum benefit of his powerful siege train. Therefore, despite numerical inferiority, the Confederates would have to attack. This was precisely the sort of audacity Colonel Ives had had in mind; to Lee it was a natural impulse. Numerical inferiority held no terrors for him. He knew of Napoleon Bonaparte's successful exploits against larger armies in Europe, and had witnessed Scott's triumph over a numerically superior Mexican army. Numbers, in Lee's opinion, were important, but not all important. Initiative, concentration of forces at a decisive point, surprise and determination counted for at least as much, and good intelligence was vital. Accordingly, on June 11 Lee summoned to headquarters his old associate from the 1859 Harpers Ferry incident, Confederate Brigadier General Jeb Stuart, the army's twenty-nine-year-old chief of cavalry.

Together with Stonewall Jackson and Lee himself, Jeb Stuart became the third member of the Virginia triumvirate that dominated post-Civil War mythology in the South. He became a legend partly because he behaved like a legend, displaying cavalier mannerisms, plumed hats, and a flair for the dramatic. The image, however, contrasted sharply with Stuart's deep piety and sound combat judgment, and Lee came to rely upon Stuart because of his shrewd intelligence-gathering and analytical abilities, not his theatrics.

Lee needed two critical bits of information before he could take the offensive against the Union army, and he wanted Stuart to secure them: first—the exact location of the enemy right flank, second—the line of McClellan's communication to the immense Federal supply depot at White House Landing on the Pamunkey River. To secure the information Stuart took 1,200 picked troopers on a two-day ride completely around McClellan's army, gathering intelligence, capturing prisoners and wagons, and outdistancing pursuers led by his unionist father-in-law, Brigadier General Philip St. George Cooke. When he returned he

told Lee the Federal right wing was "in the air"—that is, it continued several miles north of the Chickahominy River and then simply ended; it was anchored to no substantial natural obstacle. Also, McClellan's supplies were still being drawn exclusively from White House Landing. No effort had been made to change the Federal base to a forward point on the James River.

By mid-June Lee had settled upon the course he would take. His army would concentrate upon the exposed Union right flank, break it, then pitch into McClellan's rear and cut his supply lines. If successful the Federals would be forced to withdraw the way they had come, back down the Peninsula.

The idea of hitting the enemy right flank was not new. President Davis, General Johnston, and Confederate Major General James Longstreet had all proposed it at one time or another. But the details remained Lee's to figure out. In the days following Stuart's raid he devoted most of his energies to the problem.

McClellan had five corps east of Richmond but only one north of the Chickahominy. That force, the V Corps, under command of Brigadier General Fitz John Porter, had the dual mission of screening the Federal base at White House Landing and facilitating a jointure with McDowell's corps should it ever be released from northern Virginia service by the Lincoln Administration. Lee proposed to use the bulk of his 80,000 available troops to crush Porter and leave only 20,000 to hold the trenches directly in front of Richmond. When Davis first heard of the plan he naturally inquired what would happen if McClellan lunged at the weakened trenches while Lee was away. Lee responded, "If you will hold as long as you can at the intrenchments and then fall back on the detached works around the city, I will be on the enemy's heels before he gets there." Actually, Lee expected McClellan to go completely on the defensive the moment the Confederate attack opened.

On June 23, 1862, he met with the officers who would play key roles in the coming offensive. Stonewall Jackson was there, having left his troops, then en route to Richmond, and ridden fifty miles to attend the meeting. Lee gave him the vital assignment of turning the right flank of the Union's V Corps. When he had done so, the divisions of Major Generals Longstreet, Daniel H. Hill, and Ambrose P. Hill would cross the Chickahominy at Mechanicsville and attack frontally. Assailed front, flank, and rear, Porter's corps would be swept aside. The Confederates could then move on to sever McClellan's communications with White House Landing.

After presenting the plan, Lee left the room to permit his subordinates to confer privately. In particular he allowed them the privilege of determining the date of the attack based on their own intimate knowledge of the forces under their command. Since Jackson would lead the attack and had the farthest to march, the others suggested he name the day. At first, Jackson rather casually said the 25th would be fine with him. But the ever prudent Longstreet questioned this. Two days to march fifty miles and launch a major assault seemed a tall order. Ultimately, the four concurred on a day and time—the 26th about midday. As events showed, that, too, was unrealistic.

To everyone's astonishment, Jackson failed to get into position on time, nor did he report to headquarters news of his situation and whereabouts. Noon came and went on the 26th and nothing happened. Then at 3:00 p.m., A.P. Hill decided the offensive could no longer wait for Jackson. Without asking clearance from Lee, he led his "Light Division" straight for the packed cannon of the Union's V Corps. Reluctantly, Lee sent in D.H. Hill's and Longstreet's divisions to support the charge and his carefully planned offensive degenerated into a head-on slugging match. Thousands of Rebel troops fell to Union rifle and artillery fire without ever piercing the V Corps' formidable positions near Mechanicsville. Worse, the Federals learned of Jackson's belated approach and during the night conducted a skillful withdrawal to even stronger positions at Gaines' Mill, two miles east.

The 27th threatened to be a replay of the 26th with Longstreet and the two Hills again bludgeoning the Federals in brave but useless charges, while Jackson floundered about north of the battlefield. In the afternoon, however, Stonewall finally got his troops into action and by dusk the Federals were beaten. Porter successfully withdrew his battered corps south of the Chickahominy. McClellan abandoned his offensive and went over completely to the defensive, just as Lee had expected.

But Lee's own plans never quite worked out and the unfortunate battles at Mechanicsville and Gaines' Mill seemed to set the tone for the entire campaign. Time and again, bad staff work and faulty generalship scuttled spectacular opportunities to maul McClellan's army. Jackson continued to perform poorly, for reasons that have intrigued historians ever since. The most likely explanation is that physical stress—the result of weeks of intense campaigning in the Shenandoah Valley coupled with the exertions required to reach Richmond on time—finally wore Jackson into a state of extreme mental fatigue. But Jackson was not the only bungler. Another key subordinate, Major General John Magruder, found himself unable to handle large troop formations in combat,

while several lesser commanders, displayed little but mediocrity.

Still, the victory at Gaines' Mill forced the Federals to abandon their supply base at White House Landing and begin a risky withdrawal toward a new base along the James River. Lee saw the withdrawal as a gigantic chance to demolish completely the Army of the Potomac, something he had hardly dared hope for at the campaign's outset. But poor intelligence, poor use of artillery, poor tactics, and of course, poor generalship combined to prevent so decisive a result. On June 29 Magruder got into a costly but useless fight at Savage Station. The following day saw a botched attempt to envelope the Union army at Frayser's Farm. By July 1 McClellan had nearly made good his withdrawal and Lee was beginning to lose his much-vaunted composure. When a subordinate expressed concern lest McClellan escape, Lee snapped, "Yes, he will get away because I cannot have my orders carried out!"

At Malvern Hill, McClellan placed most of his field artillery to cover the final stage of his retreat. Swamp land on either side of the hill offered no chance to turn the position and it looked much too formidable to be taken by a frontal assault. Lee, with a stubbornness that would emerge on other battlefields later in the war, refused to concede McClellan's escape. He ordered a frontal assault. Lines of Confederate soldiers went forward against the black Yankee guns packed along the crest. They were shattered as Union artillery tore their ranks to shreds. D.H. Hill said all that needed to be said of the battle when he declared, "It was not war, it was murder."

But The Seven Days, as the battles between June 26 and July 1 became known, resulted in the salvation of Richmond, which was all most Southerners cared about. Lee became a hero. The Army of the Potomac, beaten though not seriously hurt, cowered along the banks of the James at Harrison's Landing. Of the 85,500 Confederates engaged, 20,141 had become casualties, a loss rate of nearly 24 percent. The Federals, by contrast, lost only 15 percent of their own force—15,849 from an army of about 105,000.

Many historians have since questioned the wisdom of Lee's costly offensive strategy. But the real question is whether he could have saved Richmond in any other way. And although conceivably the Confederates could have relocated their capital elsewhere, the loss of Richmond would have opened the entire eastern Confederacy to attack by the Federals. If the South could not successfully defend Virginia, where the gap between sea and mountains was only 100 miles wide, how could it hope to defend the much more open regions farther south?

The Battle of Malvern Hill, July 1, 1862. Lee's troops charged across a 900-yard field into the fire of more than 25 well-positioned Union artillery batteries. (Library of Congress)

No sooner did the Army of Northern Virginia dispose of one threat to Richmond than the Lincoln Administration produced another. On June 26, 1862, it activated a new "Army of Virginia" composed of three corps under McDowell, Banks, and Frémont, and led by Major General John Pope. Pope came from the war's western theater and had made a name for himself through the capture of Missouri's Mississippi River fortress at Island Number 10. Conceited, pompous, and boastful, he was an easy man to dislike. When, early in the war, a trio of Confederate generals appraised the old West Point classmates they might meet on the battlefield, they broke into a chorus of derisive remarks when Pope's name came up. "Oh, he'll never amount to anything," one of them quipped, "he's too vain and silly for anything except a ball room." Ultimately, these same men took great pleasure in causing Pope's downfall, a downfall that Pope himself seemed to have dimly seen coming. When ordered east he was unhappy about the transfer and to a friend's chirruped "And so you are going to Virginia?" he replied glumly, "Yes, to the grave of military reputations."

Pope's mission was threefold: to protect Washington, to assure Federal control of the Shenandoah Valley, and, by operating against the Confederate rail center at Gordonsville, Virginia, to draw Confederate strength from Richmond and thereby assist McClellan's operations. Hindered by the wide dispersion of his forces, his newness to the eastern theater, and

his matchless knack for alienating almost everyone, Pope ultimately became the victim of one of Lee's deftest bits of offensive-defensive strategy.

Lee shaped his planning step-by-step, constrained by the knowledge that McClellan still lay within striking distance of Richmond. As information accumulated, however, and McClellan's quiescence showed no sign of change, Lee felt assured enough to detach three divisions against Pope's Army of Virginia. These he entrusted to Stonewall Jackson, together with the curt injunction, "I want Pope to be suppressed."

The braggart from the West had already earned Lee's contempt by publishing a series of punitive orders against Virginia's civilians. Although by contemporary European standards the orders were not unusual, they violated Lee's rather chivalrous conception of war. From then on he considered Pope a "miscreant." In a letter to Mary Lee, discussing a nephew who had taken arms with the North, he noted that the lad had become a staff officer in the Army of Virginia. He concluded with cool reproach, "I could forgive his fighting against us, but not his joining Pope."

After a preliminary battle between Jackson's and Banks' men at Cedar Mountain, Virginia, on August 9, Lee brought most of his army north to join in the struggle against Pope. McClellan temporarily posed no threat, because Washington authorities had withdrawn his army from Harrison's Landing. For nearly two weeks Lee sparred with Pope amid the rolling countryside of the Rappahannock Valley, fruitlessly trying to bring him to bay before McClellan's army reentered the picture. A Confederate cavalry raid on Pope's headquarters netted a number of useful military documents which established the size of the Army of Virginia at 45,000 men and pointed toward its early reinforcement by McClellan's army. If Lee still hoped to defeat Pope, he would have to do it soon.

He did not feel strong enough to attack Pope directly, but neither did he feel like abandoning the attempt and retreating. Instead he elected to maneuver, hoping to cut Pope's communications, threaten Washington, and avoid a general engagement. On August 24 he called Jackson to his headquarters at Jeffersonville and instructed him to sever the Orange & Alexandria Railroad, Pope's principal line of communications. To accomplish the mission Jackson was given 23,000 troops, leaving Lee with only 32,000 to hold the upper Rappahannock crossings and fix Pope's attention. The division of the army in such a manner violated conventional wisdom, but Lee saw no alternative. The disparity in numbers between the contending forces rendered the risk unavoidable.

Jackson's execution of the operation gave proof that the military brilliance he displayed in the Shenandoah had not been lost. In a remarkable forced march of fifty-seven miles in two days, Jackson placed his swift infantry, his "foot cavalry," squarely upon Pope's line of communications, cut the Orange & Alexandria Railroad, and demolished a gigantic Union supply depot at Manassas Junction. As a finale, he disappeared into a secluded and defensible position near Groveton to await developments.

Aware only that Jackson lurked somewhere to his rear, Pope abandoned his Rappahannock line and began beating about the countryside in a disorganized attempt to locate Stonewall's forces. Lee, meanwhile, disengaged from the Rappahannock line as well and began a circuitous march aimed at a jointure with Jackson.

Crucial to this jointure was Thoroughfare Gap, a pass through the Bull Run Mountains separating the two Confederate forces. If Pope had sent a sizable detachment to hold the gap he might well have been able to fend off Longstreet while destroying Jackson's isolated divisions. On the 28th word reached Lee that the gap was indeed occupied.

It was a critical moment, but Lee exhibited no tension. Instead, he fired off a brisk series of orders to outflank the Union position, then went off to dine at the house of some local admirers. While the fate of the campaign was decided, Lee coolly exchanged small talk with his hosts.

After several hours of skirmishing, Thoroughfare Gap fell into Confederate hands. Late the next morning, August 29, the army was reunited as Longstreet's divisions assumed positions just southwest of Jackson's line. Jackson's troops had been in a fierce stand-up battle the day before at Groveton, and Pope assailed them again early on the 29th. But the Federals were unaware Longstreet later arrived in the vicinity. Lee saw an opportunity to crush the unprotected Union left flank and on three occasions tried to prod Longstreet into attacking, but Longstreet did not feel ready to do so. Lee decided to heed his subordinate's misgivings, a decision that reflected his willingness to respect the judgments of his officers. This established a fateful, perhaps poor precedent. From then on Longstreet seldom hesitated to resist Lee's orders if he disagreed with them.

On August 30, still blissfully unaware that Longstreet had arrived on the battlefield, Pope struck Jackson again. For a time the situation became critical; several Confederate units ran out of ammunition and were forced to hold their lines by wielding bayonets and even throwing rocks. Then Longstreet's five divisions broke from their cover and smashed the exposed Union left, sending the Federals in wild retreat until their officers could rally them for a stand around Henry House Hill on the old field of First Manassas. There, repeated Confederate attacks failed to dislodge them.

It made no difference. Stung by repeated reverses, Pope elected to withdraw his demoralized forces toward Washington. At a cost of 9,500 men, Lee had inflicted 14,500 casualties upon the Federals and had cleared northern Virginia of any major Union army. The miscreant Pope had been suppressed. More importantly, in twelve weeks of campaigning Lee had reversed the tide of the war in the East.

Lee's Mode of Warfare

With Pope beaten and McClellan's army withdrawn behind the Washington fortifications, Lee believed it was time to carry the war into enemy country—it was time to invade Maryland. Three major considerations impelled the move. First, the Union armies were weakened and demoralized, creating an opportunity to seize the initiative. Second, it might cause Maryland, a divided "border state," to secede and even lead Britain and France to grant diplomatic recognition to the Confederacy (although personally Lee doubted either event would ever occur). Third, and most important, it would permit the army to forage in Maryland and give Virginia the chance to harvest its crops unmolested.

Supplies gave an army strength, just as much as numbers or ammunition, and so throughout the war the hard realities of logistics constantly shaped Lee's strategy: if he could not feed his army, he could not fight it. He realized the army was not properly equipped for an invasion of enemy soil. It lacked sufficient artillery, transportation, and horseflesh. And the campaigns of the spring and summer had worn the troops' uniforms into rags. Thousands of them did not even have shoes. "Still," Lee concluded, "we cannot afford to be idle, and though weaker than our opponents in men and military equipments, must endeavor to harass, if we cannot destroy them."

Lee's ultimate objective, however, seemed to embody something more than mere harassment. He wanted to destroy the major railroad bridge across the Susquehanna River at Harrisburg, Pennsylvania, depriving the Union of one of its major lines of communication between East and West. A second line, the Baltimore & Ohio Railroad, already lay in Confederate hands. Destruction of Harrisburg's Pennsylvania Railroad bridge would leave the North with only the circuitous Great Lakes route as a means of communication. And Lee's strategic vision did not end there. He hoped, eventually, to attack one of the North's major coastal cities, possibly Philadelphia, Baltimore, or Washington.

A campaign of such magnitude would challenge even an army of 200,000, much less Lee's ragged and ill-equipped veterans. But Lee was developing an almost mystical regard for the prowess of the Confederate soldiers he led. Time and again he asked them for the impossible, and incredibly, they often gave it to him. He grew convinced there had never been soldiers like them. He also formed a correspondingly dismal picture of the Union forces and, especially, of Union leadership. When a subordinate seemed dubious about his sweeping strategic schemes, for example, Lee blandly explained that McClellan's caution made them quite practical.

Before Lee could take on the work of severing Federal supply arteries he first had to make certain of the strength of his own. In September 1862, as his army concentrated around Frederick, Maryland, it became obvious his communications required modification. The Confederates' supply line lay exposed to Federal cavalry and needed to be shifted westward, beyond the sheltering rim of the Blue Ridge Mountains. That, however, created another problem; two Federal garrisons at Harpers Ferry and Martinsburg in western Virginia could molest this new line. Lee

planned to eliminate the two garrisons as soon as possible.

Lee issued an operational directive named *Special Order Number 191*. It called for the division of the army into four major parts, three of which, under Jackson's command, would move against the enemy garrisons. The fourth part, consisting of divisions commanded by Longstreet, now a lieutenant general, a semi-independent division under D.H. Hill, and Stuart's cavalry, would proceed to Boonsborough, Maryland, where they would await completion of Jackson's operations.

When the Confederate army left Frederick on September 10, it broke into pieces—like a shell exploding in slow motion. Unfounded reports of Federal units operating around nearby Chambersburg, Pennsylvania, prompted the force to split into five parts instead of four: Longstreet's command continued to Hagerstown, Maryland, leaving only D.H. Hill's division near Boonsborough. Jackson's forces took longer to get into position than anticipated; not until September 13 did they drive the Martinsburg garrison into Harpers Ferry and besiege the combined Union force. When they did so, the fate of the town was sealed. With Confederate guns sited on areas surrounding the town, its surrender became a mere matter of time.

The Confederates did not have time. General Lee had miscalculated McClellan's response to the invasion. After the Federals' debacle at Second Manassas, the Virginian believed it would take three or four weeks for the one-time railroad executive to prepare the Army of the Potomac for new offensive operations. McClellan did the job in less than seven days. As Jackson's units sewed up Harpers Ferry, the main Federal army arrived in Frederick, just one day's hard march from the scattered Confederate army. If the Union general realized the exposed state of Lee's forces, the situation would become critical. And that is precisely what occurred.

By incredible coincidence, two Federal soldiers found a copy of *Special Order Number 191* in a field near Frederick, wrapped around three cigars. These "Lost Orders" sped up the Union chain of command to McClellan, who took one look at them and became understandably ecstatic. "Here," he exulted to one of his generals, "is a paper with which if I cannot whip Bobbie Lee, I will be willing to go home. Tomorrow we will pitch into his centre and if you people will only do two good, hard days' marching I will put Lee in a position he will find hard to get out of."

McClellan's euphoria showed how well he understood the opportunity presented by Lee's divided army. A swift thrust would put the Federals between the various Rebel forces and allow them to be beaten one by one. Unfortunately for the Union cause, McClellan lacked the killer instinct needed to capitalize upon the situation. Instead of insisting on an immediate advance and providing the solid, driving leadership required, he sent his columns forward at a leisurely pace that contrasted strangely with his spoken remarks. He gave Lee just enough time to retrieve the situation.

Lee heard about McClellan's dangerous advance near midnight on September 13. From a Confederate sympathizer in Frederick he also learned of the "Lost Orders." Longstreet received instructions to move at once toward Turner's and Fox's Gaps, two important passes through the barrier ridge of South Mountain. If the Confederates could hold the South Mountain gaps, they could perhaps fend off McClellan long enough to reunite their army.

The crucial struggle began at dawn, September 14. Elements of the Union's I and IX Corps struck D.H. Hill's division at Turner's and Fox's Gaps; farther south the Federal VI Corps attacked a Confederate force guarding Crampton's Gap. The Rebels had a bad time of it. One of Hill's brigades was nearly wrecked and all were severely pressed; only the timely arrival of Longstreet's men prevented a total rout. The Battle of South Mountain, as this action became

known, effectively ended Lee's hopes for an invasion of the North. From then on he was strictly on the defensive.

As evening fell on September 14, Lee gave orders for his army to regroup at Sharpsburg, a modest farm town miles to the west. Nestled in a "V" formed by the Potomac River to the west and Antietam Creek to the east, Sharpsburg seemed a strange place to make a stand. True, it offered high ground and the welcome barrier of Antietam Creek, but in case of defeat the army might well be trapped against the Potomac and destroyed.

Lee's decision to fight at Sharpsburg remains one of the most controversial of his career. Early 20th-century British military theorist J.F.C. Fuller felt it owed to "Lee's excessive contempt for his enemy; further, his personal pride could not stomach the idea that such an enemy could drive him out of Maryland." That statement seems overstrong, although Lee possessed an undeniable streak of stubbornness. The political damage of a quick retreat from Maryland so soon after entering the state as "liberators" may also have been a factor. What is most likely, however, is that Lee underestimated McClellan and overestimated the strength and prowess of his own forces. He fought at Sharpsburg, not from pride, but because he thought he could somehow win.

The Battle of Antietam: Federal soldiers clash with Lee's troops in front of the Dunker Church, near Sharpsburg, Maryland, on September 17, 1862—the "bloodiest day" in American military history. Lee fought an army twice the size of his own to a standstill, then retreated back to Virginia. Painting by T. de Thulstrup. (Seventh Regiment Fund, New York)

It is now known that the Army of Northern Virginia suffered tremendously from straggling and exhaustion during the Maryland Campaign. Thousands of shoeless soldiers fell out of ranks with torn and bloody feet; others were so hungry they temporarily disappeared in search of food. A sizable number did not believe in the moral justice of a Northern invasion and refused to cross the Potomac. If Lee was unaware of the full magnitude of these problems, he may well have thought the army he led was comparable in size to the force that had beaten Pope two weeks before. Actually it was smaller by nearly 25 percent.

The coming fight would be called the Battle of Antietam by the Federals, the Battle of Sharpsburg by Confederates. The wisdom of Lee's decision to make a stand there is questionable, but his conduct of the battle was magnificent. During the 16th his force managed to coalesce among the low ridges east and north of the town, although when the Federals attacked at dawn on September 17 Lee's Army of Northern Virginia was still understrength by thousands of troops. The initial Union assault crumpled several of Jackson's brigades guarding the left flank, then the fighting progressed toward the right as additional Federal units entered the battle in piecemeal fashion. The "bit-by-bit" nature of the Union tactics permitted Lee, acting as a sort of military choreographer, to shift his own units from one threatened point to another.

General Lee's command of the situation was virtually flawless, but the Union pressure became overwhelming. Outwardly calm, Lee was under tremendous strain. When he saw a straggler making off with a pig while his comrades were dying by the hundred, his temper exploded violently and he ordered the man to be sent to Jackson with instructions to have him shot. (Jackson, who needed every man he could lay hands on, placed the man in the thickest of the fighting instead.)

By late afternoon Lee's army was all but fought out, and still the Federals came on—this time striking the Confederate right flank. Lee had no more troops to meet the new attack. As he contemplated impending disaster, a column of marching men hove into view behind the Confederate flank. If they were Federals, the Army of Northern Virginia was lost. Quietly Lee inquired after their identity. An officer squinted through his telescope and reported, "They are flying the Virginia and Confederate flags." Lee nodded. "It is A.P. Hill from Harpers Ferry," he said.

Left behind by Jackson to complete the paroles of 11,000 Union prisoners seized at Harpers Ferry, Hill had finished up the job and then driven his Light Division to Sharpsburg in killing heat. When he unleashed them against that final Union thrust, the day was saved.

The Army of Northern Virginia had held its ground, but at tremendous cost: 13,700 casualties against Union losses of 12,350. The Battle of Antietam, one of Lee's most costly battles, is remembered as the bloodiest single day of the Civil War.

Lee maintained his troops in position throughout September 18, stubbornly defying McClellan to renew the attack. Then he withdrew across the Potomac into Virginia on the 19th. He spent much of the autumn months in the lower Shenandoah Valley, resting, refitting, and reinforcing his bedraggled army. Two corps were officially created: the First under Longstreet, the Second under Jackson. For Lee personally, it was a hard autumn. His hands, severely injured during a fall from his horse on August 31, did not heal until mid-October. Near the close of that month he learned that Annie, his second oldest daughter, had died in North Carolina. To his eldest daughter, Mary Lee, he wrote an eloquent testimony of paternal anguish: "In the quiet hours of the night, when there is nothing to lighten the full weight of my grief, I feel as if I should be overwhelmed. I have always counted, if God should spare me a few days after this Civil War was ended, that I should have her with me, but year after year my hopes go out, and I must be resigned."

Much to the disgust of the Lincoln Administration, McClellan tamely remained in Maryland during this period. Eventually this general called "Little Mac" crossed the Potomac toward Warrenton, Virginia, but Lincoln had had enough of his excessive caution and on November 7 relieved him of his command. Lee expressed regret at his adversary's departure. "We always understood each other so well," he explained to Longstreet. "I fear they may continue to make these changes till they find someone whom I don't understand."

McClellan's replacement was Major General Ambrose E. Burnside, an amiable, modest soul who had enjoyed some success in amphibious operations against the Carolina coast. When offered command of the Army of the Potomac, he tried to decline the job because he felt unequal to the responsibility. Events would swiftly and amply prove him correct. But, initially he did rather well, and within a week of assuming command he started the Union army upon a new "On to Richmond" campaign. This one aimed at sliding past Lee's right flank and crossing the Rappahannock River at Fredericksburg, about fifty miles north of the Confederate capital. Lee had to move rapidly to counter the move; initially he even felt he might have to fall back to a position along the North Anna River, halfway between Fredericksburg and the capital. Burnside, however, soon lost control of the situation and wound up giving Lee the easiest victory of his career.

Burnside's plans required a prompt crossing of the Rappahannock into Fredericksburg before the Confederates could oppose him in force. Unfortunately for him, the necessary pontoon bridges failed to arrive until well into December, giving Lee ample time to concentrate in and around the town. The Army of Northern Virginia took well-nigh impregnable positions on Marye's Heights behind the community, and continued their line for two miles to Hamilton's Crossing. Burnside foolishly persisted in his now pointless plan of campaign, and on December 11 two Confederate signal guns announced that the Federals were attempting a crossing.

Lee was unfazed. He wanted the Northerners to attack. With his troops posted on Marye's Heights, defeat was out of the question. The only unknown factor was the ultimate size of the Union casualty list. The entire Army of Northern Virginia had the same absolute certainty regarding the battle's outcome. Longstreet asked one of his artillerists about an idle cannon, only to be told that other Confederate guns already covered the ground so well its use was academic: "A chicken could not live on that field when we open fire on it."

The Federals succeeded in getting into Fredericksburg. Lee made no serious attempt to impede them. On December 13 Burnside made six major assaults against Marye's Heights. All failed. Massed Rebel infantry and artillery scythed them down by the hundred. Something of the exaltation men sometimes find in war welled in Lee's chest. "It is well war is so terrible," he confided to Longstreet. "We should grow too fond of it!"

The Battle of Fredericksburg ended as it was destined to end—in a cheap Confederate victory. Although Federals lost over 12,500 men, Southern losses totalled fewer than 5,500. But the confining battlefield of Fredericksburg offered Lee no scope for a counterattack. He had to content himself with watching the wounded enemy retire to the river's far bank. "We had really accomplished nothing," he later commented, "we had not gained a foot of ground, and I knew the enemy could easily replace the men he had lost."

After Fredericksburg both armies went into winter quarters, and the Confederates fortified a twenty-five-mile stretch of Virginia between Banks'

Ford on the Rappahannock and Port Royal. In January 1863 Burnside was replaced as commander of the Army of the Potomac by Major General Joseph Hooker, an ambitious opportunist and combative, competent soldier. Hooker restored the morale of the Army of the Potomac and prepared it for another offensive, while in the Southern camps a religious revival led to thousands of conversions and lent a temporary aura of spirituality to a normally profane environment. In March Union and Confederate cavalry sparred along the upper Rappahannock fords. The Federal horsemen, as usual, came off second-best against Stuart's magnificent troopers, but they seemed to be improving ominously. Then, on March 30, Lee went down under the first blow of the heart disease that would eventually kill him.

For most of his life Lee had enjoyed excellent health and flourished even among the miasmic climes of Cockspur Island and Veracruz. That spring, however, the pain that slashed his arm, chest and back took him by surprise and forced him into bed. He remained courteous toward his physicians, but the role of patient did not suit him; the doctors, he complained, kept "tapping me all over like an old steam boiler before condemning it."

As always the idea of the offensive continued to intrigue him. He expected Hooker to try to take the initiative by May 1. But Lee intended to grasp it himself and strike toward the Shenandoah Valley. A Union commander in that area, Major General Robert Milroy, had been acting with a heavy hand toward the civilian population and Lee wanted him driven from the valley. Besides serving as retribution, such a move might open the door to a second try at a Northern invasion, a project much to Lee's liking.

Hooker moved first. The resulting campaign, called Chancellorsville, often considered Lee's greatest, brought into play all the classic features of Lee's generalship: his obsession for the offensive, his unwillingness to allow circumstances to stampede him, his reliance upon Jackson, his enormous stubbornness, and his ability to capitalize upon an opponent's weakness. It also marked nearly the last time he was successful in the mode of warfare he preferred.

On the morning of April 29 one of Jackson's staff officers awoke Lee with word that the Federals were crossing the Rappahannock below Fredericksburg under cover of a heavy fog. Lee took the news calmly, almost jocularly. "I thought I heard firing," he said, "and was beginning to think it was about time some of you young fellows were coming to tell me what it was all about. Tell your good general that I am sure he knows what to do. I will meet him at the front very soon."

Lee and his generals. Among them, at far left, Braxton Bragg. Front left, Pierre G.T. Beauregard. With hat raised, Joseph E. Johnston. Behind the rear of Lee's horse, facing the artist, James Longstreet. With his back to the artist, Stonewall Jackson. Right of Jackson: John H. Morgan, Richard S. Ewell, Leonidas Polk, John S. Mosby. (Library of Congress)

The general rode to a hill from which he could see two Federal corps massing on the Confederate side of the river. Strangely, they did not advance but merely began entrenching beneath the protecting guns of their artillery posted across the stream. As the day brightened word came from Jeb Stuart of another crossing at Kelly's Ford, some twenty-five miles to the northwest. By evening Lee knew Hooker's main body had forded the Rapidan River at Germanna and Ely's Fords and that two large Federal forces threatened him front and rear.

Worse, with two of his best divisions temporarily detached and eighty miles away, Lee had just 59,500 troops with which to oppose an enemy almost twice that size. The Union corps below Fredericksburg contained 40,000 effectives under command of Major General John Sedgwick. Hooker—who had boasted that God must have mercy on Lee, for he would have none—had 57,000 more men in the main body of his army. In effect, Hooker had prepared a gigantic trap for Lee and conventional wisdom dictated a quick withdrawal before its jaws could spring shut. Lee, however, seldom thought conventionally. In his mind

Sedgwick's thrust represented a mere diversion; the situation as a whole was simply his big chance to hit Hooker's army while it was divided. He began planning accordingly.

For the next two days Lee sorted out the situations, weighed alternatives, and decided to concentrate against Hooker's main body. Leaving 10,000 Confederate troops under command of Major General Jubal Early to watch Sedgwick, Lee moved west into the thickets around Chancellorsville, a crossroads clearing just west of Fredericksburg surrounded by a dense second-growth forest locally called "The Wilderness." Stuart's cavalry, meanwhile, performed valuable scouting functions and prevented Hooker from finding out much about Lee's forces. So, by the evening of May 1 Lee knew two important things about the Union army. First, Hooker had stopped advancing and his men were felling trees to reinforce defensive fieldworks (implying a temporary halt in the Federal offensive). Second, the extreme right flank of Hooker's army lay "in the air," anchored to no natural obstacle and so inviting an attack.

As a pallid moon rose over the gloomy Wilderness

thickets, Lee and Jackson, by then a lieutenant general, settled down to plot their next move. Sitting on cracker boxes, they conferred for several hours, finally deciding that Jackson would take 28,000 men on a circuitous march across Hooker's front and ultimately strike that exposed right flank. Lee, meanwhile, would demonstrate with his 14,000 remaining troops and dupe Hooker into thinking he intended a frontal assault.

As in the Seven Days, if Hooker realized the true state of affairs he could turn Lee's gamble into a catastrophe. But in Lee's reckoning Hooker's construction of fieldworks indicated an abdication of the initiative. And, whereas Lee had retained his own cavalry to serve as the eyes of the army, Hooker had detached his on an extended but largely fruitless raid against the Confederate supply lines. He therefore lacked the intelligence-gathering force necessary to grasp sudden changes in the strategic picture.

Although Jackson's flank march culminated in triumph, it did not go off without a hitch. It began three hours late and was not carried off in complete secrecy. Federal pickets spotted Jackson's column as early as 9:00 a.m., and by early afternoon scattered musketry betrayed skirmishing between Yankees and Confederates along the line of march. Hooker, however, reacted cautiously and Jackson refused to panic. Despite a foray made by the Union's III Corps against his artillery trains, Jackson continued the advance and by 5:15 p.m. had drawn up his forces astride the Orange Turnpike, west of Chancellorsville, and faced them almost due east. Ahead lay the exposed end of the Union's XI Corps line, partially alerted but still largely unprepared.

Jackson gave the order. Suddenly the gnarled thickets filled with the banshee Rebel Yell, and the Confederates went crashing forward in the diminishing light. The XI Corps attempted to make a stand, with units here and there rallying in an attempt to stem the Rebel tide, but their tactical situation was hopeless. Jackson pumped additional divisions into the fight as soon as they arrived. By 8:30 p.m. the Confederates had driven two miles, folding Hooker's lines into a "U" centered upon the large, isolated house called "Chancellorsville," the house that gave the clearing and the battle its name. There resistance stiffened and the Confederate attack lost impetus in the gathering darkness.

Jackson, accompanied by a cavalcade of staff officers, rode forward to reconnoiter. A band of Confederate North Carolinians mistook his party for Union cavalry and opened fire, wounding him dangerously in the left arm. Compounding the mishap, Jackson's senior division commander, A.P. Hill, fell to

enemy fire at almost the same moment. Not until midnight did a replacement commander, Jeb Stuart, assume control of Jackson's corps, and Stuart had almost no idea of Jackson's plans to continue the attack. Lee received the news of Jackson's wounding almost as a physical blow. When a staff officer told of the circumstances under which Jackson had been borne to the rear, bleeding and in great pain, Lee cut him off. "Don't talk about it," he told the man, "thank God it is no worse!"

Attacks against Hooker's main body continued throughout May 3, without great success. The psychological blow had already been dealt, however. By noon Hooker withdrew his force into an enclave north of Chancellorsville. Meanwhile, Sedgwick's wing at Fredericksburg had shoved aside Early's 10,000 and was moving west at last. But an afternoon Confederate counterattack near Salem Church, about three miles west of Marye's Heights, blunted his advance.

Lee realized he had to turn his full attention to this other threat. Leaving 25,000 troops under Stuart to contain Hooker, the general threw the rest of his army against Sedgwick's two corps. The Confederates, however, could not get into attacking positions until 5:30 p.m. on May 4. Sedgwick simply used this extra time to withdraw to safety across the Rappahannock at Banks' Ford, north of Salem Church and west-northwest of Fredericksburg. Subsequently, on May 5, Lee reconcentrated against Hooker and planned an assault for the following day.

This last decision reflected Lee's tremendous stubborn streak in battle, for Hooker had had plenty of time to prepare his lines against precisely the frontal attack Lee was so determined to make. The implications were stunning; Lee seriously planned to attack an entrenched army numerically superior to his own. He seemed utterly resolved to wreck Hooker's force and blind to the fact that it simply could not be done. Fortunately for the Army of Northern Virginia, the Federals withdrew during the evening. Daybreak found them safely across the Rappahannock. Lee, enraged, vented his wrath against the general who brought the unwelcome news. "Why, General Pender!" he said, "That is the way you young men always do. You allow those people to get away. I tell you what to do, but you don't do it! Go after them," he added furiously, "and damage them all you can!"

Hooker, however, had long since moved out of reach. It remained only to tally the losses and bury the dead: 13,000 Confederate casualties this time against a total of 17,000 Federals. The Army of Northern Virginia had won again, but had absorbed

20 percent casualties in the process and the South could ill-afford to replace such losses. Nor could it replace one loss in particular.

On May 10 Lieutenant General Thomas Jonathan "Stonewall" Jackson died of complications following the removal of his wounded arm. Lee was unprepared for his trusted lieutenant's death. "God will not take him from us," he insisted, "now that we need him so much." But God did take him, and for the rest of the war Lee had to do without the one subordinate who could make his audacious strategies take fire.

Frictions of War

The history of a military commander must necessarily view his career through the lens of strategy, reducing the chaos of combat into orderly progressions of units "attacking," "defending," or performing other generalized functions. The commander himself must view warfare largely in these same terms or he cannot function. His whole task is to manage violence and produce from it certain rational, useful outcomes. But such an approach can be taken too far. War is not a game of chess, nor were the units Lee commanded mere pieces labeled "Jackson" or "Stuart." They consisted of men, and horseflesh, and equipment. And almost every component part could influence a battle's outcome. Karl von Clausewitz, the renowned 19th-century German military theorist, called the phenomenon "frictions of war." It affected Lee as it did every other commander, producing garbled orders, clashing personalities, exhausted troops. It takes great strength of will to minimize these frictions of war.

Although a general may be described as the head or brain of an army, such clinical analogies disguise the complexity of his role. He is a human being leading other human beings under the severest of conditions. He rewards men, inspires men, punishes men, instructs men. So to view Lee's generalship as the motion of units across a map is to see something useful, but incomplete. The way he actually conducted himself in war needs to be examined.

To modern eyes, the most striking thing about Lee's activities during the Chancellorsville Campaign is the extent to which he performed actions now allocated to staff officers. But this is not to say that Lee had no staff. Like most Civil War generals, Lee possessed both a general and personal staff, the former in charge of the various departments (quartermaster, ordnance, etc.), the latter working closely with the general largely to facilitate his paperwork. But the modern staff system of officers trained to monitor operations, devise strategy, sift intelligence reports, and perform other vital duties, did not emerge widely until after the Prussian victory over France in 1870. Lee's staff officers amounted to hardly more than clerks. None was a professional soldier, and none ever played a significant role in shaping Lee's strategic designs. At Chancellorsville, Lee conducted an average of two personal reconnaissances a day. He analyzed all intelligence reports, and not only developed broad strategy, but even conducted interviews with persons who may have known the best roads for a given movement. He came to distrust normal communication channels and, whenever possible, gave his battle commanders their orders in person.

For the most part, Lee gave his subordinates a great deal of latitude in tactical matters. "You must know our circumstances," he told a Prussian observer, "and see that my leading in battle would do more harm than good. It would be a bad thing if I could not then rely on my brigade and division commanders. I plan and work with all my might to bring the troops to the right place at the right time; with that I have done my duty. As soon as I order the troops forward into

Lee helped direct the Confederate attack on General Sedgwick's VI Corps at Chancellorsville, May 4, 1863. Sedgwick's efforts to overcome the attack, which was mainly directed against his left, were futile, and he had to retreat toward Bank's Ford. Sketch by Edwin Forbes. (National Archives)

battle, I lay the fate of my army in the hands of God." To a large extent this conception remained in force at Chancellorsville. Not only did Lee trust Jackson's independent judgment in the execution of the May 2 flank attack, he also permitted Jackson a major role in planning it. But Lee did not totally abandon his army to God. He retained direct control of two infantry divisions throughout the campaign, visited key commanders frequently, and on at least three occasions personally supervised the deployment of brigades and artillery batteries.

On the battlefield itself Lee acted merely as an observer. He led no attacks, exhorted no troops, and never drew his pistol from its holster, cultivating instead a demeanor of stoic detachment calculated to reassure those around him. During the fighting on May 3 one officer observed him "looking as calm and dignified as ever, and perfectly regardless of the shells bursting round him and the solid shot ploughing up the ground in all directions."

Although the general displayed no fire or dash, his mere presence on a battlefield could set off thunderous demonstrations by the rank and file. Late on May 3 at Chancellorsville, for example, he rode among his men as they swarmed victoriously around the blazing Chancellor house, which had been the center of the Federal position. They cheered him lustily, the wounded as well as the uninjured. A staff officer remembered the scene with awe: "He sat in the full realization of all that soldiers dream of—triumph; and as I looked upon him . . . I thought that it must have been from such a scene that men in ancient times rose to the dignity of gods."

Godlike he may have seemed, but beneath his majestic figure lay a mortal and increasingly fragile human being. At age fifty-six his health had begun to falter, and throughout the campaign he still felt lingering discomfort from his recent illness. The strains of combat and command tore at him. He spent many hours each day on horseback and many more making non-stop decisions under extraordinary pressure. When he slept it was usually on the ground, but often he did not get to bed until after midnight and awoke at dawn. In between, staff officers could and usually did rouse him to receive urgent reports and dispatches. Such stress occasionally led to a foul temper, usually when troop movements proceeded too slowly. But for the most part, Lee mastered his mood and displayed a suprising generosity of spirit. At Chancellorsville he bantered with those around him, fixed breakfast for a hungry courier, and fretted constantly for the wounded Jackson, on at least two occasions issuing specific instructions for Jackson's removal to safety.

Stonewall Jackson going forward on the Plank Road in advance of his line of battle. (Battles and Leaders of the Civil War)

Clausewitz's views on military genius make an interesting yardstick for measuring Lee. Physical and moral courage, the Prussian believed, were the first requirements. He thought that some men's physical courage stemmed from simple indifference, while in others it came from such positive motives as ambition or patriotism. The one he regarded as more reliable; the other produced greater boldness. It seems certain that Lee's courage was of the second variety—that it stemmed from an obsessive concern for his duty and not from indifference to danger. On one occasion, when he berated a subordinate for exposing himself to fire, the subordinate ventured that Lee himself was similarly exposed. Lee would have none of it. "It is my duty to be here."

The same obedience to duty that placed him near the firing line when necessary, compelled him to accept responsibility with equal verve. Clausewitz specified a particular cast of mind was necessary in a military genius, in addition to courage. Generalship involved making continual decisions on the basis of missing or conflicting information. "If the mind is to emerge unscathed from this relentless struggle with the unforeseen," Clausewitz wrote, "two qualities are indispensable: first, an intellect that, even in the darkest hour, retains some glimmerings of the inner light which leads to truth; and second, the courage to follow this faint light wherever it may lead." Lee's conduct at Chancellorsville embodied these qualities exactly. He not only grasped the opportunity in Hooker's very real threat to his army, he worked unceasingly to exploit it despite all obstacles.

Strength of will formed the third necessary characteristic Clausewitz prescribed, for when conditions become difficult an army begins to balk. "The machine itself," he noted, "begins to resist." The resistance need not be deliberate. It flows from the impact of the ebbing of moral and physical strength, from the heart-rending spectacle of the dead and wounded. These things a commander must learn to withstand, first in himself, and then in those he leads. Strangely, this seems one characteristic that Lee did not always display. Although he had a powerful temper he seemed ashamed of it and never realized that it could be used as well as abused. He had trouble rebuking his officers and had a helpless tendency to soften the blow, almost to apologize for it. Perhaps that is one reason why he needed Jackson so much. Not only could Jackson carry out his strategic designs with such brilliance and élan, he had more strength of will to overcome the inevitable resistance.

Finally, Clausewitz prescribed as necessary in a great general a longing for honor and renown. "Other emotions may be more common and more venerated," he wrote,"—patriotism, idealism, vengeance, enthusiasm of every kind—but they are no substitute for a thirst for fame and honor." Did Lee possess such ambition? One wonders; certainly nothing in his extensive correspondence reveals that he ever considered himself as anything but a man doing a necessary, unhappy job. That he possessed a streak of Caesar in himself is beyond credibility. Fame did not interest him. *Honor*, however, was a different matter. It stood beside *Duty* in its near religious importance to him; that it formed a strong motivating factor seems quite likely. Honor had been lost in the Lee family, lost by a debt-ridden father and by an adulterous half-brother whom Lee never mentioned. And honor occupied a signal place in the value structure of Lee's society. When Lee wrote of his decision to join the Confederates, "I only did what my duty required, I could have followed no other course without dishonor," he touched points that formed the core of his ethos.

To say that Lee was a military genius on the basis of Clausewitz's prescriptions alone would be trite, but military genius *is* what he possessed. Even after Jackson has received his full measure of credit, Lee's conduct at the Battle of Chancellorsville is considered a virtuoso performance. There he displayed his

full mastery of the military art. But great as the victory was, Lee had essentially beaten just one man, the commander of the Army of the Potomac. In later life Hooker would shrug and say of his defeat, "I just lost confidence in Joe Hooker." Lee's triumph lay greatly in helping him lose it.

After the Battle of Chancellorsville, the Union army remained intact. In a matter of months, even weeks, it could come boiling across the Rappahannock crossings again unless Lee acted quickly to prevent it. In the general's mind that meant a new attempt to invade the North. But an invasion required major strategic commitments, and it took no small effort to persuade the Richmond government to make them, for affairs in the Confederacy as a whole did not reflect the brilliance of Lee's achievements in Virginia. Tennessee was virtually lost, New Orleans had fallen, and a Union army commanded by Major General Ulysses S. Grant had besieged Vicksburg, the last major stronghold on the Mississippi River. The loss of Vicksburg would cut the Confederacy in two. To prevent such a disaster, many thought the Army of Northern Virginia should forego a Northern invasion, stand on the defensive, and send reinforcements to succor the troops in the western theater. President Davis, Confederate Secretary of War James Seddon, and even General Longstreet concurred. Lee, on the other hand, believed that only a vigorous offensive in the East could solve the Confederacy's problems, and to that end requested reinforcements of his own. After victory at Chancellorsville he enjoyed sufficient influence to carry the debate and the government reluctantly accepted his proposal. As June began, Lee's army embarked upon its greatest test.

"It's All My Fault"

The general spent the interval between Chancellorsville and the upcoming invasion reorganizing his army into three corps of three infantry divisions each. The three-corps concept acknowledged a new, unpleasant reality. With Jackson gone, Lee had no officer capable of handling half the army. Longstreet, recently back from an abortive foray to south Virginia, retained command of the First Corps. To command of the Second Corps Lee appointed Lieutenant General Richard S. Ewell, and for command of a newly formed Third Corps he appointed A.P. Hill, then a lieutenant general. Longstreet was a known quantity, a solid, stubborn, capable, if not daring commander who could be trusted in a crisis. Lee called him with bluff affection, "my old war horse."

Ewell and Hill represented question marks. Hill had fought with the army continuously since the war's beginning, but Ewell had been out of action since losing a leg in Second Manassas. Obviously, both had been outstanding division commanders or Lee would not have picked them for corps command. But leading a corps involved new problems, new ways of handling troops, and new responsibility. No one could accurately predict their performances.

In crossing the Potomac River and heading north once more, Lee had four major objectives: to break up Union plans for a summer campaign, to clear Virginia of Northern troops, to gather supplies in Maryland and Pennsylvania, and, if possible, to gain a decisive victory over the Army of the Potomac. On June 3 his army began its advance, generally moving in such a way that one corps covered the others as they marched. It slid slowly toward the west, slipped into the Shenandoah Valley, and on June 15 Ewell's corps smashed a reinforced Federal division at Winchester, capturing nearly half the defenders and opening the Shenandoah Valley as a highway of invasion.

That same day Rebel cavalry splashed across the Potomac near Williamsport, Maryland.

Lee's movements forced the withdrawal of Hooker's army from the Rappahannock line. The Federals began moving northward, east of the mountains, paralleling the Confederate advance. Rebel dispositions behind the Blue Ridge mountains remained hidden; Rebel cavalry held the gaps and Federal scouts could learn nothing. By June 26 Hill and Longstreet had crossed into Maryland, en route to Chambersburg, Pennsylvania. Ewell's corps had already passed through the town and fanned out across the southern counties of the state; by June 28 his units ranged from Carlisle to Wrightsville. Stuart's cavalry was also busy. After a bruising fight with Union horsemen at Brandy Station, Virginia, on June 9, he seized upon a new mission from Lee as a means of restoring the pre-eminence of his cavalry. Lee's orders were to contact Ewell and protect his right flank. And he was given discretionary authority to pass around Hooker's army as one means of getting into proper position. On June 25 he disappeared with three brigades of cavalry on

Lee on his best-known mount, Traveler, who survived the war and his owner. (National Archives)

what promised to be another glorious ride around the Army of the Potomac.

The Confederate army, meanwhile, politely but thoroughly plundered Pennsylvania. Foraging parties took almost anything the army could possibly use: shoes, hats, cattle, grain, horses, chickens, hogs, milk, butter, even sauerkraut (which the Rebels credited as a cure for diarrhea). But they paid for everything in crisp Confederate scrip, and if Pennsylvania merchants grimaced at such dubious currency they could at least console themselves with the knowledge that Lee would permit no stealing by his soldiers. Heaven, he informed a subordinate, would not prosper their cause if they violated its laws: "I shall, therefore, carry on the war in Pennsylvania without offending the sanctions of a high civilization and of Christianity."

The vow revealed how close Lee came to being an anachronism in his own time. Already during the war soldiers had taken and shot hostages and thrown men into jail without the chance to face their accusers. Crops had been confiscated, undefended towns had been shelled, and within a year the deliberate devastation of whole regions would become Federal policy.

In some respects Lee understood total war. He believed, for instance, that "the whole nation should . . . be converted to an army, the producers to feed and the soldiers to fight." But its indiscriminate violence remained anathema to him. Hatred was growing, however. And not even Lee's no-stealing policy could satisfy a populace embittered by invasion. At Chambersburg, a steely woman descended upon him demanding food for her neighbors who faced hunger because of the massive foraging. Lee told her she might send a miller to tell his commissary officers how much flour would be needed to weather the emergency, and was taken aback when the hostile woman suddenly requested his autograph.

"Do you want the autograph of a Rebel?" he asked dryly.

"General Lee," she snapped back, "I am a true Union woman and yet I ask for bread and your autograph."

Scrawling "R.E. Lee" on a slip of paper, Lee told her pointedly, "My only desire is that they will let me go home and eat my own bread in peace."

By June 28 Lee became increasingly worried by the absence of any word from Stuart. He had retired for the night, still bewildered, when at 10:00 p.m. a major on Longstreet's staff rapped at his tent pole. Apologizing for the disturbance, he told Lee that Harrison, a spy in Longstreet's employ, had returned with word that the Union army had crossed the Potomac. Lee was skeptical. "I do not know what to do," he said with weary candor, "I cannot hear from General Stuart, the eye of the army. What do you think of Harrison? I have no confidence in any scout, but General Longstreet thinks a good deal of Harrison." The major kept a diplomatic silence and at length Lee consented to interview the spy. Harrison, bearded, well-dressed, but tired and travel-stained, reported the presence of three Union corps at Frederick, Maryland, and two more near the base of South Mountain. He added that the Lincoln Administration, fed up again with one of its commanders, had relieved Hooker and replaced him with Major General George Gordon Meade.

Lee had no choice but to order an immediate concentration, lest Meade strike at fragments of his army. At Gettysburg, twenty-four miles east, a spidery road network made it the logical place to draw the army together. The orders went out; the separate corps began to converge. Unknown to Lee, the Army of the Potomac was also concentrating in the area and on July 1 a collision occurred in the hills west of the town. This began the Battle of Gettysburg.

Elements of Hill's corps ran into Federal infantry and cavalry; before long a sizable battle rocked and swelled amid the tidy farm lots north, west, and south of the town. Both sides fed additional troops into the fight as soon as they arrived, but the Confederates had the advantage: their troops were closer and came onto the field more rapidly. Two of Ewell's divisions happened upon the Union right, north of Gettysburg, and pitched into it furiously. The Federal line cracked under the pressure. By late afternoon the Confederates had routed one corps, pummelled another, and driven the survivors through Gettysburg. Hundreds of Northerners surrendered to closely pursuing Rebels while the remaining Federals withdrew south of the town to Cemetery Ridge.

Lee arrived on the field shortly after noon July 1, but found the action so fluid and confused that he refrained from giving any orders. As daylight waned, however, he made two fateful decisions. First, he elected to fight a general engagement around the fields and hills below Gettysburg, despite earlier doubts that the army was strong enough to fight a pitched battle against the larger Union army. Second, although he instructed Ewell to capture Cemetery Hill "if practicable," he failed to insist upon it. Ewell did not consider the move practicable and therefore did not attack, with the result that the Federals used Cemetery Hill, the northernmost point on Cemetery Ridge, as the foundation on which they constructed their entire defensive line.

If Lee felt convinced that Gettysburg was the place

to fight a general engagement, Longstreet felt equally convinced it was not, and in the gathering darkness of July 1 he took advantage of his close working relationship with Lee to propose a radical change of strategy. "All we have to do," he told Lee, "is to throw our army around their left, and we shall interpose between the Federal army and Washington. We can get a strong position and wait, and if they fail to attack us we shall have everything in condition to move back tomorrow night in the direction of Washington, selecting beforehand a good position into which we can put our troops to receive battle next day. Finding our object is Washington or that army, the Federals will be sure to attack us. When they attack, we shall beat them, as we proposed to do before we left Fredericksburg, and the probabilities are that the fruits of our success will be great."

To Lee this sounded much like wishful thinking and he replied flatly, "If the enemy is there, we must attack him." Behind this simple assertion lay many factors: the moral impetus of a triumphant first day's battle, the patent impossibility of Longstreet's proposal given the dearth of reliable intelligence concerning Union dispositions, and Lee's almost mystical belief in the prowess of his troops. But if he thought his response had settled the matter he was wrong, for Longstreet clung to his own opinion.

"If he is there," Longstreet pressed, "it will be because he is anxious that we should attack him—a good reason, in my judgment, for not doing so." He continued to talk and Lee affected to listen, but when he had finished Lee blandly pursued his original conception: to fight a full-scale battle at Gettysburg and to do so offensively.

A conference that evening with key generals in the Second Corps convinced Lee that Ewell should not make the main attack the next day. Since Hill's corps had already suffered heavily, that left Longstreet's corps for the assignment. Only two of its divisions had arrived on the field but Lee thought them sufficient to strike the Union left flank to the south. When they did, the other corps would demonstrate vigorously, pin down the rest of the Federals, and prevent their shifting troops from meeting Longstreet's thrust.

During the night both sides received reinforcements as additional units took their places in the battle lines. The Union line south of Gettysburg began to take on its famous "fishhook" appearance: the barb at Culp's Hill southeast of the town, the curve at Cemetery Hill, and then a long shank that ran for a mile or so south down Cemetery Ridge. The Confederate Second Corps faced Cemetery and Culps hills, the Third Corps occupied the northern half of Seminary Ridge to the east. The First Corps lay behind it, awaiting the morrow's attack.

The Confederate army's performance on July 2 contrasted strangely with the Battles of Second Manassas and Chancellorsville. Nothing worked as planned. Longstreet took all day to get into position and launched his attack only at 4:30 p.m. The assault, when it came, was poorly conceived and made without proper reconnaissance, but initially it did make headway. In severe fighting the divisions of Confederate Major Generals John Bell Hood and Lafayette McLaws smashed a poorly positioned Federal corps and plunged onward up the steep, rocky slopes of Little Round Top, a hill at the end of the Union's left flank. Only last-minute Union reinforcements beat back the Confederates there and restored the front. On the battlefield's opposite end, Ewell failed to begin a secondary attack until dusk and won little but casualties for his pains. The Union position had proven too strong, the Confederate thrusts too late or too weak.

Lee remained determined to continue the offensive. The great stubbornness that displayed itself at the Seven Days, Sharpsburg, and Chancellorsville dug in at Gettysburg. Despite the failures of July 2 Lee heard amid the reports glimmerings of potential success: good artillery positions *had* been seized, charging divisions had *almost* broken through, probing brigades had come *close* to breaching the Union center. Then reinforcements arrived in the form of an infantry division under Major General George Pickett and Stuart's long-lost cavalry. Morale remained good and Southern valor could still be counted upon. Lee ordered Longstreet to renew the attack on July 3.

Longstreet, however, tried again to peddle his own concept. "General," he informed Lee the next morning, "I have had my scouts out all night, and I find that you still have an excellent opportunity to move around to the right of Meade's army, and maneuver him into attacking us." Lee again listened courteously, then instructed him to attack the Union right with the divisions of Hood, McLaws, and Pickett. Longstreet responded that Hood and McLaws could neither disengage nor attack from their present positions. Lee accordingly revised his battle plan: Pickett would attack the Union center, supported by Major General Henry Heth's division and two brigades from Hill's corps.

After a long preliminary bombardment by Confederate artillery, the climactic attack began on the afternoon of July 3. Fifteen thousand Rebel soldiers in battle lines that stretched nearly a mile from flank to flank surged from the wooded crest of Seminary Ridge and headed toward a clump of trees on Cemetery Ridge that marked the center of the Union line. They charged bravely, those gallant men in whom Lee vested such outsized confidence: they charged bravely, and died bravely, and never had a chance.

136

Napoleonic assaults of that sort could no longer win against veteran troops firing rifles that could kill at ranges of 300 yards or more. Nor could they prevail against canister rounds, artillery loads made up of lead slugs that transformed cannon into gigantic shotguns. Valor was not at issue, and a general who helped lead the charge need not have been doubted when he claimed, "If the troops I commanded could not take that position, all Hell couldn't take it." What lay at issue were the tactical realities of 1863. By that time the balance of strength had tilted sharply from the offensive to the defensive form of warfare.

The survivors of what became known as "Pickett's Charge" came streaming back across the field, leaving their dead and dying comrades strewn across the shallow valley that separated the rival positions. Lee rode among the returning troops, shaken, saddened, and moved to a strange, almost wistful tenderness. When an artillery officer began whipping a recalcitrant horse he enjoined, "Don't whip him Captain, don't whip him. I have just such another foolish horse myself, and whipping does no good." When a wounded prisoner gathered breath to shout "Hurrah for the Union" as he rode by, Lee dismounted, walked up to the boy and shook his hand. "My son," he said, "I hope you will soon be well." To General Pickett he spoke soothingly, "Your men have done all that men could do; the fault is entirely my own."

In conversation with other officers Lee repeatedly and explicitly blamed himself for the defeat. "It's all my fault," he would tell Longstreet, "I thought my men were invincible." To a British observer he tried to be philosophical: "This has been a sad day for us, Colonel, a sad day; but we can't always expect to win victories." To a cavalry general that evening he revealed something of the depth of his disappointment and sorrow: "I never saw troops behave more magnificently than Pickett's division of Virginians did today in that grand charge upon the enemy." Lee's voice held a sudden excitement, remembering the moment when those 15,000 men had boiled up the slope of Cemetery Ridge. "And," he continued, "if they had been supported as they should have been—but for some reason not yet fully explained to me, were not—we would have held the position and the day would have been ours."

Lee paused. The memory of that terrible aftermath took hold of him. "Too bad!" he cried. "Too bad! Oh, too bad!"

"I Would Rather Die"

Lee lost nearly 20,000 men at Gettysburg; during the retreat he nearly lost his entire army. Summer storms caused the Potomac to rise, barring passage to retreating Confederate forces. With the fords unusable and the bridges long since destroyed, the beaten Confederates faced annihilation if Meade's Federals caught up with them and launched a determined assault. Meade, however, pursued cautiously. Minor skirmishing developed but no major attack. While engineers built a pontoon bridge and a jury-rigged ferry boat shipped across handfuls of men, Lee wrote Mary that he hoped God would not desert them. The bridge, a crazy patchwork of planks, scows, and barges, was completed on July 13. The wagons crept across it and the infantry waded to safety through chest-high water. The Army of Northern Virginia was saved, scarcely twenty-four hours before Meade had planned a belated attack.

The failure at Gettysburg brought Lee under the most intense criticism of his military career. On August 8, from the army's new encampment near Orange Court House, Virginia, he wrote a letter of resignation to President Davis which Davis lost no time in declining. But as time went on Lee became less inclined to blame himself for the defeat. Officially he refused to criticize his subordinates; privately he intimated that the performances of Longstreet and Ewell had disappointed him. After the war he told a friend, "If I had had Stonewall Jackson with me, so far as man can see, I should have won the battle of Gettysburg."

In the decades that followed, as it became clear that Gettysburg rang the death knell of the Confederacy, it became increasingly important to Southern writers to establish that Lee was not responsible, that others had failed him. Accusing ink pens were pointed at Ewell and Longstreet, especially the latter, for not only had Lee's "war horse" allegedly undermined Lee's authority at Gettysburg, he later found the temerity to criticize him in print. That was unpardonable. Admittedly Longstreet got carried away on occasion. He wrote, for example, that Lee was "excited and off his balance" during the first day at Gettysburg and that "he labored under that oppression until enough blood was shed to appease him."

Bad taste, however, hardly made Longstreet guilty of losing the battle. The fact remains that nothing much could have won the battle for the South. Had Ewell seized Cemetery Hill with his battle-worn troops, fresher Union forces might well have seized it back. Had Longstreet attacked on July 2 at 10:00 a.m. instead of 4:30 p.m. he would have encountered as many Federals posted on ground as good if not better than the position he finally attacked. He would have fought with fewer troops of his own because one brigade did not arrive until mid-day. Certainly Pickett's Charge contained the seeds of disaster from its inception. In short, a search for scapegoats is unavailing, for Lee lost Gettysburg as far as any single hu-

Tennessee's Rutledge Rifles, a group of Confederate artillerymen who fought in the terrible bloodbath of Shiloh in early 1862. (Tennessee State Library and Archives)

man being can lose a battle. He lost it through the same stubbornness that resulted in the disastrous Seven Days fight at Malvern Hill and that led to that amazing decision to storm Hooker's fortified lines at Chancellorsville. Lee himself admitted he blundered by considering his troops invincible and that he had misused them tactically. When Lee confessed, "It is all my fault," he spoke the truth exactly.

The Pennsylvania defeat ended forever the Southern army's days as an offensive weapon. Too many veterans had died, too few recruits took their places in the battle line, and worse, the heavy loss in field officers proved irreparable. Autumn 1863 brought several reversals that underscored the army's weakened abilities. In October A.P. Hill blundered into a trap at Bristoe Station, Virginia, and lost 1,300 men. The following month Union forces gobbled up an exposed salient at Rappahannock Bridge, resulting in the capture of 1,200 more. At the end of November the Army of the Potomac launched a Virginia offensive at Mine Run and, although it fizzled, the Federals withdrew unscathed despite Lee's intense desire to strike them. "I am too old to command this army," he remarked in sad frustration, "we should never have permitted those people to get away."

Old or not, he at least managed to defend the sector entrusted to him. The same could not be said for the Confederacy's other major commanders. In Mississippi Lieutenant General John C. Pemberton lost Vicksburg and 30,000 defenders in July 1863.

The following November, despite briefly holding a serious advantage over the enemy, Confederate General Braxton Bragg lost Chattanooga, Tennessee. In both cases the chief architect of Northern victory was Major General Ulysses S. Grant. A quiet, taciturn man sixteen years Lee's junior, the Virginian had known him slightly in Mexico. Grant was summoned to Washington in March 1864. The Lincoln Administration promoted him to lieutenant general, gave him command of all Union armies, and expected him to destroy the Confederacy. From then on he became Lee's chief antagonist.

Unlike previous Union commanders, Grant saw the war as a whole, and he devised a policy of simultaneous attack all along the military frontier to maximize Northern numerical troop superiority. Without the manpower to meet each thrust blow-for-blow, the Confederacy would succumb to attrition if nothing else. Federal armies prepared to drive into Louisiana's Red River Valley and against Georgia's rail center, Atlanta. In Virginia Lee faced not one but four offensives, three of them secondary but all of them dangerous. The main threat would come from Meade's army, whose operations Grant would personally supervise. Lesser armies would strike objectives in southwestern Virginia, the Shenandoah Valley, and the Richmond and Petersburg areas.

Lee believed that the coming struggle would be more severe than any previously, and that his army would have difficulty meeting it. Reduced in numbers and bled of many good officers, it also suffered from inadequate supplies. Clothing issues had dwindled and the meat ration had been severely curtailed. (Lee himself by then ate meat just twice a week; he generally dined on a head of boiled cabbage and a piece of corn bread.) He had one consolation, the First Corps, many months serving far away in Tennessee under Bragg, returned. In a solemn ceremony on April 29, 1864, Lee reviewed Longstreet's veterans. The men cheered him alone; the rest of the time they maintained an almost reverent silence that an observer likened to "a military sacrament." Including Longstreet's corps Lee had about 65,000 men with which to face the revitalized Army of the Potomac, 120,000 strong.

Early in May 1864 the Union army broke camp and began slicing toward the Rapidan River fords east of Lee's position near Orange Court House, Virginia. As they crossed the river the Federals entered the Wilderness, that gloomy expanse of dank undergrowth, deep ravines, and second-growth timber near Chancellorsville, ground Lee regarded as good terrain in which to precipitate a battle. There the dearth of good roads would reduce the enemy's numerical advantage while the dense thickets would give the superior Union artillery little scope for employment. On May 5 Lee threw his Second and Third Corps into action along the two main roads that entered the Wilderness from the west. The fighting soon grew chaotic as the choking undergrowth confused troops, hid the enemy, and slowed attacks. Initially successful, the Confederates fell on the defensive as the tangled vegetation drained their momentum and the Federals counterattacked. Neither side could see the other; the smoke and endless trees hid everything. Men simply blazed away at jets of flame that pierced the permanent twilight. As evening fell the woods caught fire and injured men screamed, begging for help as the flames licked closer to them. Those still unhurt could only listen to the shrieks of the dying in impotent horror because anyone who exposed himself was shot within seconds.

At the end of the day Longstreet's corps had not yet reached the field and Lee learned that a confusion of orders would delay it still longer. He accepted the news quietly, but at dawn the Federals launched a fierce attack against Hill's corps. The lines began to crumble, and Hill's commanders pleaded repeatedly for help. But Lee could only ask them to hold until Longstreet came up. Ordering the wagon trains readied for instant withdrawal should the Federals break through, Lee hurried to the front. The extent of the debacle staggered him; some of his best troops were streaming to the rear. To a veteran brigadier he exclaimed, "My God, General McGowan, is this splendid brigade of yours running like a flock of geese?"

The men needed only a place to re-form, the general assured him, but Lee knew that they would never find it unless the Federals were stopped.

In that critical moment the famed Texas Brigade of Longstreet's corps came onto the field and deployed for action. Lee saw their determined, dust-stained faces and realized the crisis had passed; the lines would hold now. Relief gave rise to euphoria. "Hurrah for Texas!" he yelled, waving his hat, losing his reserve, and surging into the midst of these veterans. He attempted to lead them in person but the men refused to permit it. "Go back, General Lee, go back!" they screamed, and would not charge until he complied. Reluctantly Lee subsided, the Texans attacked, and Lee ran into Longstreet who bluntly told him he should go farther to the rear.

For a time it seemed as if the great days of Chancellorsville had returned. The First Corps' counterstroke reversed the situation and soon it was the Federal line that was in danger of buckling. But terrain again thwarted the Confederates, slowing their attack and disorganizing their battle lines, and finally two of Longstreet's units lost their way, collided, and mistakenly opened fire. Longstreet himself went down in the crossfire dangerously wounded. The attack collapsed.

On May 7 both armies huddled behind hastily constructed trenches and breastworks separated by 1,200 smoldering yards of the Wilderness. It had been a new kind of battle, devoid of much maneuvering or tactical finesse, and a contemporary writer called it simply "the fierce grapple of two mighty wrestlers suddenly meeting." By the standards of previous encounters the Confederates had won a victory in this battle; they had struck hard, inflicted 17,000 casualties against a loss of 8,000 Rebels, and halted the Federal offensive in its tracks. The year before, punished with equal severity, Hooker had withdrawn. Grant, however, elected to slide around Lee's right flank and continue toward Richmond. He would not permit the Confederates to keep the initiative.

Grant's decision unmasked the psychological nature of Lee's previous victories. The Seven Days, Second Manassas, and Chancellorsville had broken the will of the enemy commander, not the enemy army. Suffering reversals at the hands of the Confederates, McClellan, Pope, and Hooker had not known what to do next. Grant knew, and though beaten in the Wilderness by Lee, he simply recovered and tried things a different way. He understood how to use engagements and managed to exploit this tactical defeat nearly as well as he might have followed up a victory. The character of the war had changed, become fiercer, more unrelenting. From then on the armies remained in contact from day to day and, with the exception of a short break in June, would do so until the final campaign, Appomattox.

When Grant moved around Lee's flank he headed straight for Spotsylvania Court House, a strategic crossroads that would place him between Lee and Richmond. Fortunately for the Confederates, the Army of the Potomac advanced clumsily and the Army of Northern Virginia moved with alacrity; the Confederates won the race to Spotsylvania, took up new positions, and immediately began to entrench. Such field fortifications became a staple of battlefields during 1864–65, for veterans on both sides had realized that trenches could mean survival.

"The great feature of this campaign is the extraordinary use made of earth-works . . . ," wrote a Union officer. "When our line advances, there is the line of the enemy, nothing showing but the bayonets, and the battleflags stuck on top of the works." At Spotsylvania these Confederate entrenchments cut the countryside like a jagged, inverted V. For nearly two weeks the Federals probed and pummelled it and tried to pierce it. And they came close to success; on May 12 two Union corps punched through a salient called the "Mule Shoe" and looked for a time as though they would split the Confederate army in two.

As in the Wilderness, in this battle Lee tried to lead the counterattack in person. Again his troops refused to allow it. After turbulent fighting the Confederates restored the line and a few days later Grant attempted another move around Lee's right flank. The Confederates blocked him just as before, this time from prepared positions behind the North Anna River, and their entrenchments appeared so formidable that Grant made no effort against them but slipped for the third time around the Confederate right, crossing the river.

These turning movements, although never decisive, demonstrated the new reality: Lee no longer had the strength to seize the initiative. His days as an offensive commander had ended. For the rest of the war he would not mount more than a local attack. But the master of the offensive proved even more formidable on the defensive, blocking every thrust, exacting a high price in Northern blood and creating a virtual stalemate. After the Federals' crossing of the North Anna, the Confederates raced again to block the enemy's way to the capital. At the Battle of Cold Harbor on June 3, by his skillful use of terrain and entrenchments, Lee defeated Grant handily. There, just a few miles short of his goal, Grant abandoned his plans to strike at Richmond. The Federal general instead would seek a new strategy by which to destroy the Army of Northern Virginia.

Other troubles then arose to challenge Lee's abilities. On June 5 a small Union army under Major General David Hunter routed an even smaller Confederate force at Piedmont in the Shenandoah Valley and occupied Staunton the following day. This forced Lee to detach 14,000 veteran infantry from his army. Led by Lieutenant General Jubal Early, the 14,000 managed to drive Hunter into western Virginia and even marched down the Shenandoah Valley to threaten the Union capital, thereby forcing Grant to send 40,000 of his own troops to repulse them. Early did not capture Washington, but his foray more than offset the weight of his departure from Lee.

Early's successful campaign, however, created a large secondary theater for Lee to watch and direct. He also had to guard against a sizable Union force that had landed at Bermuda Hundred, Virginia, south of Richmond early in May, and against persistent raids by the now-formidable Federal cavalry. At the Battle of Yellow Tavern in mid-May, Jeb Stuart died while trying to parry one of these raids and the news of his death dealt Lee a heavy blow—Jackson was gone, Longstreet was wounded, and now Stuart was dead at age thirty-one. "He never brought me a piece of false information," Lee later said quietly.

Meanwhile, Grant had seized upon a new plan and in mid-June 1864 began operations against Petersburg, an important rail center south of the capital whose trunk lines connected Richmond with the rest of the Confederacy. At nightfall on June 12 the Army of the Potomac began funneling south toward an immense pontoon bridge Grant's engineers had built across the mile-wide James River estuary. Lee had predicted a Federal attack on Petersburg and moved deftly once he was sure of Grant's objective, but Grant cloaked the movement skillfully and Lee did not fully discern the altered military picture until June 18. By that time the Union army came close to seizing Petersburg. Only Northern fumbling and a courageous stand by 9,000 Confederates under command of General P.G.T. Beauregard gave Lee time to get his ragged veterans into the Petersburg trenches for what ultimately became a siege of ten months.

Although the only move available, the decision to defend the town held the elements of ruin. With no more room to maneuver, the Confederate army would be ground to powder. "However bold we might be," wrote a Confederate officer, "however desperately we might fight, we were sure in the end to be worn out. It was only a question of a few months, more or less."

Lee came to Petersburg to defend its railroads and they became his primary concern. He planned to hold the exposed Petersburg-Weldon Railroad as long as possible, then concentrate on retaining the vital Southside Railroad. If the Southside were lost no further supplies could reach Lee's army and disaster would result. Aggressive spoiler attacks in the latter part of June helped check further Union encroachments, but Lee knew he lacked the resources for a counter-offensive. Instead he hoped Grant would be foolish enough to attack the Petersburg trenches directly, for a defensive battle offered Lee his only serious means of damaging the enemy.

During July the Confederates began to suspect the Federals were planting an explosive mine beneath their works. Southern engineers sank counter-shafts and established listening galleries* but discovered nothing; before long the mining rumor became a kind of running joke. Then, at 4:44 a.m. on July 30, 1864, an 8,000-pound gunpowder charge blew apart "Elliott's Salient," a weak point in the Confederate trench system very close to Union lines. The explosion hurled men, guns, and debris high into the air and left a mammoth crater some 100 feet in diameter and 30 feet deep.

By the time Lee arrived on the scene, the crater had filled with thousands of Union attackers who threatened to crack the Confederate line wide open. He organized an immediate counterattack. A Confederate brigadier general named William Mahone was in temporary command of the nearest infantry division and he spearheaded a charge with headlong ferocity. The Confederates waded into the hapless Federals, shooting, stabbing, and clubbing them; soon they had cleared the crater, repulsed the Federals, and sealed the gap in the Confederate trenches. A grateful Lee named Mahone to permanent command of the division and from then on the scrappy little fighter became one of Lee's hard-hitters.

The "Battle of the Crater," as this bizarre fight was known, served notice that the Army of Northern Virginia still packed a whallop. Then at Reams Station, Virginia, along the Southside Railroad in August, A.P. Hill provided additional proof of this by giving the Yankees battle and by capturing 2,000 Federals at a cost of only 600 Confederates. And then in September, Confederate Major General Wade Hampton led the celebrated "Beefsteak Raid" in which his cavalry rode around to the Union rear and made off with an entire herd of Yankee cattle.

These were only bright spots in an increasingly stormy sky. In mid-August Lee was forced to abandon the Petersburg-Weldon Railroad and disasters on other fronts became daily news. In August a Union

fleet captured Alabama's Mobile Bay and in September Atlanta, Georgia, fell to Union Major General William T. Sherman's veteran troops. And during September and October 1864 powerful Union forces under command of Major General Philip Sheridan smashed Early's army in the Shenandoah Valley and torched and vandalized the entire region.

Lee, pinioned against the Richmond and Petersburg defenses, lamented the steady attrition and began to feel that "Richmond was the millstone dragging down this army." To protect it the Confederates had to stretch their weakly held lines to meet Grant's continual encroachments on their right flank. The lack of sufficient Confederate manpower became an obsession with Lee that even crept into his family correspondence. "Tell the young women to send me all their beaux," he wrote Mary. "I want them at once."

As the Confederacy collapsed on other fronts, Union forces penetrated deep into the Southern heartland. Confederate veterans who had faced many battles without shrinking began to desert by the hundreds in order to look after their families in war-ravaged areas. In a one-month period desertions claimed nearly 8 percent of Lee's effective strength.

By the beginning of 1865 the South had clearly lost the war. But the Confederate Government held on, desperately hoping for a miracle, and in February placed Lee in charge of all its armies. But the time had passed when anything much could be done. Roughly 50,000 troops remained to defend the Richmond-Petersburg area, while 15,000 more men under command of General Joseph Johnston struggled ineffectually against Sherman's armies in North Carolina. These troops, plus a handful of other minor forces, comprised the Confederacy's remaining military strength.

Strategy degenerated into a simple struggle to delay the inevitable. On March 5, 1865, on Lee's orders, Major General John B. Gordon's division struck Grant's army at "Fort Stedman," a seige fort on the eastern Petersburg trench lines, hoping that a surprise blow would cause Grant to contract his lines and permit the detachment of men from the Army of Northern Virginia to reinforce Johnston's army. The operation failed completely; the Federals scarcely realized it had been intended as a serious attack.

Four days later a powerful Union force under Philip Sheridan shattered the Confederate right flank at Five Forks. Grant followed up the success with a general attack all along the line, and the Petersburg fortifications cracked at last. Federal troops roamed throughout the entrenchments as Lee's army withdrew; a party of them, or perhaps just a straggler,

*A listening gallery is a shaft sunk to a point in advance of one's defensive lines. Observers there literally listen for the subterranean sounds of approaching enemy miners.

142

found A.P. Hill and killed him. Lee heard the news of Hill's death as he made preparations for a general evacuation to the west. "He is at rest now," Lee said, "and we are the ones who are left to suffer."

The whole world seemed to collapse in chaos and flames. Lee withdrew from Petersburg on April 2, taking 15,000 remaining troops. President Davis fled South with most of his Cabinet to Danville, Virginia, before continuing his flight into the Deep South. Richmond fell; the few surviving Confederate units north of the James River struck out westward to join Lee's army. The only hope lay in reaching Johnston's army. But without food and nearly exhausted, Lee's gaunt veterans fell out of ranks by the hundreds and were scooped up by Federal cavalry. Powerful columns of infantry and horsemen pursued them ceaselessly. Lee headed first to Amelia Court House, hoping to find rations for his hungry troops, but none materialized. He continued toward Farmville, still hoping for rations, but now doubting he could ever reach Johnston.

At Sayler's Creek on April 6, superior Union forces destroyed Robert Lee's rear guard and took thousands of prisoners. "My God, has the army been dissolved?" the general cried when he heard the news. By the following evening the Federal army had nearly caught up with the rest of his force and Grant sent him a summons to surrender. Wordlessly, Lee passed the message to stolid, blunt-spoken Longstreet, who merely grunted, "Not yet."

The Civil War ends for the defeated Army of Northern Virginia and its commander, Robert E. Lee: "They crowded about him as he went, their eyes wet with tears." Drawn by George Varian, this originally appeared in McClure's Magazine, *April 1901.*

The retreat continued throughout the 8th to a small spot called Appomattox Court House. It was a heartbreaking march, hemmed in by Federal pursuers, and increasingly pointless. A spokesman for several of Lee's generals approached and suggested it was time to think about surrendering. "Surrender?" Lee echoed coldly. "I have too many good fighting men for that!" But evening brought word that Northern cavalry blocked the way ahead. The general met with Gordon, Longstreet, and his nephew Fitzhugh Lee outside Appomattox to discuss the situation. With a calm born of deep weariness and resignation, the four decided to attempt a break-out in the morning. Longstreet's surviving troops would cover the rear while Gordon's and Fitzhugh Lee's men engaged the troops in front. If they met only cavalry they would knock it aside and continue toward Lynchburg, Virginia, but if they encountered infantry, they would have no choice but to surrender.

Although duty required such an attempt, Lee doubted its chances of success. When he appeared on the morning of April 9 he wore his best dress uniform. "I have probably to be Grant's prisoner," he explained, "and I thought I must make my best appearance." At 5:00 a.m. he rode through Appomattox Court House while his troops attempted their all-or-nothing breakthrough. It did not last long. Fitzhugh Lee managed to escape with most of his cavalry, but Gordon's infantry never had a chance. When one of Lee's staff officers rode up to observe the situation, Gordon shouted at him above the din of gunfire, "Tell General Lee I have fought my troops to a frazzle, and I fear I can do nothing unless I am heavily supported by Longstreet." When Lee heard this he knew further resistance was impossible: Longstreet, three miles away, was preparing to receive a major Federal attack and could offer no help at all.

"Then there is nothing left me but to go and see General Grant," Lee said mournfully on hearing the news, "and I would rather die a thousand deaths."

After some difficulty, a temporary cease-fire was arranged and at 1:30 p.m. Lee and Grant met at the McLean House in Appomattox Court House. Grant brought with him a coterie of generals and staff officers anxious to observe the surrender. Lee brought only Colonel Charles Marshall, his military secretary.

The surrender meeting is so well-known as to bear almost the character of a play. Lee and Grant spoke quietly, courteously about the required terms. The Federal commander stipulated only that the troops must agree not to take up arms again until properly exchanged. He permitted officers to keep their sidearms, personal mounts and baggage, and allowed enlisted men to retain any horses they might own. At

Lee's request, Grant ordered the dispatch of 25,000 rations to feed the hungry Confederates.

The familiar motif of Southern chivalry meeting Northern modernity, so often favored by tellers of the Appomattox story, is nonsense. In many ways Lee formed the antithesis of the cavalier tradition and had a rather Puritanical cast of mind. Grant, a middle-class tanner before the war, had grown up in and loved the rural and small-town America that industrialization would destroy forever. Both men, in their own ways, resisted the traditions from which they sprang; both displayed more compassion than the societies that bred them. And in a world where civil wars commonly end with firing squads and penal camps, the grandeur of those two men is something a more modern age cannot claim as its own. It can only look back on them with humility and awe.

Marching out of Step

After the war Lee survived just five more years, until the heart disease that first assailed him in 1863 killed him in 1870. Following his surrender, he went first to Richmond and rejoined his family at a house on Franklin Street rented by his son Custis. He had nowhere else to go. Arlington was gone, confiscated by Federal authorities for non-payment of taxes. Its spacious lawns now held the graves of thousands of Northern soldiers. The other Custis properties lay in ruin and Lee's first desire became to find a permanent home. "I am looking for some quiet place in the woods," he wrote, "where I can procure shelter and my daily bread if permitted by the victor."

The whims of "the victor" remained heavily on Lee's mind. Federal President Abraham Lincoln had been murdered on April 14 by a thespian possessed of passionate Southern sympathies, John Wilkes Booth. The assassination only increased the North's desire for vengence and a hard peace. Union authorities captured Jefferson Davis, flung him into prison, and in June 1865 indicted Lee for treason. Through Senator Reverdy Johnson of Maryland, a unionist friend who favored reconciliation with the South, Lee asked Grant to help him. The terms of his parole at Appomattox, he maintained, stipulated that he would not "be disturbed by the United States authority."

Grant agreed to help and angrily threatened to resign from the army if Federal authorities arrested Lee. In a letter to Grant, Lee enclosed his application for the restoration of his citizenship; Grant forwarded it to President Andrew Johnson and asked that he quash the indictments against Lee and other Confederate prisoners. Although the Johnson Administration declined to do so, it nevertheless suspended Lee's

After the war, Lee accepted the presidency of Washington College, later renamed Washington & Lee. (CWTI Collection)

prosecution and he was never arrested, brought to trial, nor, during his lifetime, restored to citizenship.

In applying for citizenship Lee established a precedent that greatly influenced other Southerners. Captain George Wise, a son of Confederate Brigadier General Henry Wise, angrily protested to Lee that he did not think the terms of his parole obliged him to take the oath of allegiance and he would sooner leave the country than do so. Lee told him quietly, "Do not leave Virginia. Our country needs her young men now." Captain Wise signed the oath.

"You have disgraced the family!" thundered General Wise when he heard of it.

His son blandly responded, "General Lee advised me to do it." The old man was instantly mollified.

"Oh, that alters the case," he gruffed. "Whatever General Lee says is all right, I don't care what it is." Thousands felt the same way. In postwar days, at St. Paul's Episcopal Church in Richmond, a black man came forward to receive Holy Communion. The congregation, accustomed to racial segregation, froze in horror until Lee walked up to the chancel rail and knelt not far from the man, whereupon they too came forth and the service continued.

During the summer of 1865 Lee moved his family to Derwent, a secluded if dilapidated house in the Virginia countryside offered for his use by friends. The dwelling gave him some semblance of a home, but what he really needed was a job. During a visit to Staunton, Lee's daughter Mary happened to say as much. The remark intrigued the man who heard it. He belonged to the Washington College Board of Trustees. The college had few students, less income, and no president. At the next board meeting, this man made a novel proposal: elect Robert E. Lee to serve as president of the college. If he came, students and funding would certainly follow. The board liked the idea and voted Lee in on the spot. Then they packed off a representative to Derwent to see whether Lee would accept.

Lee thought over the college's offer for three weeks. He had no educational background beyond his tenure as superintendent of West Point over ten years before. He was still under indictment for treason and his past might bring harm to any institution with which he might associate. Worse, his health had begun to decline and he did not think he could perform more than administrative duties. But the cause of Southern education had strong appeal. "If I thought I could be of any benefit to our noble youth," he informed a friend, "I would not hesitate to give my services." He therefore accepted, subject to the condition that he would undertake no active teaching that might jeopardize his health. Overjoyed, the trustees officially installed him as president in mid-September 1865.

Washington College had its campus in Lexington, Virginia, the same town where the Virginia Military Institute (VMI) was located. Lee embarked at once upon his duties as college president and helped redefine the curriculum to reflect the South's need for men who could rebuild her. Metallurgy, engineering, and other practical skills were emphasized. He also wrote dignified letters that solicited financial help for the college and letters that encouraged students to resume their studies after spending years in the war. One veteran told him, "I am so impatient to make up for the time I lost in the army." Lee cut him off sharply. "Mister Humphreys!" he snapped. "However long you live and whatever you accomplish, you will find that the time you spent in the Confederate army was the most profitably spent portion of your life. Never again speak of having lost time in the army."

If Lee expected pride in having served the Confederacy, he also expected loyalty to the re-established Union. Again and again, he hammered away at the need for reconciliation and peace. "I need not tell you," he wrote to General Beauregard, "that true patriotism sometimes requires of men to act exactly contrary, at one period, to that which it does at another, and the motive which impels them—the desire to do right—is precisely the same . . . History is full of illustrations of this: Washington himself is an example of this. At one time he fought in the service of the King of England; at another he fought with the French at Yorktown, under the orders of the Continental Congress of America, against him. He has not been branded by the world with reproach for this, but his course has been applauded." To the widow of a Confederate soldier Lee spoke frankly, "Madam, do not train up your children in hostility to the government of the United States. Remember, we are all one country now. Dismiss from your mind all sectional feeling, and bring them up to be Americans."

Civilian life had great appeal for him and he shucked off the regimentation of his military years with genuine relief. In a letter to General Ewell he remarked that he had wasted the best years of his existence and he told a professor, "The greatest mistake of my life was taking a military education." On ceremonial occasions when the students and faculty of Washington College marched with those of VMI, Lee deliberately marched out of step.

As a national figure, politics occasionally lumbered into his life despite his continued distaste for it. Sometimes the intrusions were benign if somewhat bizarre, as in 1868 when the New York *Herald* proposed that the Democratic party nominate him for U.S. President. Other times they proved necessary in the interests of sectional harmony, as when he assisted former Union Major General William S. Rosecrans in organizing support for the 1868 Democratic ticket.

Occasionally, however, the intrusions proved wholly unwelcome. In 1866, for example, a Congressional subcommittee summoned him to testify upon the suitability of Virginia and the Carolinas for readmission to the Union. Lee candidly informed the members that Southerners would probably object to giving Blacks the vote; that most felt as he did that the decisions of their states to secede had bound them personally; and that Northern attempts to blame him for the deaths of Union prisoners neglected to consider Grant's late war refusal to allow prisoner exchanges. In November 1867 a Richmond grand jury ordered him to testify during the legal proceedings against Jefferson Davis, and the prosecution attempted to wrest from him an admission that he had conducted military operations at Davis' behest. Lee, however, refused to be drawn. "I am responsible for what I did," he declared frankly, "and I cannot now recall any important movement I made which I would not have made had I acted entirely on my own responsibility."

The harsh "Reconstruction Acts," punitive legislation affecting the property and lifestyles of ex-Confederates, outraged many Southerners, including Lee's wife. Of the Northern "carpetbaggers" and Southern "scalawags," unionists who wielded postwar power in the South, she fumed: "It is bad enough to be the victims of tyranny, but when it is wielded by such cowards and base men . . . it is indeed intolerable. The country that allows such scum to rule them must be fast going to destruction."

Robert Lee, however, believed ever more firmly in the preservation of harmony and kind feelings; his yearly vacations at White Sulphur Springs, Virginia, became annual campaigns for sectional friendship. Each summer the springs, a fashionable spa, drew the rich and well-connected to taste the waters and be seen with one another. Lee himself went for the sake of his deteriorating health; once there he worked unceasingly to persuade the élite of the South to behave with courtesy toward those of the North. Yet even his mountainous reputation could not always prod his compatriots to overcome their enmity toward Yankees. On one occasion at the springs he searched in vain for a Southern belle to introduce him to Andrew Curtin, Pennsylvania's war-era governor who had been instrumental in the struggle against the Confederacy. Sternly he told a group of young ladies that he would introduce himself if they would not, adding that he would be glad to present any who would accompany him. Finally one rose and said, "I will go, General Lee, under your orders."

"Not under my orders," he replied, "but it will gratify me deeply to have your assistance." Taking her arm, he led the girl across the ballroom floor toward Governor Curtin and his party, but halfway across he paused and spoke softly, urgently.

"He told me," she later remembered, "of the grief with which he found a spirit of unreasoning resentment and bitterness in the young people of the South, of the sinfulness of hatred and social revenge, of the duty of kindness, helpfulness and consideration of others."

"But, General Lee," she said, "did you never feel resentment towards the North?"

Lee replied he was neither bitter nor resentful. "When you go home," he added, "I want you to take a message to your young friends. Tell them from me that it is unworthy of them as women, and especially as Christian women, to cherish feelings of resentment against the North. Tell them that it grieves me inexpressibly to know that such a state of affairs exists, and that I implore them to do their part to heal our country's wounds." With that he led her on to Curtin's party and graciously made the introductions.

Robert E. Lee died on October 12, 1870, at the age of sixty-three. Neither his visits to the springs nor a trip to the Deep South made for the sake of his health could save him from the heart that finally failed him. On a rainy autumn night he returned from a meeting of the college board, haggard and unable to speak. The doctors that rushed to his bedside diagnosed what amounted to cerebral thrombosis coupled with a throat infection and his ever-present heart disease. He succumbed a few days later. It was not given him to die a civilian. In the last hours of his life the delirium overtook him, the smoke of war returned, and he uttered commands to generals long in their graves. "Tell A.P. Hill he *must* come up!" Lee said at one point, and finally, "Strike the tent."

Dying words are dramatic, yet so often unrevealing of the man who gives his final breaths to utter them. Real greatness is never found on a battlefield, and if Lee was a great captain that did not automatically make him great as a man. Real greatness must at last be found in humanity, in the slow, stubborn will to behave with compassion and decency no matter the circumstances or cost. In the life of Robert E. Lee

Edward Valentine's recumbent statue of Robert E. Lee. (Washington and Lee University)

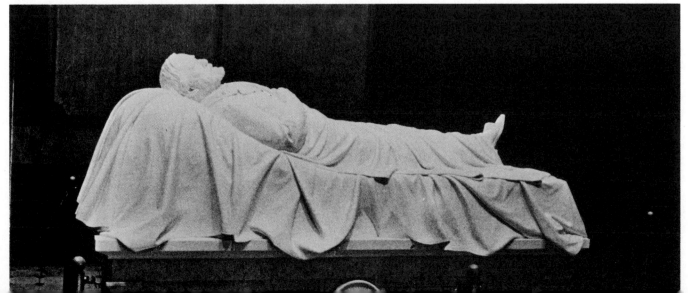

Lee Chapel in Lexington, Virginia, on the day of the general's funeral in October 1870. Lee's widow and all his children also repose in the chapel. (Washington and Lee University)

many moments could be found to capsulize his essence and point at least vaguely toward the human greatness he possessed. Perhaps none characterizes him quite so well, however, as another incident that occurred at White Sulphur Springs.

A young woman at the resort remained solitary and shunned by her Southern peers. She was a West Virginian; her father, a unionist during the war, had stayed away from the fighting and instead made a fortune as a profiteer. She became very lonely at the resort and finally began to avoid the dances and social events that only increased her sense of being ostracized and despised.

The resort had a custom called "the Treadmill," a grand promenade in which small parties of guests sailed slowly up and down a long parlor, pausing to introduce new acquaintances and chat with old ones.

Afterward the hotel staff removed most of the dining room tables to create a large ballroom in which nightly dances were held. Shunned, the young woman could participate in neither the Treadmill nor the dances; she spent the festive evenings reading books and trying to forget the romance and pleasure that swirled just a few rooms away. One evening, when she was seated in a parlor some distance from the Treadmill, a quiet, dignified figure paused in front of her. Tremulously, she looked up to see who it was.

An old man gazed down upon her. He smiled. Behind the white beard the same dark eyes that had attracted women since his youth met hers with kindness and concern. He spoke quietly to her, then with a graceful gesture proffered his arm. She rose and accepted it, and Robert E. Lee led her toward the bright music of the dance.

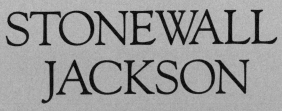

STONEWALL JACKSON

by Mark Grimsley

They laid him in state in a reception room of the Executive Mansion, a room fragrant with bright, delicate scents from the hundreds of flowers that graced his coffin. His widow, dressed in black, came for a final glimpse of him, but they had sealed his coffin and she could see his face only through a glass plate, a view, she said, that was "disappointing and unsatisfactory." The next morning an escort of generals solemnly transferred his body to the Confederate House of Representatives, where it reposed while 20,000 mourners filed by. The bells of the city tolled, cannon crashed in salute, and all government offices and businesses were closed. A day later the coffin left Richmond aboard a special train, and two days afterward the dead soldier's friends and townspeople buried him in Lexington, Virginia.

At the time of his passing, May 1863, no Confeder-

Thomas Jonathan "Stonewall" Jackson at Winchester in February 1862, during the Shenandoah Valley campaign in which his daring, clever tactics gained him fame. (Library of Congress)

ate—indeed, no soldier or statesman in either the North or South—enjoyed a greater reputation than Lieutenant General Thomas Jonathan Jackson. In the South and to the world at large, he was "Stonewall" Jackson, and an aura of genius and invincibility surrounded the name. Jackson always won. Or so it seemed. No matter how large the enemy's force, no matter how slender his own resources, Jackson always found a way to victory. When he died, the entire South plunged into mourning; shocked, benumbed, but with enormous pride, it gave him a funeral worthy of a warrior out of legend. In later years, after the Confederacy itself had perished, the South kept his memory alive and grieved for what might have been if fate had spared him. A prominent ex-Confederate wrote in 1877: "The star of Confederate destiny reached its zenith on the 2nd day of May, when Jackson fell wounded at the head of his victorious troops; it began to set on the 10th of May, when Jackson was no more."

His combat record read like a litany of the South's glittering military achievements. On the grassy plain at Manassas, Virginia, in July, 1861, Jackson's handling of an untested infantry brigade reversed the tide of the battle. Eight months later, with only a few thousand troops at his disposal, he inaugurated a classic campaign in which his little army ranged up and down Virginia's Shenandoah Valley, defeating several enemy detachments and dislocating the Union's entire strategy in the Eastern theater. Afterward, as army commander General Robert E. Lee's most trusted lieutenant, he turned in brilliant performances at the Battles of Second Manassas, Antietam, Fredericksburg, and Chancellorsville, until a tragic accident ended his life at the age of thirty-nine.

The Life of a Confederate Hero

He was born in Clarksburg, Virginia (now West Virginia), on January 21, 1824, the third of four children born to Jonathan Jackson, an aspiring but penniless lawyer, and Julia Neale Jackson, a frail schoolteacher. Poverty and death dominated his early years. Jackson lost his father and an older sister when he was barely two. His mother remarried but died in childbirth four years later. Even before her death, bad finances and Julia's poor health made it necessary to place Jackson and his surviving brother and sister with relatives. Shuttled from one kinsman to another, he did not enjoy a stable environment until he was nearly twelve, when he settled down at the home of Cummins E. Jackson, his father's brother. The lack of security during these childhood years left him stiff, overcontrolled, and rigidly logical, as if by sheer force of reason he could ward off further catastrophe.

He had little formal schooling, but in the still-raw mountain country of western Virginia this proved no handicap. During his teen-age years Jackson worked briefly as an engineering assistant and town constable; his success at these vocations encouraged him to take a competitive examination for admission to the U.S. Military Academy at West Point in 1842. He lost, but did well enough so that when the successful candidate quit the academy after only a few weeks, Jackson was sent in his place.

His lack of education hurt him then. While better-prepared cadets grasped their course work without serious difficulty, Jackson had to struggle just to keep from flunking out. Night after night, month after month, he stayed awake well after "lights out," reading his lessons by the dim glow of a small, coal-fired room heater. As a classmate aptly noted, Jackson literally "burned" knowledge into his brain.

After a hellish first year, Jackson's grades began to improve and he even found time to reflect on a philosophy of life. Into his notebooks went any number of moral guidelines, all couched in the most unyielding terms. Some were heroic: "Sacrifice your life rather than your word." Some were prim: "Speak but what may benefit others or yourself; avoid trifling conversation." All reflected a young man who took life with extreme seriousness. One self-composed epigram became a motto he lived by all his life: "You may be whatever you resolve to be."

Above all else, Jackson resolved to be a graduate. At the end of his first year he stood only fifty-first in a class of seventy-two, but by graduation he had risen to seventeenth, and respectful classmates declared that if the course had run a year longer, Jackson would have graduated ahead of them all. Because of his good showing, Jackson was able to select the artillery as his branch of the service, and shortly after graduation he went off to join the war in Mexico.

There he became a hero. At the Battles of Contreras and Cherubusco in August 1847, Jackson's gallantry under fire won him the permanent rank of 1st lieutenant as well as a brevet promotion to captain. During the fighting around Chapultepec on September 14, his courageous handling of an exposed section of artillery won the entire army's admiration. When Mexican cavalry charged down a causeway toward an isolated American storming party, Jackson's guns ripped their attack to shreds, an incident of such cold-blooded precision that it earned an unusual ges-

ture from General Winfield Scott himself. At a reception given shortly after the fall of Mexico City, Scott pointedly clasped his hands behind him when introduced to Jackson. "I don't know that I shall shake hands with Mr. Jackson," he said stiffly. "If you can forgive yourself for the way you slaughtered those poor Mexicans with your guns, I am not sure that I can." Much taken aback, Jackson blushed violently until Scott broke from the pose and warmly pumped his hand.

For his performance at Chapultepec, Jackson won promotion to the brevet rank of major, but the war's end cut short any chances for further advancement. In the months that followed he served with the occupation force in Mexico City, learned some Spanish, and kindled an interest in Christianity. His immediate superior, Captain Francis Taylor, was a devout Episcopalian who convinced Jackson that a personal study of religion was an obligation every young man owed himself. Impressed, the serious young officer looked into several Christian denominations and began a program of regular Bible study and prayer, although for a long time he felt no satisfaction "stronger than that of having performed a duty."

Eventually his depth of faith increased, fueled in part by a concern for his health that grew prominent in his mid-twenties and remained a striking personality trait for the rest of his life. Jackson worried chiefly about his digestion; he believed he suffered from "dyspepsia," a 19th-century term that referred to all sorts of stomach and intestinal complaints. After consulting a number of physicians, he resolved to drastically alter his diet, which thereafter consisted of the plainest foods possible: stale bread, unseasoned meat, bland vegetables and fresh fruit. (His digestive woes evidently gave him a fair measure of pain at times. In later years he would remark that if anything could drive a man to suicide, it was dyspepsia.)

A strong believer in an omnipotent God, Jackson viewed his defective health as no accident. "My afflictions," he wrote his sister Laura, "I believe were decreed by Heaven's sovereign, as a punishment for my offenses against his Holy Laws and have probably been the instrument of turning me from the path of eternal death, to that of everlasting life." Convinced of this, on April 29, 1849, he accepted baptism at an Episcopal church near Fort Hamilton, New York.

The following year, Jackson, received an assignment that took him to Fort Meade, a malarial outpost near Tampa, Florida. As company quartermaster and commissary officer, he initially did well, but soon clashed with the post commander, Brevet Major William H. French. Both men shared responsibility

Virginia Military Institute in Lexington, Virginia, where Jackson was a professor of physics and artillery tactics until the outbreak of the war. (New Market Battlefield Park)

for the squabble. Jackson, for his part, conducted his duties with unwarranted autonomy, while French was heavy-handed and overbearing. Enmity that began over jurisdictional disputes escalated when Jackson heard—and investigated—rumors of sexual impropriety on the part of his commanding officer. When French learned of the investigation he grew furious and ordered Jackson's arrest. So blatant an over-reaction did not escape official attention; the order was reversed and French's career was crippled. But although Jackson appeared at least nominally vindicated, he feared his role in the unsavory affair had tarnished his future with the service. When an opportunity came to exit gracefully, he took it.

His chance came when the Virginia Military Institute, a military college run by the commonwealth, offered him a position as professor of natural and experimental philosophy (the discipline now called physics) and artillery tactics. Although anything but an educator by temperament or ability, Jackson lost no time in accepting the job, for it offered good pay and a measure of prestige. In the summer of 1851, he resigned his commission and journeyed to Lexington, Virginia, home of the institute, to begin his new duties.

Jackson found Lexington a well-scrubbed village of about 1,700 inhabitants, nestled in the southern reaches of the Shenandoah Valley. It boasted two major seats of learning: the recently founded Virginia Military Institute (VMI) and its more established neighbor, Washington College. The two schools helped make Lexington a somewhat elitist community with more than its share of learned persons, and without exception, Jackson chose his closest associates from this group. He seems to have identified little, if at all, with his backwoods origins.

As a professor, Jackson never amounted to much. He had no teaching ability, a narrow intellect, and an awful method of instruction: he first memorized a given lesson and then recited it, verbatim, to his glassy-eyed students. If asked a question, he seldom extemporized an answer. Instead, he simply backed up in his recital and repeated, word for word, the entire lesson up to that point. Such atrocious teaching made him notorious among the cadets, one of whom recorded the heartfelt impression that Jackson was "a hell of a fool."

He cut an equally eccentric figure in Lexington society. When seated in someone's parlor he habitually sat bolt upright, legs uncrossed and rigidly

The Jackson dwelling in Lexington, a village with some 1,700 inhabitants in 1851. (Harper's New Monthly Magazine)

clamped together, a posture, he said, designed to keep his alimentary canal in proper alignment. As if this were not enough, his religious convictions made him excessively scrupulous. When, for instance, a speaker remarked, "You remember, Major, that at this period Lord Burleigh was Queen Elizabeth's great counselor—", Jackson could not permit even this rhetorical courtesy to pass uncorrected. "No," he blurted, "I don't remember, for I did not know it."

Despite such grotesqueries, Jackson made a number of lasting friendships in Lexington, particularly among the town's influential Presbyterian congregation. Shortly after his arrival he met Daniel Harvey Hill, a former West Pointer who taught mathematics at Washington College. When Jackson presented himself as someone deeply interested in Christianity, Hill urged him to consider Presbyterianism, whose Calvinist doctrines seemed in keeping with Jackson's own religious leanings. Jackson read the Presbyterian Shorter Catechism, had a number of discussions with Hill and the local pastor, liked what he heard, and on November 22, 1851, officially joined the Presbyterian church.

A year or so later, Jackson came to Hill with a problem of a different kind. It involved Miss Elinor Junkin, daughter of George Junkin, a prominent minister and the president of Washington College. He had known Elinor for quite a while, Jackson said, but until recently had given her little thought. "I don't know what has changed me," he told Hill. "I used to think her plain, but her face now seems to me all sweetness." Hill guffawed. "You are in love," he laughed, "that's what is the matter." Jackson mumbled that he thought as much, and in his stolid, logical way he set out to marry Miss Junkin.

Elinor reciprocated Jackson's interest, and on August 4, 1853, after a courtship of about eight months, the two were married in the parlor of the Junkin home. Because houses in Lexington were very scarce, the newlywed couple accepted an offer to live in a wing of the Junkin residence, and for Jackson it was like suddenly acquiring the family life he had never known. He liked and respected the distinguished Reverend Junkin, became close friends with his sister-in-law Maggie, and adored Mrs. Junkin, whose maternal and spiritual qualities greatly impressed him.

Then, in October 1854, Ellie died, together with the unborn child she carried. The loss devastated Jackson. To those around him he displayed considerable stoicism, but behind this veneer was a man paralyzed by grief. "I can hardly yet realize that my dear Ellie is no more," he wrote, "that she will never again welcome my return—no more soothe my troubled spirit by her ever kind, sympathizing heart,

Jackson circa 1855. His wife's death devastated Jackson, who sought comfort in his religion. (National Portrait Gallery)

words, and love. . . ." Tortured by his loss, he turned ever more steadfastly to religion, seeking in the fierce benedictions of God a comfort and a reason for the arbitrary tragedies that had shattered his childhood and now ripped from him the only love he had ever known. In keeping with this philosophy, Jackson increased his religious service, becoming both a church deacon and the district coordinator for a Bible society fund-raiser. He also began a Sunday school for Blacks, despite mutterings that he was in violation of a state law prohibiting mixed racial assemblies. Jackson ignored the objections. Early suspicions gave way to acceptance, even cooperation, and emboldened by Jackson's example, the Lexington Presbytery eventually spearheaded a campaign to give religious instruction to other Blacks as well.

In the summer of 1856, Jackson secured a leave of absence from the institute to make a five-month tour of Europe. While there he visited half a dozen countries, fell in love with the natural and artistic treasures of the Old World, and acquired an itch to remarry. He even settled upon a candidate: Mary Anna Morrison, a sister-in-law of D.H. Hill whom he had known socially in the days before his marriage to Elinor. Anna lived in North Carolina, but that scarcely deterred a man just returned from overseas. He wrote her a letter from Lexington expressing his "blissful remembrances" of the times they had shared several summers before, then followed it up with a visit to her home.

His visit was brief—only a few days—but apparently it accomplished its purpose. On July 16, 1857, Jackson and Mary Anna Morrison were married. Their union had a mature, more subdued tone than his earlier marriage. But like the first, it was steeped in religion, from the tenor of Jackson's pre-nuptial love letters ("When in prayer for you last Sabbath . . . I realized an unusual degree of emotional tenderness"), to their post-honeymoon pastime, memorization of the Shorter Catechism. Anna became pregnant almost immediately and on April 30, 1858, delivered a daughter whom the Jacksons named Mary Graham, in honor of Anna's mother. The child took sick with jaundice, however, and died within a month.

In the winter of 1858 the couple bought a house on Washington Street in Lexington, an old, over-sized, drafty residence that was intended as a temporary home until something better became available. Jackson set to work repairing it, however, and sent away to New York for the finest furnishings money could buy, while Anna worked hard to make it a domestic paradise.

They had considerable help. Over the years, Jackson acquired at least six slaves. Like most Southerners of his generation, he accepted slavery as part of the natural order of things, an arrangement sanctioned by God and taught in Scripture. But unlike many, he found the "peculiar institution" troublesome and, according to his wife, would have preferred to see Blacks set free. He had nothing but scorn for the notion that slaves were mere chattel property, not people. They were indeed people, he treated them as such, and was not afraid to risk the disapproval of others for holding such a view. At the same time, he shared the common view of the period that Blacks were a backward race, unable to fend for themselves and in need of supervision from Whites.

Some had very different opinions. In October 1859 abolitionist John Brown and a party of followers attacked Harpers Ferry, a Virginia community scarcely 100 miles from Lexington. They killed several people and attempted to foment a slave insurrection, but a Marine detachment led by Colonel Robert E. Lee of the U.S. Army soon quelled the revolt and captured Brown. Virginia tried the anti-slavery man for treason and sentenced him to hang, and, to ensure order, summoned hundreds of militiamen to attend the execution. Among those called was a contingent of VMI cadets, commanded by Major Jackson; and in this way Jackson witnessed one of the most famous executions in American history.

"I was much impressed," he wrote Anna, "with the thought that before me stood a man in the full vigor of health, who in a few moments must enter eternity.

I sent up the petition that he might be saved. Awful was the thought that he might in a few minutes receive the sentence, 'Depart, ye wicked, into everlasting fire!' I hope that he was prepared to die, but I am doubtful. He refused to have a minister with him."

Brown's aborted revolt and his swift execution foreshadowed the secession crisis looming on the political horizon. Although an entrenched states' rights Democrat, Jackson viewed the prospect of disunion with alarm and hoped God would not allow war to erupt and "interfere so materially with the Christian labors of this country at home and abroad." As the 1860 presidential election brought political tensions to a high level, Jackson pursued every recourse in his limited power to avert bloodshed. He voted for John Breckinridge, believing his election might calm the situation. When this failed, he joined eleven Lexington citizens in calling for a county assembly to discuss alternatives to war. "People who are anxious to bring on war don't know what they are bargaining for," he warned his nephew; "they don't see the horrors that must accompany such an event."

But as the country continued to drift toward war, Jackson's utterances began to lose some of their peace-loving flavor. "I am in favor of making a thorough trial for peace," he wrote his nephew, "and if we fail in this, and the state is invaded, to defend it with a terrible resistance." At an assembly of VMI faculty and cadets he announced, "The time for war has not yet come, but it will come, and that soon; and when it does come, my advice is to draw the sword and throw away the scabbard."

Jackson the Strategist

On April 12, 1861, Confederate forces opened fire on the U.S. Army garrison at Fort Sumter in the harbor of Charleston, South Carolina. Three days later, President Abraham Lincoln called for 75,000 troops to suppress the rebellion in the Southern states. Unwilling to remain in the Union under such conditions, Virginia seceded on April 17 to join a new nation, the Confederate States of America. Shortly afterward, state authorities summoned a contingent of VMI cadets to the capital, Richmond, there to join with other militia for the defense of Virginia.

Professor Thomas J. Jackson, late of the U.S. Army, commanded the column. It left Lexington on April 20, a Sunday. Before his departure, Jackson quietly led his wife to their bedroom. There, he asked God to protect Anna and prayed for peace for the country. Then he departed to take part in what would be called the Civil War or the War Between the States. The next time he returned to Lexington, it was to be buried there.

Jackson's first assignment in the war took him to Harpers Ferry, the scene of John Brown's raid and now one of the places where Virginia gathered troops to defend her far-flung borders. Armed with a commission as a colonel in the state's forces, Jackson arrived to assume command of the town on April 29. He found it filled with untrained troops led by gaudily attired militia officers, their encampments laid out as casually as a county fair. In keeping with Virginia's policy of disbanding her militia in favor of a system of state volunteers, Jackson released the militia units and deposed all militia officers above the rank of captain. His measures created resentment and some confusion, but Jackson's autocratic style brooked no interference. The surplus officers left his camp, the soldiers mustered in as state troops, and the encampment swiftly assumed a military appearance.

Next on his order of business was the Baltimore & Ohio Railroad, a vital east-west supply artery for the enemy. The line's tracks ran directly through Harpers Ferry. And, though hostilities had existed between the United States and the Confederacy for nearly a month, the Rebels at Harpers Ferry, anxious to avoid antagonizing the adjacent border state of Maryland, still permitted the B&O's trains to pass through the town unmolested.

At first Jackson did nothing about the situation except to complain to the railroad's management about traffic at night. Nervous rail officials obliged him; the nocturnal traffic abruptly ceased. A few days later, Jackson amended his request: he now asked that rail traffic be confined to the hours of 11:00 A.M. to 1:00 P.M. Again the B&O's officials agreed, and for two hours each day the trains of the mighty railroad rolled through Harpers Ferry almost without pause. Once this new pattern was established, Jackson acted. He blocked both ends of a thirty-mile stretch of track at the height of this noontime rush, confiscated all the rolling stock, and handed over to the Confederacy a total of fifty-six badly needed locomotives and over 300 cars.

It was neatly done. But Harpers Ferry was too important a post to leave to a mere colonel. Early in June a full general, Joseph E. Johnston, arrived to assume command.

Johnston respected his predecessor and when he organized the troops at Harpers Ferry into three brigades he gave the first of them to Colonel Jackson. Composed of the 2d, 4th, 5th, 27th and 33d Virginia regiments, the 1st Brigade was destined to soon make its mark in the war, and Jackson took pride in it from the very outset. "I am very thankful to our heavenly Father for having given me such a fine brigade," he wrote Anna.

As spring gave way to summer, the strategic picture in Virginia began to assume a focus. By the end of June, Johnston commanded 10,500 men, with more gradually arriving. Dissatisfied with the terrain at Harpers Ferry, he had abandoned the town in mid-June and reconcentrated his force near Bunker Hill, a more defensible location about twenty miles to the southwest. From this point, Johnston could cover the Shenandoah Valley and remain within striking distance of the Baltimore & Ohio Railroad. Sixty miles to the east, a second and larger Confederate army had assembled near Manassas under the command of Confederate General Pierre Gustave Toutant Beauregard. Between them, the two forces guarded northern Virginia against invasion.

The Union also had two armies in the region. The largest, under Brigadier General Irvin McDowell, remained encamped around Washington, D.C. Its forces outnumbered Beauregard's and it was expected to take the field soon. A second army, under Brigadier General Robert Patterson, had already done so. Early in July it splashed across the Potomac River near Williamsport, Maryland, and gingerly approached Johnston's force.

Everyone knew what to expect. McDowell's army would presently leave its camps around Washington and go forth to do battle with Beauregard. When that happened, Johnston would have to bring most of his forces east to reinforce the Confederates at Manassas, for Beauregard could not stave off McDowell's larger army without assistance. Patterson's objective, naturally, would be to so occupy Johnston's attention that the required shift could not be made. As the month of July wore on, both sides waited for this great drama to begin.

In the meantime, Jackson kept busy. On July 2 his brigade opposed Patterson's crossing of the Potomac in a spirited rear guard action at Falling Waters, then withdrew to Johnston's main position at Bunker Hill. There Jackson learned that he had been appointed a brigadier general in the provisional Confederate army. Pleased with the promotion, Jackson affected to be surprised by it. But he knew his political supporters in the Confederate capital, Richmond, had lobbied for the promotion for several weeks.

On July 16, the first great offensive of the war began. Thirty thousand Union soldiers marched from Washington to attack Beauregard's 20,000 defenders at Manassas Junction. Beauregard alerted Johnston at once, and Johnston, true to the agreed plan, prepared to come to his colleague's assistance. In this he received enormous help from his opponent,

Union General Patterson, who behaved with supine acquiescence. Leaving only a cavalry screen to cover his movements, Johnston started his troops eastward on July 18. The next day he placed them aboard trains at Piedmont, a station on the Manassas Gap Railroad, and hustled them down the line to Manassas Junction, some thirty-five miles away.

Beauregard positioned his forces behind Bull Run, a sluggish, steep-banked stream that flowed to the north and east of Manassas. By the time Johnston's troops began arriving, the Federal army had reached Centreville, a village about a mile or so in front of Beauregard's line. Fortunately for the Confederates, McDowell spent several days preparing his attack, an interlude that permitted most of Johnston's units to reach the field before the battle started. As it happened, Beauregard contemplated an offensive of his own against the Northerners, and had therefore weighted his forces very heavily to his right. His left flank was nearly unprotected.

The long-expected battle—called Bull Run in the North, Manassas in the South—materialized on July 21, 1861, a day of sun and smoke and waves of humid heat. McDowell's forces launched the first blow, swinging around the Confederate left flank at a little creek crossing called Sudley Springs Ford. The Rebels spotted the move shortly after daybreak. Confederate Colonel Nathan G. Evans pluckily shifted eleven companies of infantry to meet it, but his small force could not hold the Federals long. Reluctantly, Beauregard dispatched two brigades to guard his left, but held most of his army in place to mount his offensive, an offensive that never materialized. Beauregard's decision merely allowed the Federals' flank attack more time to develop.

As a result, the two brigades sent to protect the left found themselves outnumbered and in several hours of bitter fighting the Federals chewed them to pieces. Confederate Brigadier General Barnard Bee, the senior officer on that portion of the field, struggled without success to rally his men, who began streaming toward the rear. By mid-morning, it became apparent to everyone that the Confederate left was in real danger. Jackson, apparently without awaiting orders, began marching his brigade toward the sound of the firing. Three other brigade commanders did the same.

Jackson's men were the first reinforcements to arrive, making their way through the clots of stragglers that grew more numerous as they neared the battle. About 11:30 A.M., the brigade reached Henry House Hill, a grassy ridge that overlooked the carnage then in progress to the north. Another commander might have pressed onward, moving into line beside Bee's men, but Jackson recognized that to do so would only add his brigade to the rout already looming ahead of

A rather idealized image of Jackson at First Manassas. Though shown in full Confederate regalia, he actually wore an old blue U.S. Army uniform in the fight. (CWTI Collection)

him. Better to halt on the hill, create a rallying point, and stand firmly on the defensive. This Jackson did, directing his five regiments to form a line of battle on the rear slope of the hill, where they would be out of the Federals' direct line of fire. He also commandeered a passing battery of artillery and placed it just in front of his infantry. As more artillery entered the sector, Jackson posted them as well; eventually he had some 26 guns banging away on his front.

As the first of these cannon arrived, Bee approached Jackson on horseback and waved his sword despairingly. "General," he said, "they are beating us back."

"Sir," Jackson responded, "we'll give them the bayonet."

Bee returned to his troops, swung them into line beside Jackson's fresh brigade, and shouted, "There is Jackson standing like a stone wall. Let us determine to die here, and we will conquer. Follow me!" A Federal bullet killed Bee a short time later, but he had given the South a name to conjure with. From then on, Thomas Jackson became "Stonewall" Jackson.

Jackson's decision to stand on Henry House Hill probably saved the Confederates from defeat. Beauregard and Johnston constructed a defensive line on the foundation he provided. In time, the Southern line held more firmly as additional units swung into line on either side of Jackson's. During the afternoon, more reinforcements swelled the Southern ranks to a point where a counterstroke seemed in order. Around 4:00 P.M., Beauregard ordered a general advance. Jackson turned to his men and shouted, "[G]ive them the bayonet; and when you charge, yell like furies!"

The attack slammed into the Federal line, rocked it, crumbled it. The Union offensive dissolved into retreat, the retreat became a rout, and soon the entire Northern army was reeling back toward Washington. Much to Jackson's displeasure, Johnston and Beauregard elected not to pursue. In this they were probably correct—the Confederate forces had lost some of their organization, the troops were exhausted by the day's fighting and not nearly experienced enough to shift immediately from defensive operations to a headlong pursuit. Such considerations, however, seldom weighed heavily on Jackson's mind. To an astonishing degree, he believed in the primacy of bold aggressiveness over material factors, and on many future battlefields he would demonstrate what sheer offensive spirit could do.

The battle ended. Jackson went off to receive medical attention for a minor wound—a bullet had clipped the middle finger of his left hand.

According to Dr. Hunter McGuire, who dressed the wound, both he and Jackson noticed a gaunt,

vaguely familiar figure riding into the throngs of stragglers who swarmed in the rear areas. "I am President Davis," the man was yelling. "Follow me back to the field!" Sure enough, Jefferson Davis himself had arrived on the field, grimly certain that so many stragglers must signal some kind of military disaster. Dr. McGuire told Jackson what the Confederate president was saying. Jackson rose and tried to set Davis straight. "We have whipped them!" he squalled. "They ran like sheep! Give me 5,000 fresh men and I will be in Washington City tomorrow!"

The high command, of course, had a different perspective. Instead of pursuing McDowell's broken army, the Confederates contented themselves with an advance to Centreville, where they spent the next eight months. Jackson termed this period of inaction the darkest of the war. In the aftermath of the Manassas victory, a smug self-assurance permeated the Southern forces; it bred a spirit of indolence and complacency, he believed; it might ultimately result in disaster.

Nothing like complacency appeared in Jackson's 1st Brigade, however. The general refused to allow it. He drilled his troops incessantly, maintained the tightest discipline, and granted few leaves of absence. If the men grumbled at his strictness, they also understood that he was making them soldiers. "His brigade," one man acknowledged, "was a good school of war."

On October 7 Jackson was promoted to major general, and shortly afterward received new orders. A military district had been created in the Shenandoah Valley; Jackson would command it and leave the men of the 1st Brigade behind. It pained him to bid them farewell. In a valedictory address to his troops on November 4, he told them, "[Y]ou are the First Brigade in the affections of your General; and I hope by your future deeds and bearing you will be handed down to posterity as the First Brigade in our second War of Independence."

The troops responded with a wild, discordant yell. Jackson waved his battered forage cap at them, swung his horse around, and rode off.

Rolling, green, and prosperous, in 1861 the Shenandoah Valley was one of the most productive agricultural regions in North America. Tidy farmlands and fat barns alternated with picturesque towns and villages along a corridor, 100 miles long and 30 miles in width, that stretched from the Potomac River to the headwaters of the River James. The Shenandoah River wound over the valley floor, a romantic stream the Indians had called "Blue-eyed Daughter of the Stars." On either side of the valley the ancient, regal Allegheny and Blue Ridge Mountains rose up, their tree-clad, granite slopes standing against the sky. The

156

valley had a quality that captured the heart, and it had long possessed Jackson's. A ten-year resident of Lexington, he loved the region as he loved no other place on earth.

But, if it had qualities that captured the heart, the valley also had qualities that arrested the strategist's eye. Its verdant farmland produced food and was one of the Confederacy's main sources of horses. The Baltimore & Ohio Railroad ran across its northern reaches, with the result that any Confederate force in full control of the valley also controlled the Union's single most important east-west communications link. And the sheltering mountains on either side made the valley a natural avenue of invasion; its northern tip opened directly into Maryland and Pennsylvania. For these reasons, Federals and Confederates wanted control of the region.

Despite a desire to hold the valley, in November 1861 the Confederates had almost no forces available to defend it. When Jackson established his headquarters at Winchester, Virginia, on November 5, he discovered his new Valley District boasted just 1,651 militiamen and 485 spirited, but undisciplined cavalry. Against this meager force the Federals could send out 18,000 troops from western Maryland, men under Major General Nathaniel P. Banks. Another 5,000 Union troops were in Romney, Virginia, just forty miles from Winchester; 22,000 Federals occupied the mountain country beyond the Alleghenies.

Fortunately, the approach of Winter and the generally cautious nature of the Union high command made it unlikely that the Federals would advance before Spring. Equally fortunate, the Confederate high command soon recognized the Valley District's denuded state and dispatched reinforcements. The identity of these reinforcements gave Jackson a good deal of pleasure: it was his former command, the 1st Brigade, now known universally as the Stonewall Brigade. With this welcome addition, Jackson's forces grew to about 5,000.

During the next two months, Jackson organized and trained his soldiers, conducted a couple of minor operations, and made plans for a winter expedition. His objective was Romney; holding this town would give Confederates control of the crop-rich South Branch Valley and sever communication between Federals posted in Maryland and western Virginia.

On New Year's Day, 1862, Jackson led this slender command from its camps around Winchester and hiked into the Allegheny Mountains. With him on the march were 6,000 reinforcements from the Army of the Northwest, a division-sized unit led by Brigadier General William W. Loring. But the operation proved less than auspicious. In fourteen days of stren-

uous marching in the ice-swept mountains—sometimes in temperatures that dipped to −20° Fahrenheit—Jackson managed to capture Romney with little bloodshed, losing just four killed and twenty-eight wounded. Many more men, however, succumbed to the elements and disease. Worse, Jackson's callous use of his troops produced a serious collapse of morale. Loring denounced the expedition as "the damndest outrage ever perpetuated in the annals of history."

When the expedition concluded, Jackson returned to Winchester with the Stonewall Brigade and left Loring's division at Romney. Loring and many of his officers complained bitterly: the town was too bleak, its location too exposed to a counterthrust by the Federals. Sick of Romney and sick of Jackson's intransigence, they sent a petition to Richmond asking permission to return to Winchester, and Loring used political influence to get the Confederate Secretary of War to approve the move. Jackson, when he discovered this, coldly asked to be returned to the Virginia Military Institute or else be allowed to resign. "With such interference in my command," he wrote the Secretary of War, "I cannot expect to be of much service in the field."

The Confederacy seemed on the brink of losing one of its finest officers. Fortunately, a number of individuals, including General Johnston and Virginia Governor John Letcher, appealed to Jackson and persuaded him to withdraw his resignation. Loring and his men were removed from the Valley District, and in the end, Jackson seemed content to say goodbye and good riddance. But the affair revealed a prickly side to Jackson. Unlike many Civil War commanders, he never got used to the politicking and occasional informality that attended a struggle which engaged virtually the whole population. He always kept a stern, "regular army" attitude. It produced trouble with Loring; it would produce trouble again.

In other respects, Jackson had a fine winter. Early in December Anna came to join him at Winchester; the couple took an apartment at the residence of the Reverend James Graham, pastor of a local church. They called the place their "war home" and in later years Anna would recall it as one of the most pleasant times of her life. The Jacksons became a part of the Graham family, ate with them, played with their children. On chill evenings the general would park himself in front of the crackling fireplace and boom happily, "Oh! This is the very essence of comfort!" For weeks, Anna wrote, "we spent as happy a winter as ever falls to the lot of mortals on earth." Then in late February came word that the Federals were on the move. With active campaigning about to begin,

Jackson, who stood "like a stone wall" at First Manassas, was noted both for his steadfastness and his brilliant tactics, which enabled him to hold on to the Shenandoah Valley, thereby playing a crucial role in saving Richmond. (The Confederate Soldier in the Civil War)

Jackson reluctantly sent Anna to safety farther south. They did not see each other again for thirteen months.

Union generals performed poorly in the first months of the war. But in Spring 1862, one of them finally confronted Confederates with a strategic challenge that could do them damage. In mid-March, Union Major General George B. McClellan, who had replaced McDowell after his defeat at Bull Run, began ferrying the powerful Army of the Potomac from its Washington encampments to Fort Monroe, a Federal strongpoint on the Virginia coast about seventy miles southeast of Richmond. From there, he embarked on his celebrated Peninsula Campaign, using the tongue of land between the York and James Rivers to advance against the Confederate capital. Even before this movement began, a greatly outnumbered Johnston withdrew his army from Centreville to more defensible positions behind the Rappahannock River. In April, when McClellan's strategy became obvious, Johnston took most of this army southward to the Peninsula. Meanwhile, in late February General Banks crossed the Potomac with orders to clear the northern Shenandoah Valley of Rebel troops. Jackson's orders were to harass Banks, and, without exposing his own force to destruction, prevent Banks from leaving the valley to reinforce McClellan. It was a tough assignment: Banks had 38,000 troops, Jackson just 4,500.

Banks moved slowly, but by March 12 Jackson was forced to abandon Winchester and fall back to a safer position about thirty miles south. Satisfied that he had carried out his mission, Banks left a division of 9,000 men at Strasburg, twenty miles south of Winchester, and began transferring his remaining forces east of the Blue Ridge. Jackson had standing orders to prevent this.

On March 20, the remaining Union division, under Brigadier General James Shields, withdrew to Winchester, the logical place from which to base a long-term occupation of the lower valley. As soon as he learned of this, Jackson moved north, hoping to find an opportunity to engage the enemy under favorable conditions.

Shields, a cagey politician turned soldier, left four regiments dangling near Kernstown, just south of Winchester, while with his remaining force he affected retreat. Fooled by this ruse, Jackson's cavalry reported that an excellent opportunity existed to gobble up the four isolated regiments by a quick thrust, and on March 23, Jackson attacked.

Fought on a Sunday, the Lord's day—a fact that gave Jackson considerable discomfort—the Battle of Kernstown quickly went very wrong for the Confederates. The four regiments resisted stoutly, allowing time for the rest of Shields' nearby division to join the battle. Outnumbered and sorely pressed, the Rebel aggressors suddenly became beleaguered defenders, short of ammunition, fighting desperately. Brigadier General Robert B. Garnett, commander of the Stonewall Brigade, decided the Confederates must fall back, and, after unsuccessful efforts to locate Jackson, ordered a withdrawal on his own authority. Garnett's decision probably saved Jackson from a severe defeat, but Jackson did not see it that way. He believed the lines could have been held at bayonet-point if necessary and that Garnett had traded a drawn battle for a clear-cut loss. Within days of the Battle of Kernstown, he ordered Garnett's arrest and court-martial.

Although, tactically, a defeat for Jackson, the engagement at Kernstown bore unexpected fruit. The bold Confederate attack convinced Shields that Jackson had received reinforcements or expected them shortly. As a result, Banks returned to the valley with a second division of 9,000 men. President Lincoln ordered the detachment of a 10,000-man division from the Army of the Potomac and ordered it to join Union Major General John C. Frémont's forces in western Virginia, on the theory that if Jackson was strong enough to attack Shields he might threaten Frémont as well. Nor was this all. Because Banks was now unavailable to defend Washington, D.C., during McClellan's germinating Peninsula Campaign, Lincoln withdrew an entire corps—40,000 men—from McClellan's control and retained it in northern Virginia. Jackson's battlefield defeat turned into strategic success; he tied up the movements of nearly 60,000 Federal troops.

Kernstown marked the beginning of Jackson's famous Valley Campaign, a classic example of military art. But in many respects his success there was made possible by the enemy's ineptness; the Federals completely misread the situation. It may be argued that Jackson's military genius truly began to bloom during the four weeks his troops spent in camp after the battle. Before that time, his incredible strength of will was evident, but very little else. Afterward he settled down, became a more clear-headed commander and quite a bit more subtle.

Jackson began by acquiring the services of Major Jedediah Hotchkiss, a thirty-three-year old ex-school teacher who was fascinated by engineering and cartography and had learned quite a bit about each. Hotchkiss had already made a few maps for the Confederate army; now Jackson instructed him, "I want you to make me a map of the Valley, from Harpers Ferry to Lexington, showing all the points of offense and defense." It was an important assignment. In the mid-19th Century few settled parts of the United States had been mapped. Those maps that did exist were usually unsuited for military use. Civil War armies frequently moved with only a limited understanding of the terrain around them. Under such conditions, the general who had a better grasp of terrain enjoyed an enormous advantage.

Hotchkiss rode forth, armed with notebooks, compass, and altimeter, to prepare detailed sketches from which his finished maps would emerge. As the work progressed, he carefully briefed Jackson on his findings. The Shenandoah Valley, it was apparent, offered superb opportunities for strategic innovation. Its most important feature, Massanutten Mountain, was a fifty-mile ridge that divided the middle third of the valley into two parts. On its western side, a hard-surfaced road called the Valley Turnpike ran from Winchester to Staunton. East of the mountain, a lesser highway paralleled the turnpike from Conrad's Store to Front Royal. Other roads connected these primary highways at either end of the ridge: between Harrisonburg and Conrad's Store in the south and between Strasburg and Front Royal in the north. This road network formed, in effect, a strategic rectangle; it would play an important role in the fighting ahead.

Only one road pierced Massanutten Mountain itself. It ran from New Market on the Valley Turnpike to Luray on the eastern highway, and held the key to the whole rectangle. Whoever controlled it could shift between the eastern and western valleys, using both main highways for attack or defense. An opponent, by contrast, could get from one valley to the other only by circling around the far-flung ends of Massanutten Mountain.

From his defensive position at Rude's Hill, just north of New Market, Jackson held this vital, center connecting road. During the first half of April, Banks marched cautiously against him, hampered by poor intelligence—he greatly overestimated Jackson's strength—rain-swollen streams, and sheer lack of military ability. Unlike Jackson, Banks had never been a professional soldier. He was a former Speaker of the U.S. House of Representatives, a former Governor of Massachusetts, and just one of many politicians Lincoln made generals in order to assure their support for the war effort. Banks meant well, but as a commander Jackson outclassed him completely. Still, in Banks' favor were his 15,000 troops; Jackson had scarcely 6,000.

As a result, on April 16 Jackson withdrew from Rude's Hill rather than fight Banks at hopeless odds. He fell back to Conrad's Store, a position from which he could threaten the flank of any continued Union advance up the valley. Banks got as far as Harrisonburg, seemed disinclined to advance, and went into

camp. By the end of April he lost track of Jackson's force, but assumed it had quit the valley. Announcing to Washington that there was nothing more to be done, he requested that his troops be allowed to rejoin either McClellan or McDowell for the campaign now in progress against Richmond. Washington responded to this suggestion by again withdrawing all but one division from the valley. Banks, to his chagrin, was left behind to command this reduced force.

In Richmond, Confederate General Robert E. Lee kept the situation in the valley under scrutiny. As military adviser to President Davis, he had broad if vague powers, which he began using in an effort to influence the course of events. On April 21, he wrote Jackson suggesting a preferred course of action in which Jackson, reinforced by a division led by Major General Richard S. Ewell, would attack Banks' division at Harrisonburg.

Jackson responded that even with Ewell's help, he would still need an additional 5,000 troops to attack with any chance of success. When Lee could not furnish the extra 5,000, Jackson proposed a modified plan: instead of striking Banks, he would unite with the 2,800 troops under Brigadier General Edward "Allegheny Ed" Johnson, soldiers charged with guarding the Staunton-Parkersburg Turnpike against Union Major General John C. Frémont's troops in western Virginia. After meeting with Johnson, Jackson would hit Frémont's advance guard, which was encroaching upon the valley from the west. Then, using both Ewell and Johnson, he would attack Banks. Lee approved the plan on May 1, and Jackson began his preparations.

As a first step, he brought Ewell's division to Swift Run Gap, a short distance from Conrad's Store, where it would remain while Jackson's Confederates marched to join with Johnson's. Then, to everyone's surprise, Jackson began the movement by marching entirely out of the valley. Once east of the Blue Ridge Mountains, he took his troops to Mechum's River Station on the Virginia Central Railroad. There he placed them aboard cars and shuttled them west to Staunton, to the relieved delight of the townspeople, who feared that Jackson had abandoned them. From Staunton he marched to West View, linked up with Johnson's brigade, and continued west to Bull Pasture Mountain near the village of McDowell. On May 8, his combined force beat back a determined but ill-advised attack by Frémont's advance guard under Brigadier General Robert H. Milroy. Milroy fell back toward the town of Franklin, and Jackson wired Richmond: "God blessed our arms with victory at McDowell."

Banks, aware of his reduced strength (now down to 8,000), unsure of Jackson's whereabouts, and fearful that the Confederates might materialize in his exposed rear, withdrew to Strasburg on May 13. Jackson, now reinforced to about 10,000, advanced to New Market, while Ewell, with 7,000 more, moved up as far as Luray. The stage was set for a decisive strike against Banks when an unexpected problem arose: Joseph E. Johnston, Ewell's direct superior, ordered him to return east of the Blue Ridge and link up with the main Southern army on the Peninsula. Jackson appealed to Lee, who was able to intercede so that Ewell remained in the valley.

Then Jackson made use of the "short cut" across Massanutten Mountain. This was to be his major effort to destroy Banks' force. Leaving a screen of cavalry to shield his move, he marched to Luray, added Ewell's division to his forces, and raced north to Front Royal, a town garrisoned by 1,100 Union troops under Colonel John R. Kenly. On May 23, after deploying his forces so that the Federals would be captured *en masse*, Jackson attacked. In a brief battle, Kenly lost 904 men, including 750 prisoners; Jackson's casualties numbered just 35.

At first Banks could scarcely grasp what had occurred. His most recent intelligence had placed Jackson directly in his front, somewhere between Strasburg and New Market. Now, suddenly, he received word that Jackson had all but crushed the Union garrison at Front Royal. If true, it meant that Jackson had turned his flank and that he must retreat to Winchester at once. But so audacious a move by Jackson's whole force did not seem credible. Not until the morning of the 24th could Banks believe what had happened to him, and by that time Jackson was preparing to swoop straight into his rear.

Everything now hinged on a race to Winchester. Banks' force got there first, but was hounded on its line of march by Jackson's cavalry and artillery. When he reached the town, Banks attempted to make a stand. But Jackson pressed him so closely that in a battle on May 25 the Confederates had little trouble dislodging the Federals and sending them in headlong retreat. Banks did not stop retreating until he crossed the Potomac at Williamsport on May 26, having lost about 35 per cent of his force.

In Washington, Lincoln and advisors viewed the situation with alarm, mingled with the shrewd awareness that an opportunity now existed to trap Jackson's entire force. Having pursued Banks as far as the Potomac, the Confederate commander lingered at the lowest fringe of the valley, partly to press home his advantage, partly to rest his now-exhausted troops as much as circumstances would permit. That left him perilously exposed, and Lincoln believed the Union had ample forces available to cut Jackson off and destroy him.

At Franklin, for example, Union General Frémont had 15,000 men. A march of forty miles would place them at Harrisonburg, eighty miles in Jackson's rear. Similarly, Union General Irvin McDowell had another 40,000 men at Fredericksburg, where he was preparing to march overland to join McClellan's offensive against Richmond. Lincoln instructed McDowell to delay the planned movement and send 20,000 of his men to Front Royal, a move that would imperil Jackson's line of retreat. The main issue was whether the Union forces could move fast enough to close the trap before Jackson could escape. As Lincoln remarked, it was "a question of legs."

The plan did not work as Lincoln hoped. For a variety of reasons, Frémont failed to advance into the valley by the most direct route and instead marched northward, parallel to the valley but completely out of position to block Jackson. "What does this mean?" Lincoln moaned. By the time he entered the valley, Frémont had squandered much of his chance to trap Jackson. By June 1, using the all-weather Valley Turnpike, Jackson had out-marched both Frémont and Shields and escaped the trap.

Jackson then chose a position at Port Republic, a small village where the North and South Rivers met to form the South Branch of the Shenandoah River. Spring rainstorms had swollen these streams to the point where they could be crossed only at bridges or rare fords; by controlling the crossings at Port Republic, Jackson could concentrate against either Frémont or McDowell while denying his opponents the opportunity to join forces.

Jackson's troops reached the town on June 6. Meanwhile, Union troops under Frémont concentrated at Harrisonburg while McDowell's lead division—commanded by James Shields, Jackson's antagonist at Kernstown—advanced up the Luray Valley. June 8 fell on a Sunday. Jackson, still monitoring the approach of his enemies, expected no action that day and planned none of his own. As he told his chief of staff, "You know I always try to keep the Sabbath if the enemy will let me."

The enemy did not let him. To Jackson's great surprise, around 9:00 A.M. a regiment of Shields' cavalry slipped into Port Republic and briefly captured the all-important crossings. Jackson personally organized the counterattack that threw them back. A bit later, Frémont launched an unexpected but half-hearted attack against Ewell's division, covering the western approaches to Port Republic near a place called Cross Keys. Jackson changed his tune a bit. Turning to his chief of staff he remarked, "Major, wouldn't it be a blessed thing if God would give us a glorious victory today?"

By day's end, Ewell parried Frémont's feeble assaults and Jackson made plans to attack Shields the following morning. This engagement, called the Battle of Port Republic, began badly for the Confederates. The Stonewall Brigade advanced against Shields' two leading brigades, but soon found itself under a ripping crossfire from a six-gun battery posted near a coaling yard on the Federal left flank. Punished by the shelling, the Stonewall Brigade wavered and seemed in danger of a rout, but one of Ewell's brigades supported it in time to avert calamity. Even so, the Federals, backed by that deadly six-gun battery, kept up a tenacious resistance.

Finally, a second brigade from Ewell's division made its way around the Union left flank and, after three charges, managed to capture the enemy battery. Then the attack that until that moment had gone so poorly began to come together. The three Southern brigades charged, the Union line cracked, and Shields' men fell back in defeat. Jackson was exultant. "General," he told Ewell, "He who does not see the hand of God in this is blind, sir, blind!"

Whether Ewell viewed it that way is open to question, but military analysts have never had trouble discerning in Jackson's Valley Campaign the hand of a master strategist. With an army less than half the size of the forces opposed to him, he had managed to defeat the enemy on five major occasions, hold on to the upper third of the Shenandoah Valley, and above all, force the diversion of thousands of Union troops who would otherwise have joined McClellan's army on the Peninsula. His success in the valley played a crucial role in saving Richmond.

Jackson of the Chickahominy

Following Jackson's victory at Port Republic, the Confederate high command had two possible ways of employing the Valley army. It could shift the army to Richmond, directly reinforcing the Southern forces defending the capital; or it could give Jackson more men and send him slashing down the valley in a full-scale offensive, thereby creating such pressure on the North that McClellan would be forced to make large detachments from his own army in order to recover the situation.

Initially the Rebel brass preferred the second alternative. Even before Port Republic, Lee (now commander of the Army of Northern Virginia after Johnston's wounding at the Battle of Seven Pines) had written President Davis, "I think if it was possible to reinforce Jackson strongly, it would change the character of the war. . . . Jackson could in that event cross Maryland into Pennsylvania." However, it soon became apparent that an invasion was simply too ambitious. Not only did scant opportunity exist for

Jackson to raid the North successfully, it did not even seem practicable for Jackson to destroy Frémont and Shields—a prerequisite for any more far-reaching operation. Accordingly, planning quickly turned to the first alternative. Jackson would come to Richmond.

Telling no one, not even his own staff, of the destination, Jackson began his march on June 18. While his army made its way eastward, Jackson rode on horseback to Richmond for a conference with Lee. On June 23, after a ride of fifty-three miles in just over twelve hours, he met the army commander at his headquarters, along with Major Generals James Longstreet, Ambrose Powell Hill, and Daniel Harvey Hill, his friend from Lexington. Together with Jackson, these men would bear the chief responsibility in the impending battle against McClellan's Army of the Potomac, now just five miles east of Richmond. And with the exception of D.H. Hill, who would leave the north Virginia theater in January 1863, Jackson would spend the rest of his life in constant professional contact with them.

Jackson had known Lee by reputation since at least the Mexican War. He respected the man immensely; at the war's outset he had written Mary Anna that he considered Lee a better officer than Winfield Scott. Lee, for his part, knew how magnificently Jackson had performed during the Valley Campaign and had, of course, played no small role in shaping the course of that operation. In a real sense, Jackson and Lee were already military partners.

Longstreet, the group's only non-Virginian, was the Army of Northern Virginia's most experienced combat commander. Longstreet did not rattle, did not tire, and did not easily impress. Although respectful of Jackson's abilities, Longstreet never accorded Jackson the element of genius that others so often saw in him. The two men would work effectively together, but with little sense of camaraderie.

D.H. Hill was Jackson's relative by marriage, and of course the two knew each other well. But A.P. Hill, a thin, red-bearded general from Culpeper, Virginia, was an officer whom Jackson knew only from brief acquaintance in the weeks before the Battle of Manassas. Neither realized it at the time, but Jackson and A.P. Hill were destined to clash in one of the war's most bitter personal antagonisms, a running feud that would end only with Jackson's death. Not even Lee would be able to mediate effectively between these two strong personalities, the one proud, quick-tempered, and sensitive, the other cold and unyielding as the grave.

At the conference, Lee outlined his plan for defeating the Federal army in front of Richmond. Most of the Union forces lay south of the Chickahominy River, a swampy, steep-banked stream that flowed northeast of the Confederate capital. But a single Union corps under Major General Fitz John Porter had taken up a position just north of the river behind Beaver Dam Creek. East of the Union line and perpendicular to it, McClellan's supply route traced its way to White House Landing on the Pamunkey River. From Brigadier General J.E.B. Stuart, his cavalry leader, Lee had learned that Porter's solitary corps was vulnerable. Although strongly entrenched in front, its right flank lay "in the air," anchored to no natural obstacle and easily attacked. If Lee's forces could turn this flank and strike powerfully at Porter's corps, they could destroy it, cut McClellan's supply line to White House Landing, and force the Federals either to fight under severe disadvantage or retreat very quickly.

Lee assigned 20,000 men to hold Richmond's entrenchments while the turning movement took place. That left 60,000 soldiers available for the strike across the Chickahominy, a move that would begin a bloody week-long push known in history as the Seven Days' Battles.

Convinced that this move—splitting his force in the face of the enemy—was a gamble worth taking, Lee had not called the conference to debate the plan's merits. He met with Jackson, Longstreet and the two Hills because together these generals would lead the army's striking force. And Jackson would play the most important role. His still-distant forces would establish contact with the left flank of the Army of Northern Virginia, then continue eastward, curling around Porter's exposed flank. When Jackson had gotten into position, the rest of the army would begin its attack.

The timing of the offensive therefore rested with Jackson. After Lee excused himself to attend to some administrative business, Longstreet turned to the valley commander. "You have distance to overcome," he pointed out, "and in all probability obstacles will be thrown in the way of your march by the enemy. As your move is the key to the campaign, you should appoint the hour at which the connection may be made cooperative."

Without hesitation, Jackson replied, "The morning of the 25th."

That hour was scarcely forty hours away, and Longstreet dryly observed that Jackson's estimate might be too optimistic, given the sweltering weather and the fifty miles of farmland that stood between the valley army and its assigned objective. Jackson concurred, but shifted his timetable just twenty-four hours. His troops would attack on June 26. The other commanders agreed to this. Lee returned, was told of the decision, and adjourned the conference.

Author Mark Boatner III, in his invaluable reference book *The Civil War Dictionary*, includes an un-

usual entry: "Jackson of the Chickahominy." It is a phrase, he writes, "used to distinguish the brilliant 'Jackson of the Valley' from the ineffective Stonewall Jackson who failed five times during the Seven Days' Battles."

Nothing in Jackson's military history confounds the student more than this strange interlude in his otherwise magnificent career. From the time he left the Shenandoah Valley until the close of the climactic upcoming Seven Days' battles around Richmond in late June 1862—a period of about twelve days— nothing Jackson did showed exemplary or even average competence.

Jackson did not rest himself after his long ride and his meeting with Lee. He plunged into the saddle at once and negotiated the long miles that separated his troops from Lee's army. When he arrived, he was utterly exhausted. True to his penchant for secrecy, he told no one of the impending offensive, but neither did he give any sign that the army, now detrained near Fredericks Hall, must march to Richmond as soon as it possibly could. Jackson simply went straight to bed, leaving his chief of staff to manage on his own.

Even after Jackson awoke, he seemed strangely apathetic. The march went poorly; the troops covered barely a mile per hour on the rutted back-country roads in the humid heat. Jackson seemed grumpy about the poor progress, but in an unfocused, impotent way. He took little action to rectify matters. Darkness fell on June 25 with his forces still five miles short of their objective. Jackson did not seem to care, nor did he bother to inform Lee of his whereabouts.

June 26, the promised day of battle, rose sunny and hot. Along the southern bank of the Chickahominy, the bulk of the Army of Northern Virginia waited for "Stonewall" Jackson. And waited. At length, when the hands of his watch passed 3:00 P.M., Major General A.P. Hill took matters into his own hands. He decided not to wait for Jackson any longer.

Hill gave the order, and the six brigades of his Light Division rose up and crossed to the Chickahominy's far bank. Longstreet and D.H. Hill helplessly followed suit, for now that A.P. Hill had opened the offensive they had no choice but to support him with their own divisions. After Hill's skirmishers drove Federal pickets from the tiny crossroads hamlet of Mechanicsville, his brigades swung eastward and late in the afternoon struck Porter's well-prepared battle line at Beaver Dam Creek—the line that Jackson was supposed to have already outflanked. In a sharp frontal assault, Hill's division lost 1,200 men within minutes. Two miles away, Jackson heard the crash of musketry, knew not what to make of it—after all, he was supposed to launch the offensive—and ordered his troops into bivouac for the night.

Such murky judgment only got worse the following day. Now warned of the Rebels' intentions, Porter withdrew to an even stronger position behind Boatswains' Swamp. Lee believed that Porter's new line still followed a north-south axis. If so, Jackson still had a shot at slipping around the enemy flank. In reality, however, Porter had drawn his lines in a semicircle. This arc covered his vulnerable flank, so that the opportunity to turn it no longer existed. None of this seemed to matter much, however, since on this second day of battle Jackson's column floundered as badly as before.

In the Shenandoah Valley, Jackson relied on Hotchkiss and his invaluable, accurate maps. But in the Chickahominy bottoms, Jackson not only lacked the services of Hotchkiss, who had remained in the valley, he lacked maps of any kind, and his fatigue-muddled brain was slow to grasp the lay of the land. When a local guide attempted to help, Jackson's habit of secrecy hurt him. He instructed the guide to lead the column to Cold Harbor, the jumping-off point for his attack on Porter, but neglected to tell the guide his intentions. As a result, the guide led the column by the most direct route, which happened to run too close to Porter's lines. Upon discovering the mistake, the entire column had to countermarch, amid great confusion and loss of time.

As before, A.P. Hill opened the day's fighting, and as before, he was forced to strike Porter head-on. This time, however, Jackson got his forces into action, albeit very late in the afternoon. Called the Battle of Gaines's Mill, the struggle that ensued was one of the fiercest of the war, fought not only against the Federals but against the clock. By the time the Confederates launched their major attack, just one hour of daylight remained. Porter had to be beaten before nightfall; otherwise he could be reinforced or might withdraw intact.

Stimulated by the excitement of battle, Jackson seemed to emerge from his strange apathy, but by then control of the combat had passed into the hands of his division and brigade commanders. He became little more than a high-ranking cheerleader. As the fighting got under way, someone handed him a lemon—a fruit that Jackson highly prized. The general bit a small chunk from the skin and sucked on the lemon throughout the action, sometimes waving it like a baton or to emphasize an order. At length, he summoned his staff officers and said he wanted a message sent to his division commanders. "Tell them this affair must hang in suspense no longer; sweep the field with the bayonet!"

The fiery order inspired those around Jackson, but had almost no practical effect on the battle. By nightfall, the Confederates had won the struggle, but won it by the stand-up valor of the average soldier and the tactical leadership of the brigade and division commanders, not by any higher direction from Jackson. Porter retreated south of the Chickahominy that night; the following day McClellan began a "change of base"; he would establish a new supply depot on the James River farther south.

During the next four days, Lee's Army of Northern Virginia made repeated efforts to destroy McClellan's forces as they withdrew. But bad staff work and bad generalship combined to prevent a decisive result, and Jackson deserved a full share of the blame. At the Battle of Savage's Station on June 29, his troops simply failed to show up—they were delayed in rebuilding bridges across the Chickahominy River. The following day, much the same thing happened at the Battle of Frayser's Farm. Jackson alternated between fuming and falling asleep. On the evening of June 30, after yet another failed day, his staff watched as Jackson's head drooped forward at dinner. He had dozed off with a biscuit in his teeth. Momentarily he awoke, gazed dully around, and said, "Now, gentlemen, let us at once to bed, and rise with the dawn, and see if tomorrow we cannot do something!"

By July 1, McClellan had nearly made good his escape. His forces made a stand on Malvern Hill, an exceedingly strong position protected on either side by almost impassable marsh land. Nevertheless, Lee decided to attack, but as happened so often during the Seven Days' Battles, his plans miscarried. Packed Federal cannon virtually wiped out the few Confederate units that attempted to charge the hill; most of the Rebel army never even got into proper position. It was a clear-cut defeat for the Army of Northern Virginia. That night Jackson, Ewell, and D.H. Hill met for a brief conference, and Ewell said with conviction, "If McClellan knows what he is about he will take the aggressive in the morning; and I tell you we are in no condition to meet it."

In the pause that followed, "Jackson of the Chickahominy" made his one prescient comment: "Oh no, McClellan will clear out in the morning."

So it was to prove. The next day the Army of the Potomac completed its retreat to the James. The Army of Northern Virginia followed, then took up positions to keep an eye on its enemies. The Seven Days' Battles ended. Out of 80,000 to 85,000 Confederates, over 20,000 had become casualties. The Federals, with 105,000 men, lost just under 16,000. The cost had been exorbitant, but Lee and his men had managed to remove the threat to Richmond. Not for another two years would a Federal army come so close again.

As for Jackson's strange behavior, it disappeared soon after the campaign's close. No complete explanation for it has ever emerged. Lee seemed content to trace the Valley general's poor performance to cir-

Composite of wartime photographs of Stonewall Jackson and his staff. (Library of Congress)

cumstances beyond Jackson's control—to "unavoidable delays" of one sort or another. Jackson's staff officers emphasized their chief's physical exhaustion, a point to which later historians have turned repeatedly. In *Lee's Lieutenants*, noted biographer of Confederate generals Douglas Southall Freeman agreed that such exhaustion was "the basic explanation of Jackson's inability to meet the demands of the campaign." Historian Clifford Dowdey, in a 1964 study of The Seven Days, went even further, identifying Jackson's problem as "stress fatigue," an ailment that occurs when the human body's resistance reactions to stress are strained beyond capacity.

In the weeks of relative calm that followed, Jackson renewed his worn-out body and soon rekindled his old aggressiveness. Early in July he summoned to his quarters Colonel A.R. Boteler, an aide-de-camp who also happened to serve as a Confederate congressman. Without preamble, Jackson inquired starkly, "Do you know we are losing valuable time here?"

"How so?" the congressman replied.

"Why, by repeating the blunder we made after the battle of Manassas, in allowing the enemy leisure to recover from his defeat and ourselves to suffer by inaction." The Army of the Potomac, he went on, was beaten, and the Federals would not renew their offensive unless heavily reinforced. Until then, Richmond was safe and the opportunity should be seized to mount an invasion of the North. He wanted Boteler to present the scheme to President Davis.

"What is the use of my going to Mr. Davis," Boteler asked, "as he'll probably refer me again to General Lee. So, why don't you yourself speak to General Lee upon the subject?"

"I have already done so."

"Well, what does he say?"

"He says nothing," Jackson replied, adding quickly: "Don't think I complain of his silence; he doubtless has good reasons for it."

"Then," Boteler said, "you don't think that General Lee is slow in making up his mind?"

"Slow?" Jackson echoed. "By no means, Colonel! On the contrary, his perception is as quick and unerring as his judgment is infallible. But with the vast responsibilities resting on him, he is perfectly right in withholding a hasty expression of his opinions and purposes.

"So great is my confidence in General Lee that I am willing to follow him blindfolded," Jackson continued. "But I fear he is unable to give me a definite answer now because of influences at Richmond, where, perhaps, the matter has been mentioned by him and may be under consideration. I therefore want you to see the President and urge the importance of prompt action."

Boteler went to President Davis as requested. Davis, however, proved as unwilling as Lee to agree to an immediate invasion of the North. A new threat had materialized, requiring prompt attention.

Jackson the Victorious

On June 26, the Lincoln Administration created a new army from the unfortunate units under Frémont, Banks, and McDowell, named it the Army of Virginia, and placed it under command of Major General John Pope, an officer imported from the western theater. With his new force of 47,000 men, Pope was instructed to protect Washington, secure the Shenandoah Valley, threaten the Confederate rail system in central Virginia, and force Lee to detach troops to oppose him.

This Lee did. On July 13 he sent Jackson with 10,000 men to Gordonsville, a strategic railroad junction fifty miles north of Richmond. Several weeks of quiet ensued, during which Jackson refitted his soldiers, took stern measures to strengthen discipline, and began court-martial proceedings against a number of his officers. Garnett, the Stonewall Brigade commander who had allegedly failed him at Kernstown, was among those tried, and so were several others, on charges ranging from insubordination to cowardice under fire. Jackson pressed so many charges that at one point he reported that all of his subordinate generals were on court-martial duty.

Jackson's zest for legal solutions reflected his greatest weakness as a commander. He was not a good administrator. His style of leadership tended to be authoritarian, secretive, and exceptionally unforgiving; it sometimes created undue strain among his key subordinates. "[B]e ye sure," vowed Brigadier General Alexander R. Lawton, "it was bitter hard work to keep up with Stonewall Jackson. . . . He gave his orders rapidly and distinctly and rode away. . . . 'Look there. See that place. Take it.' When you failed, you were apt to be put under arrest. When you reported the place taken, he only said, 'Good.'"

The arrival of A.P. Hill's division in the Gordonsville area in early August brought Jackson's force to a total strength of about 28,000; with these men he began active operations against Pope, a Yankee who had aroused much indignation in the South because of his punitive measures against civilians. On August 7, spies brought word that a portion of Pope's Army had reached Culpeper Court House, about twenty-five miles northeast of Gordonsville. Jackson decided to strike this segment at once while the Federals were divided. His forces moved out that evening, but the advance went badly, slowed to a near-crawl by hot weather, poor planning, and Jackson's continued penchant for secrecy. With no knowledge of their destination, his division commanders could do little to sort out the mess that faulty staff work had created. Jackson refused to see it that way, however. He blamed his commanders, particularly A.P. Hill, and noted darkly that the poor march had severely compromised the operation.

On August 9, Jackson's troops neared Cedar Mountain, a tall wooded hill rising above a network of farmland. About mid-morning his lead brigade encountered enemy cavalry; indications pointed to the presence of infantry as well. Jackson, however, made the mistake of underestimating his opponent. Intelligence reports revealed that once again he faced Union General Banks, his old Valley antagonist who he joked was always ready for a fight "and generally gets whipped."

Although most of his forces were still on the road, unable to support an attack, Jackson advanced the two leading divisions with little prior reconnaissance. These struck Banks' Federals around 2:00 P.M.; a lively engagement soon began. But the unionists put up a surprisingly stiff resistance, inflicting a high rate of casualties and killing Brigadier General Charles S. Winder, the latest commander of the Stonewall Brigade and a favorite of Jackson's. Then, around 5:45 P.M., a turning movement by Banks crashed into the Confederate left. Southerners broke and fled toward the rear; Jackson himself dashed in among them, yelling furiously. "Rally, men! Remember Winder! Where's my Stonewall Brigade? Forward, men, forward!"

Hill's division succeeded in regaining the field, and by evening enough additional Confederates arrived to force Banks' retreat. At best, however, the Battle of Cedar Mountain was no better than a draw, and in one important respect Banks had won. Despite losing more men than Jackson—2,381 versus 1,276—he prevented Jackson from attaining his intended objective, the destruction of a chunk of Pope's army. The Confederates' poor approach march, hasty attack, and near-disaster at Cedar Mountain made it seem as if Jackson was about to repeat the performance that had muddled the Seven Days' Battles. But this was not the case.

By mid-August, it became obvious to Lee that Mc-Clellan's Army of the Potomac was under orders to withdraw from the Peninsula. Disillusioned with the Union commander, the Lincoln Administration, backed by Major General Henry W. Halleck, the recently appointed Federal general-in-chief, instructed McClellan to abandon his camps on the James and return to northern Virginia. Accordingly,

Lee shifted the bulk of his forces to confront Pope, hoping to defeat him before McClellan's army could join the active campaign.

From August 15 until August 24, Lee and Pope sparred with one another along the Rappahannock River, Lee looking in vain for an opening that would allow him to strike Pope a decisive blow. Finally Lee resorted to a daring expedient: he proposed Jackson make a wide turning movement that would go around Pope's right flank and plunge deep into the Union rear. He hoped the move would force Pope into a retreat that would widen the distance between the Army of Virginia and the approaching Army of the Potomac, which by then was debarking from vessels at Aquia Creek. With any luck, the resulting strategic ferment would also yield an opportunity to strike Pope on favorable terms.

The march was made with Jackson's usual regard for secrecy. Major General William B. Taliaferro, a division commander during the operation, stated unequivocally that no one but Jackson knew their destination. "The orders to his division chiefs," wrote Taliaferro, "were like this: 'March to a cross-road; a staff officer will inform you which fork to take; and so to the next fork, where you will find a courier with a sealed direction pointing out the road.'"

Crossing the Rappahannock River above Waterloo Bridge, Jackson's 25,000 troops moved rapidly northwest; Federal cavalry spotted the column from a distance, but Pope erroneously supposed Jackson must be heading for the Shenandoah Valley. Lee, meanwhile, used Longstreet's forces to make a series of vigorous demonstrations against Pope, designed to hold him in place. By the evening of August 25, Jackson's fast-marching infantry reached the Manassas Gap Railroad at the village of Salem, having covered a total of twenty-five miles.

As dusk approached, Jackson clambered atop a large boulder and watched his men file past. Although weary from the day's march, the soldiers were in high spirits and cheered the sight of their commander. Jackson silenced them with a friendly gesture, then directed a staff officer to tell the men they must remain quiet lest the enemy should hear. The men obeyed, but smiled and waved their hats in silent homage. The demonstration highly pleased Jackson. "Who could not conquer," he asked his staff, "with such troops as these?"

The next day Jackson's forces swung east, marching through the Bull Run mountains directly into Pope's exposed rear. By afternoon they struck the Orange & Alexandria Railroad near Bristoe Station, placing themselves squarely astride the Federals' line of communications. It did not take Pope long to learn what had occurred. Three trains attempted to pass through Bristoe Station on the afternoon of the 26th. The engineer of the first saw hordes of Confederate soldiers, reversed his locomotive's engines, and backed away toward Washington, D.C. The second train was less fortunate; Rebel troops managed to derail it before it could escape. The third, like the first, backed away—this time toward Pope's army. Around 8:00 P.M., the telegraph line linking Pope's headquarters with Washington went dead, and by early next morning scouts reported for certain what Pope had already begun to suspect: Jackson was deep in his rear.

With that realization began three days of tense drama. Both Confederates and Federals enjoyed tremendous advantages and equally severe disadvantages. Jackson was squarely in Pope's rear and on the Federal supply line, but was also inferior to Pope in numerical strength and far removed from the rest of Lee's army. Pope, for his part, had an opportunity to crush half of the Army of Northern Virginia, but he did not know exactly where Jackson was and was himself off balance because the enemy sat on his supply line. The victor in this drama would be the commmander who could respond with the greater vigor, intelligence, and coolness.

On August 27, Jackson left one division at Bristoe Station and moved his remaining two divisions to Manassas Junction, which the Federals had converted into a gigantic supply depot. At first he hoped he might be able to keep control of the valuable stores until Lee could arrive with the rest of the army to distribute or remove it, but he soon realized this was impractical and gave orders for the depot to be destroyed. The men, he said, could take anything they wanted—with the exception of alcohol, which Jackson prudently instructed should be poured onto the ground. The soldiers remembered that day until they died. The abundance at Manassas included not only military stocks but also sutlers' stores, filled with an incredible variety of food. "It was hard to decide what to take," wrote one soldier. "Some filled their haversacks with cakes, some with candy, others oranges, lemons, canned goods, etc."

With Pope rapidly approaching from the south and other Union forces making appearances from the direction of Washington, Jackson needed to find a strong defensive position where he could make a stand until Lee arrived with the rest of the army. That evening he marched his troops to Sudley Mountain, a low ridge near the village of Groveton not far from where the Battle of Bull Run had been fought the year before. On August 28, his divisions reached a hidden position along the line of an unfinished spur of the Manassas Gap Railroad.

At Groveton late on August 28, Union gunners and infantry face Jackson's forces, whose positions along the edge of the woods on the other side of the Warrenton Turnpike are indicated by gunsmoke. (Battles and Leaders of the Civil War)

Pope, still thinking Jackson near Manassas, moved to cut him off from Longstreet's column, which Pope knew to be approaching from the northwest. During the late afternoon a lone Union division, completely unaware of Jackson's location, marched along the Warrenton Turnpike directly in front of the position that Jackson had chosen. Stonewall decided to attack, if feasible: he hoped to draw Pope toward him, to keep the Federals in the open where Lee might have a chance to crush them. To make certain an attack was viable, he rode forward to reconnoiter the Union division in person. Half in admiration and half in alarm, his officers watched as their commander rode a full quarter mile in front of his troops' position and casually trotted back and forth along the flank of the enemy column. When he returned, Jackson said quietly, "Bring up your men, gentlemen."

Men remembered the resulting Battle of Groveton as one of the severest of the war. Confederates, 4,500 of them, battled about half their number in a furious stand-up struggle that resulted in many casualties. Still, Jackson succeeded in his objective: Pope was alerted to Jackson's location.

The Federal commander promptly brought up most of his army to assail Jackson, hoping, he told the Lincoln Administration, "to bag the whole crowd!" During the next two days he launched repeated attacks against the Confederates along the railroad line, which beleaguered the rebels but did not break them. At one point, Confederate soldiers who ran out of ammunition threw rocks at their enemies rather than abandon their ground.

On the afternoon of August 29, Longstreet arrived on the field, having retraced the line of Jackson's march into the Federal rear, and Pope still had scant idea that the rest of Lee's army had come up. He paid the price. The following day, as Pope unleashed another charge against Jackson's men, Longstreet suddenly attacked with his entire force, smashing into the Federal army. Jackson joined the assault, and Pope's men could not stand the strain. They fell back in relatively good order to Henry House Hill, made a stand that was nearly as heroic as the one made by Jackson on the same hillock a year earlier, and withdrew that evening across Bull Run to safety.

This Second Battle of Bull Run achieved much the same result as its predecessor. This time, however, the Confederates did not allow the Federals to escape unmolested. The next day Jackson put his columns on the road again, hoping once more to turn Pope's flank and pitch into his rear. On September 1, a sharp battle occurred near a large estate called Chantilly. This inconclusive fight convinced the Confederates they could do no further damage to Pope, who was closing on the Washington fortifications and being rapidly reinforced by the Army of the Potomac (some of its units had already joined the fighting). Accordingly, Lee moved north, hoping to retain the initiative.

Pope's defeat opened the way for the move Lee and Jackson had long contemplated: a raid into Maryland and Pennsylvania. A campaign on Union soil offered several good possibilities. Some of them, such as attaining foreign recognition for the Confederate nation or bringing Maryland into the Confederacy, were long shots, but at the very least an advance north of the Potomac would move the conflict away from Virginia, allowing the ravaged state a chance to harvest its autumn crops. On September 3, the Army of Northern Virginia converged around Leesburg; the following day it moved out toward the Potomac fords.

For Jackson, the march into Maryland began with what he perceived to be an infuriating example of A.P. Hill's neglect of duty. Despite his specific instructions that the divisions under his command should begin their march at an early hour, morning of September 4 found Hill's division still in camp. Worse, the separate brigades appeared to be shifting for themselves, with no higher guidance.

Once his forces began the march, Jackson kept an eye peeled for further instances of Hill's sloppy approach to march discipline. They were not long in coming. Contrary to instructions long in effect, Hill did not ride the length of his division to make sure it remained well closed, but rather stayed at the head of his column and made small talk with the staff. Subsequently, in the absence of Hill's direct supervision the division began to lose stragglers. When noon came, Hill failed to halt his men for the customary midday

respite, and Jackson decided to act. Riding up to the lead brigade, he ordered it to halt. Momentarily Hill pounded up, angrily demanding to know by whose order the brigade had stopped. The brigade commander nodded toward Jackson, who was silently observing the scene from a few yards' distance.

Hill stormed up to Jackson, unbuckled his sword and held it out to his superior. "General Jackson," he said tightly, "you have assumed command of my division, here is my sword; I have no use for it."

"Keep your sword General Hill," replied Jackson, "but consider yourself under arrest for neglect of duty." Command of the Light Division devolved upon its senior brigadier, while a smoldering Hill was ordered to march at the division's rear. A week later, at Hill's request, Jackson restored him to command for the duration of the campaign, but that scarcely mollified the tempestuous Virginian.

It was a poor day's march that ended with the army still short of the Potomac. The next day, Jackson's forces began crossing the river around 10:00 A.M. Trouble arose when several baggage wagons halted in mid-stream, their mule teams enjoying the cool water too much to budge from the current. Jackson, still irritated over his argument with Hill, instructed wagonmaster Major John Harmon to clear the ford without delay. Harman splashed into the current and belled the air with a storm of horrendous oaths. The mule drivers followed suit, although none could match the passion and originality displayed by the major. The mules, for their part, grasped the tenor of Harman's oratory and made a dash for the Maryland shore. His mission performed, Harman returned to Jackson, fully anticipating a reprimand for his abundant cursing. "Nothing can justify profanity," Jackson believed.

Harman saluted his commander and explained himself by saying, "The ford is clear, General! There's only one language that will make mules understand on a hot day that they must get out of the water." For once, Jackson let it ride. "Thank you, major," he smiled, and splashed into the river at the head of his staff.

The invasion, in many respects, was an opportunistic thrust with only vaguely defined objectives. Essentially, Lee expected to continue the operational style that had worked so well against Pope: be aggressive, look for openings, and exploit them as vigorously as possible. But before he could do much of anything, he needed to consolidate his position in Maryland, and this meant the establishment of a secure supply line across the Potomac.

The existing line, east of the Blue Ridge Mountains, was no longer tenable. Too near fortified Wash-

Jackson, a deeply religious person, stands at the left in high riding boots in this sketch by Adalbert Volck entitled "Prayer in Stonewall Jackson's Camp." (CWTI Collection)

ington, it was liable to be cut by Union cavalry. The obvious remedy was to shift the line into the Shenandoah Valley, but this raised a second obstacle, the presence of about 13,000 Union troops at Martinsburg and Harpers Ferry. Lee expected his foray north would compel these forces to withdraw (and McClellan urged his superiors to remove them), but they remained where they were, squarely in the path of the proposed supply line through the Shenandoah Valley. As a result, Lee had no choice but to remove the garrisons, a task he entrusted to Jackson and his men.

At a September 8 conference with Jackson and Longstreet, Lee outlined his plan. The army would divide into four main parts, three of them under Jackson's operational control. Longstreet would advance with the main body to Boonsboro, Maryland, beyond the sheltering rim of South Mountain, while Jackson would move with three divisions in a far-ranging sweep that would swing into Harpers Ferry from the west. The divisions of Major Generals Lafayette McLaws and John G. Walker were detached to seize the heights overlooking Harpers Ferry, hills across the Potomac and Shenandoah Rivers. Lee's ambitious timetable called for the town to be invested by September 12 and to surrender soon afterward. Longstreet seemed skeptical, but Jackson apparently was sure it could be done in the time allotted.

The operation got underway very early on September 10, and as the army marched through Frederick, Maryland, the sidewalks thronged with well-wishers and the curious. Jackson, ever true to his passion for deception, approached several civilians and made ostentatious inquiries about places he had no intention of going. That evening the army crossed South Mountain and made camp just east of Boonsboro.

The following day, Jackson's force split off from the main body and continued west, crossing the Potomac near the town of Williamsport. That evening the Confederates camped within earshot of the sunset gun at Martinsburg, a garrison town on the Baltimore & Ohio occupied by 2,500 Federals. The next day Federals at Martinsburg cleared out and Confederate troops occupied the town without a shot being fired.

Jackson ensconced himself in a private residence so that he might prepare a report for Lee. Well-wishers, however, besieged the house, and after finishing his dispatch Jackson decided to receive them. They pressed into the house, showered him with flattery, and cropped his horse's mane and tail in their frenzied quest for souvenirs. Jackson endured it all with his quiet smile. "Thank you, thank you, you're very kind," he repeated, and patiently scribbled autographs. But when one woman suggested he grant her a lock of hair—of which, one staff officer noted, he had no superabundant supply—Jackson cut short the interview and excused himself. He declined many invitations to dinner, but is supposed to have accepted an offer from the parents of one of his men, a private in the Stonewall Brigade.

Not until the afternoon of September 13, a full day behind Lee's optimistic schedule, did Jackson's forces take up their positions on Bolivar Heights overlooking the town. Across the Potomac, McLaws' division drove a Union detachment from Maryland Heights, while Walker's division bloodlessly occupied Loudoun Heights across the Shenandoah. Harpers Ferry was invested, its surrender imminent. And yet at that moment something occurred that nearly forced the abandonment of the siege.

Several days before, McClellan had assumed command of a reorganized Army of the Potomac, now reinforced by units from Pope's disbanded Army of Virginia. On September 7 he took the field, advancing at a leisurely five miles a day, uncertain of Lee's location or intentions and, as ever, extremely cautious. On September 13, the same day that Jackson's forces surrounded Harpers Ferry, Union forces reached Frederick. There, among the jetsam of an abandoned Confederate encampment, two Federal soldiers discovered a copy of *Special Orders No. 191*, Lee's directive for the Harpers Ferry operation. The dispatch sped upward through channels and reached McClellan within an hour, who is supposed to have read the document and exclaimed, "Here is a paper with which, if I cannot whip Bobby Lee, I shall be willing to go home!" In the dispatch, laid out as precisely as McClellan could wish, were the dispositions of the entire Confederate army. McClellan now knew of its divided condition, and knew in particular that Jackson's force, itself split into three components, was at that moment investing Harpers Ferry.

Early on the morning of September 14, McClellan's forces began their advance toward the South Mountain gaps. Although fighting flared around Fox's Gap as early as 9:00 A.M., poor Union planning and timidity delayed the opening of the crucial engagement at Crampton's Gap until around 4:00 P.M., when the Federals' VI Corps swept aside a much smaller detachment from McLaws' division and advanced into Pleasant Valley. Darkness put an end to their attack and the Federals halted for the night, still several miles short of Harpers Ferry. In the sector around the National Road, Union forces failed to breach the gaps, but gathered such overwhelming strength as to leave no doubt that the Rebel line could not hold a second day.

Lee's initial response was to abandon the invasion and recross the Potomac as soon as possible, but late on the evening of the 14th he received an encouraging note from Jackson: "Through God's blessing, the advance, which commenced this evening, has been successful thus far, and I look to Him for complete success tomorrow."

Buttressed by this knowledge and unwilling to abandon the siege if victory was imminent, Lee altered his plan. Instead of withdrawing into Virginia, he elected to concentrate the army around Sharpsburg, still on the Maryland side of the river and a position from which he could support Jackson if the Federals mounted a concerted drive to raise the siege. The orders went out; the movement began late that evening.

Dawn of the next day found Jackson's artillery frowning down on Harpers Ferry, and as soon as the mist burned away sufficiently the Rebel guns began plunging shells into the Federal position. Soon the white flag waved from the Union ramparts. The Confederates marched in, took possession of the town, and began the sizable administrative task of paroling the prisoners and counting up the captured supplies. The final tally read: 11,000 prisoners, 73 guns, 200 wagons, and 13,000 stands of arms, not to mention the bountiful commissary stores that were seized. Too quickly forgotten in the shadow of the battle about to occur, Harpers Ferry was a considerable Confederate victory.*

Leaving A.P. Hill's division to complete the parole of prisoners and exchange of supplies, Jackson started moving his forces to Sharpsburg. He reached the village late on the 15th, riding ahead of his three divisions, and reported to Lee at his headquarters. There Lee explained to him the army's new dispositions. The position Lee had selected lay behind Antietam Creek, on a series of hills and low ridges that offered good (though hardly excellent) ground from which to resist attack. Longstreet and D.H. Hill already held the right and center; Jackson's men were needed on the left, where the Confederate line curved toward the Potomac a mile or so away. The presence of the river in the Rebels' immediate rear formed the position's major—and possibly fatal—disadvantage. In the event of a Union breakthrough it would be impossible to extricate the army in time to prevent complete disaster.

Lee, however, counted on McClellan's cautious nature. This proved to be a good bet. The Union army failed to attack throughout the long day of September 16, when much of the Confederate army had not yet arrived from Harpers Ferry. The next day, when McClellan did launch his attack, he did so in a piecemeal fashion, so that the Confederates could shift their

---

*It marked the largest mass surrender of U.S. forces until the fall of Bataan in the Philippines some eighty years later during World War II.

outnumbered forces from place to place to meet it. Even so, for most of the day the Rebel army wavered on the brink of catastrophe.

The battle, called Antietam in the North, Sharpsburg in the South, began shortly after dawn on the 17th. Things went badly for the Confederates from the very outset. Superior Union artillery lashed out at Jackson's position from the heights east of Antietam Creek, while the I Corps under Major General Joseph Hooker launched an assault against his front. Within minutes, two understrength Confederate divisions were mauled and out of action. Jackson issued an urgent summons to Brigadier General John B. Hood, requesting that he come with his division at once. Hood did so, noticed that the Confederate line had practically disappeared, and charged, hoping his unexpected attack would throw the Union forces off balance. The counterattack succeeded in driving back Hooker's corps, but soon ran into Major General Joseph Mansfield's advancing XII Corps and was forced to halt. By 11:00 A.M. or so, the Confederates had steadied the line against the encroachments of the XII Corps and, later, the II Corps. Afterward, the fighting shifted to a sunken road in D.H. Hill's sector. By then, Jackson noted proudly, his troops had recovered their original position.

As pressure mounted on the Confederate center, Jackson received a message from Lee asking whether a way might be found to mount an attack on the Federal right flank. Jackson and the army's cavalry chief Major General Jeb Stuart were initially optimistic—Jackson even announced fiercely, "We'll drive McClellan into the Potomac." But sober inspection of the terrain revealed the scheme was impossible. Federal artillery covered the proposed line of attack too well.

During the afternoon A.P. Hill came up, launched an attack on Union Major General Ambrose Burnside's IX Corps, and ended the day's battle. That evening Lee, Longstreet, Jackson, and several division commanders met to discuss a counterattack. But taking up the offensive proved out of the question; horrendous casualties had been sustained that day. Lee decided, instead, that the army would hold its ground the following day.

McClellan failed to renew the attack. On the night of September 18–19, the Confederates withdrew, leaving the field of a drawn battle, not the site of an outright defeat. Jackson assured Lee, it "was better to have fought in Maryland than to have left it without a struggle."

The army crossed the Potomac at Boteler's Ford without serious incident and Jackson established his headquarters about four miles south of the river. Shortly after midnight, Confederate artillery chief General William N. Pendleton appeared with dire news. The Federals, he said, had crossed the river unexpectedly, brushed aside Pendleton's infantry support, and captured the army's entire artillery reserve. Without waiting for instructions, Jackson immediately ordered A.P. Hill's division to march to Boteler's Ford and drive back the Federals. Hill did so, pushing the Union troops into the river and pumping volley after volley into them as they frantically swam to safety. Lee wound up losing only four guns. After the war, D.H. Hill declared that Jackson's prompt counterstroke had saved the Confederates

Harper's Ferry, below Maryland and Loudon Heights, where Jackson made short work of the Union garrison, eliminating a threat to Lee's rear. (U.S. Army Military History Institute)

from probable ruin. Lee, he said, had been so unstrung by Pendleton's news that he had ordered a line of battle to be formed four miles south of the river, in effect leaving the guns to their captors. "The result," Hill wrote, "would have been the most disastrous conceivable. . . . I have sometimes wondered whether the Army of N. Va. would have ceased to have an organized existence but for this splendid movement."

Lee's army withdrew into the Shenandoah Valley; the Army of the Potomac remained on the Maryland side of the river. Much to the dismay of the Lincoln Administration, McClellan insisted he required several weeks of quiet to rest and refit his men before resuming an active campaign. Grateful for the breathing space, Lee used the time to reorganize his own forces.

Ever since the first operations against Pope, the Army of Northern Virginia had been informally divided into two groups of divisions. Longstreet had led one group; Jackson directed the other. A new Confederate law permitted Lee to formalize the arrangement. From October 1862 onward, the troops under Longstreet's command became the First Corps; those belonging to Jackson were designated the Second Corps. The two new corps commanders also received promotion to the recently created rank of lieutenant general.

Jackson's sterling performances at Second Manassas, Harpers Ferry, and Sharpsburg made everyone forget his bungling during the Seven Days. "My opinion of General Jackson has been greatly enhanced during this expedition," Lee wrote President Davis of the summer campaigns. "He is true, honest, and brave; has a single eye to the good of the service, and spares no exertion to accomplish his object." Others praised him even more extravagantly. His fame had become worldwide and he was frequently touted as the South's finest general.

In mid-October, British Colonel Garnet Wolseley visited the Confederate army's encampment and made it a special point to look up Jackson. Having heard of Jackson's religious intensity, Wolseley expected a puritan radical. Instead he found a pleasant Anglophile who spent most of their interview recounting his pre-war visit to England. The British colonel came away tremendously impressed. "The religious element seems strongly developed in him," he wrote afterward; "and though his conversation is perfectly free from all puritanical cant, it is evident that he is a person who never loses sight of the fact that there is an omnipresent Deity ever presiding over the minutest occurrences of life, as well as the most important. . . . With such a leader men would go anywhere, and face any amount of difficulties, and for myself I believe that, inspired by the presence of such a man, I should be perfectly insensible to fatigue, and reckon upon success as a moral certainty."

Not everyone in the Second Corps shared Wolseley's glowing picture of Jackson, however. Its best division commander, A.P. Hill, still smoldered in the wake of his confrontation with Jackson during the march from Leesburg. On September 22, Hill requested that Lee convene a court of inquiry to investigate the matter. Lee declined, stating that since he believed Hill's derelictions were unintentional and would not be repeated, he saw no point in pursuing the issue. Jackson, for his part, seemed content to drop the matter as well. But Hill could not dismiss it so easily. His honor had been impugned; he would not be satisfied until he could demonstrate Jackson's error.

Jackson, although willing to forget the matter, was not willing to back down from it if Hill insisted on making a fuss. On October 3, he sent Lee a list of eight specifications against Hill on the charge of neglect of duty—not because he wanted to, he said, but because Hill would accept nothing less. Jackson added coldly that, so far as he could see, Hill's insistence on a court of inquiry while the army remained in the field was simply yet another example of his neglect of duty.

The continuing feud between Jackson and Hill eventually forced Lee to intervene in person. One day in October he rode to Jackson's headquarters; Hill arrived shortly thereafter. The trio disappeared into Jackson's tent and did not emerge for several hours. But apparently neither Hill nor Jackson would listen to Lee's entreaties; the rift between them remained. Thereafter, the two men tried to avoid one another, and on the rare occasions when their duties required them to meet, they saluted each other with icy formality and spoke as little as possible.

By late October the Federal army had crossed into Virginia east of the Blue Ridge Mountains. Lee shifted Longstreet's corps to oppose it, but left Jackson in the Shenandoah Valley on the chance that the Second Corps might be able to turn McClellan's flank if he advanced farther. McClellan continued forward with his customary caution, but fed up with the Union general's lack of vigor, an impatient Federal government shelved him in early November. In his place they substituted Major General Ambrose E. Burnside, an affable West Pointer who thought himself unequal to so important a command and had already twice refused it. Intent on getting action, the Lincoln Administration insisted Burnside begin an active campaign at once. Burnside complied, and on November 15 began marching his army toward Fredericksburg from Washington, hoping to cross the Rappahannock River before Lee could intervene.

The plan came close to success. The celerity of Burnside's movement took Lee by surprise, and when the vanguard of the Federal army reached Fredericksburg it found only a few hundred Confederates in position to contest a crossing. Unfortunately for Burnside, the bridges at Fredericksburg had long been destroyed. Burnside knew this and had ordered pontoon bridges to be transported to the crossing site, but bureaucratic foul-ups delayed their arrival for nearly three weeks. As a result, Lee was able to concentrate his entire army on the south bank of the Rappahannock. By the 29th of November, 72,564 Confederates confronted 116,683 Federals across the river.

Jackson disliked Lee's decision to defend the Rappahannock line at Fredericksburg. The bulk of the Army of Northern Virginia was posted along a series of low ridges just west of the town, a strong defensive line, but one without enough maneuvering room to allow for a counterattack. "[W]e shall whip the enemy," he told D.H. Hill, "but gain no fruits of victory." He preferred the line of the North Anna, a stream farther south, but Lee rejected the option as too expensive in terms of the amount of territory it would give up to the enemy.

At first, the Second Corps' front included a twenty-mile stretch of the lower Rappahannock, a caution against any attempt by Burnside to cross below Fredericksburg. But by December 11 it became obvious that the Union commander intended to stick with his original plan. On that day, Federal engineers constructed six pontoon bridges near the town. Jackson hurried his four divisions to their new battle positions.

Lee posted Longstreet's First Corps on Marye's Heights directly behind the town. The Second Corps occupied a stretch of lower ground from Deep Run to Hamilton's Crossing. The Union army crossed on December 12, but stood under the protection of heavy artillery posted on the opposite bank and did not attempt an immediate attack. The next morning Jackson met with Lee, Stuart and Longstreet. Ever offensive-minded, he suggested the Confederates launch an attack of their own while the morning fog blinded the Union cannoneers. Stuart concurred, but Lee said no. Longstreet then pointed to the Federal hosts already visible on Jackson's front. "General," he inquired in a heavy attempt at humor, "don't those multitudes of Federals frighten you?"

"We shall see very soon whether I do not frighten them," Jackson replied.

"What are you going to do with all those people over there?" Longstreet pursued.

"Sir," snapped Jackson, swinging onto his horse, "we shall give them the bayonet!"

The Federal attack jumped off around 12:00 P.M. Repeated charges struck the First Corps at Marye's Heights; Longstreet's men beat them back with ease. On Jackson's front, a similarly easy victory seemed likely until a lone Union division found a gap nearly 600 yards wide in the middle of A.P. Hill's line. But the Federals did not receive enough support to exploit the gap; otherwise Jackson's position might have become dire. As it was, the heaviest Confederate losses of the battle occurred when Jackson had to launch a counterattack to force them back.

By evening, Burnside's gambit had utterly failed. Over 12,500 Federals had become casualties, compared with fewer than 5,500 Confederates. The Army of the Potomac drew back to the northern bank of the Rappahannock; the Army of Northern Virginia went into winter quarters.

The Fallen Champion

The months that followed were happy ones for Jackson. He set up headquarters at "Moss Neck," a handsome residence owned by Mr. and Mrs. Richard Corbin, whose family became as dear to him as the Grahams had been the previous winter. A religious revival swept the Confederate camp; Jackson welcomed it, and was instrumental in establishing a Chaplains' Association to better oversee the spiritual needs of soldiers. Best of all, in April 1863 his wife Anna came to visit him in camp. With her came a tiny traveling companion: Julia Laura Jackson, the general's infant daughter.

Julia had come into the world on November 23, 1862, while the Second Corps was en route to the battlefield at Fredericksburg. She enchanted her father from the first moment he saw her. He liked to hold the infant up to a mirror and exclaim, "Now, Miss Jackson, look at yourself!" and objected when well-wishers commented that she resembled him. "No," he would say, "she is too pretty to look like me." After thirty-eight years, he at last had a family of his own.

As the spring of 1863 approached, the rival armies in Virginia geared up for active operations. Beefed up by the North's ample reserves of manpower, the Army of the Potomac had more than recovered its pre-Fredericksburg level of strength; its men were well-fed, warmly dressed, and ready for a new offensive. Federal morale, which had plummeted in the wake of Burnside's disastrous leadership, surged upward under a new commander, Major General Joseph Hooker, whom Lincoln appointed to replace Burnside in January 1863. By contrast, the Army of Northern Virginia possessed excellent morale but very little else. Confederate logistics had already begun to fail; Lee found it difficult to keep his troops adequately fed and equipped and was forced to disperse them over wide swaths of countryside so that they could forage locally. Worse, a Union threat to southside Virginia had obliged him to detach Longstreet and two divisions in order to protect that region. By mid-April, Lee could count just 59,000 effectives. Hooker, in contrast, had nearly 135,000.

Early on the morning of April 29 a courier arrived with a message; Jackson was needed at the front. South of Fredericksburg, Union forces had laid pontoon bridges across the Rappahannock, perhaps intending to repeat their attack of the previous December. Quickly, Jackson gave instructions: his wife and child must go at once to Richmond, and General Lee must be informed of this new Federal activity. Later in the day Lee arrived and the two men discussed strategy. The reports of scouts on the upper Rappahannock led Lee to believe Hooker's main attack would come from upstream. If so, the Federal presence below Fredericksburg was a simple diversion. Another day passed, however, before the situation became clear. Until then, the Confederate army remained substantially in place.

Characteristically, both Lee and Jackson thought of mounting an attack of their own. Jackson briefly advocated an offensive against the Federals below Fredericksburg, but careful examination of the ground revealed the plan could not succeed; Union artillery on the opposite bank commanded the terrain too well. Lee decided to concentrate against Hooker instead. Leaving one division to contain the Federals below Fredericksburg, the rest of the army would move west until it made contact with the enemy's main body.

The Federal army had actually split itself into two halves. The main segment, commanded by Hooker in person, comprised 60,000 men and by April 30 had nearly completed a long flanking march that took it from its camps near Falmouth to a lonely crossroads called Chancellorsville, three miles south of the Rapidan River and squarely on the Confederate left flank. The other segment, with 59,000 men, was commanded by Major General John Sedgwick, whose instructions were to demonstrate in order to divert Confederate attention from the main body, then advance as circumstances permitted.

Ordinarily, an army threatened front and flank by a force over twice its size might reasonably be expected to retreat, and Hooker anticipated that Lee would do precisely that. Lee, of course, did nothing of the kind, and when he failed to do what Hooker expected, something inside the Federal commander

wilted. As he explained it later, "I just lost confidence in Joe Hooker."

The loss of confidence concealed itself in a glittering shower of bombast and self-congratulation. On the evening of April 30, Hooker announced to his troops "our enemy must either ingloriously fly or . . . give us battle on our own ground, where certain destruction awaits him." But the following day Hooker's doubts bubbled forth when he mysteriously halted his successful advance and ordered his troops to prepare defensive positions in the wooded thickets around Chancellorsville. When Hooker's second-in-command, Major General Darius Couch, questioned him about this, Hooker responded soothingly, "It is all right, Couch, I have got Lee just where I want him; he must fight me on my own ground." Couch was not fooled; he later wrote scathingly, "I retired from [Hooker's] presence with the belief that my commanding general was a whipped man."

Beyond the Federal lines, Lee and Jackson con-

Lee and Jackson discuss strategy during their famous council in a thicket of pines on the night of Friday, May 1. Drawing by W.L. Sheppard. (Battles and Leaders of the Civil War)

templated their adversary's baffling halt. Shortly before dusk on May 1, they met in a thicket of pines east of Chancellorsville. The situation offered the opportunity for a counterstroke, but where should one be made? It seemed obvious an attack against the Union left flank could not succeed—the undergrowth in that sector was too thick, the roads too few. What about the center? The commanders dispatched two engineering officers to check it out, then tentatively discussed a possible flank march against Hooker's right, a discussion that acquired especial point when cavalry corps commander Stuart arrived and announced Hooker's right was "in the air"—it simply extended west from Chancellorsville a few miles and then ended, anchored to no natural strongpoint.

"How can we get at those people?" Lee inquired.

"You know best," Jackson replied. "Show me what to do, and we will try to do it."

Lee traced a possible route for a flank attack, then said that Jackson would have charge of it. The corps

commander smiled. "My troops will move at 4 o'clock."

Returning to his headquarters, Jackson instructed his cartographer Hotchkiss to find a road around the Federal army. The engineer returned at dawn, found both Lee and Jackson warming themselves by a small fire, and made his report. From information provided by officers who lived in the area and knew it intimately, he learned that the needed route existed, passable for artillery and screened from enemy observation by the dense forests that characterized the region. He traced the route on a map. When he had finished, Lee said, "General Jackson, what do you propose to do?"

Jackson indicated the screened route. "Go around here," he said.

"What do you propose making this movement with?"

"With my whole corps," Jackson replied.

This was a new wrinkle: Lee had not anticipated a turning movement of such scale. "What will you leave me?" he asked.

"The divisions of McLaws and Anderson."

Lee paused. The proposal meant that for most of the day, until Jackson got into position, he would have just 14,000 men with which to oppose Hooker's 60,000. If the flank march failed—if the Federals spotted it, or if Hooker attacked Lee while Jackson was on the move, disaster could result. But after a moment he said simply, "Well, go on."

The march began at 8:00 A.M., a full four hours after the time that Jackson had optimistically promised the evening before. The ten-mile route wound southwest at first, then veered sharply to the northwest. It took Jackson's men most of the day to cover it, and despite their commander's care to select roads screened from enemy vision, the Union army discovered the movement almost immediately. Federal soldiers continued to spot it throughout the day, yet Hooker failed to take any real action. Instead, he convinced himself that it must be the Confederates' much-hoped-for retreat. The worst moment for the Second Corps came when a venturesome Union corps attacked some of Jackson's rear-guard, but the assault was half-hearted and two Southern brigades managed to fend it off.

Mid-morning found a confident Jackson discussing old times with three former colleagues from VMI, now members of the Second Corps. As they rode along, his thoughts turned to the Union commander whose strange caution had made the impending flank attack possible. "I hear it said," he remarked, "that General Hooker has more men than he can handle. I should like to have half as many more as I have today, and I should hurl him into the river! The trouble with us has always been to have a reserve to throw in at the critical moment to reap the benefit of advantages gained. We have always had to put in all our troops and never had enough at the time most needed."

He would have the same trouble today; he knew it. Every man in his corps would have to enter the attack, leaving nothing in reserve. The only solution would be to press the enemy as hard as possible. "[N]ever let up in the pursuit so long as your men have strength to follow," Jackson maintained; "for an army routed, if hotly pursued, becomes panic-stricken, and can then be destroyed by half their number."

The line of battle began forming around 4:00 P.M.: Major General Robert E. Rodes' division deployed first, the other two divisions formed behind it. By 5:15 P.M. the Confederates had created an attacking column a mile and a half from end to end. It aimed straight at the vulnerable Union flank, where unhurried Federal soldiers nursed small cooking fires in preparation for dinner.

"Are you ready, General Rodes?" Jackson asked his lead division commander.

"Yes, sir."

"You can go forward, then."

The Confederate charge overran the Union XI Corps, whose panicked men streamed east away from Jackson's furious avalanche of force. Here and there an isolated Northern unit attempted to make a stand, only to be smashed by the onrushing Confederates. In two hours of combat, Jackson's corps gained nearly two miles of ground. Jackson followed in the wake of his lead division, his face lit with the wild flame of battle, and one man who saw him swore that now and again the general paused like some Old Testament prophet and swept an arm skyward in supplication: Bow thy heavens, O Lord, and come down.

With the Union right flank shattered, Jackson's objective became the capture of a road leading from Chancellorsville to United States Ford, the route Hooker's army would have to use to withdraw across the Rappahannock. If that could be done, he might indeed be able to hurl the Army of the Potomac into the river. But by 7:30 P.M. the daylight had bled away and the leading units had lost all organization in the headlong assault. Rodes suggested to Jackson that A.P. Hill's division be brought up from the rear to press the attack while the units already in front paused to regroup. Jackson agreed, gave the order, and soon Hill rode up to report his division had deployed as instructed. "Press them," Jackson snapped. "Cut them off from United States Ford, Hill. Press them!"

The maze of thickets and second-growth timber in the region made it impossible to continue the advance cross-country. It also helped the retreating Federals to break off contact with the pursuing Confederates. Jackson decided he must make a personal reconnaissance in order to clarify the situation.

Accompanied by a small group of staff officers, he rode beyond Confederate front lines. When one of the officers objected that it was too dangerous for Jackson to expose himself that way, the general exploded. "The danger," he insisted, "is all over—the enemy is routed!—go back and tell A.P. Hill to press right on!"

The horsemen rode down a narrow country lane, the dank woods around them lit by the pallid gleam of a full moon. Presently they heard a noise ahead and paused to listen more carefully. The sound became distinct: a cacophony of ax blades, biting into trees to be felled for fortifications. Somewhere, a short distance up ahead, the Federals were preparing a new line of entrenchments.

The reconnaissance party swung their horses around and headed back to Confederate lines. Soldiers in the 18th North Carolina heard them coming, assumed from the direction of their approach that they must be Federal cavalry, and opened fire. "Cease firing!" cried a staff officer with Jackson. "You are firing into our own men!" But an unseen infantry officer thundered back, "Who gave that order? It's a lie! Pour it into them, boys!"

A full volley from the regiment decimated the helpless cavalcade. One bullet entered Jackson's left arm; another pierced his right hand. His horse bolted in panic; a tree limb smashed him across the face, nearly knocking him from the saddle. With difficulty he managed to control the animal, and a moment later a staff officer grabbed the reins.

Two men helped him down from the saddle and laid him on the ground. A.P. Hill appeared. "I have been trying to make the men cease firing," he said. His face creased in concern as he saw the stricken Jackson. "Is the wound painful?" Hill asked softly.

"Very painful," Jackson said, "my arm is broken."

At length, officers quieted the firing and made preparations to carry the general to safety. Command of the Second Corps devolved upon Hill, but within minutes a fragment from an exploding Union shell clipped him across the shins, bruising him so badly he could not walk. With no other division commander experienced enough to handle a corps, Hill decided to send for cavalry man Jeb Stuart, the nearest major general available.

It took two hours to get Jackson to a field hospital. Dr. Hunter McGuire, the physician who had dressed Jackson's wound at First Manassas and now the Sec-

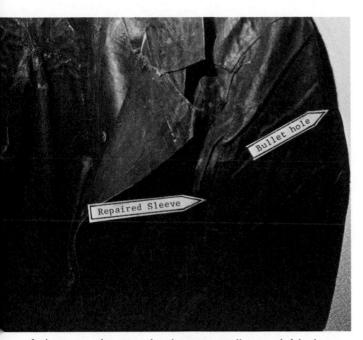

Jackson wore this coat when he was mortally wounded by his own troops at Chancellorsville. A bullet hole is still evident in the left arm of the coat. (Virginia Military Institute)

ond Corps' medical director, gave the general two additional hours to rest after the ordeal. Then Mc-Guire chloroformed the general in order to conduct a detailed examination of the wounds. He soon found what he feared would prove the case: the bone of Jackson's left arm had been shattered. There was no way to save the limb; he would have to amputate.

The operation took comparatively little time, and by 3:30 A.M. Jackson had come out from under the chloroform. Oddly, the effects of the drug made him garrulous; he told Lieutenant James Smith chloroform was a great boon to medicine. It had numbed all sensation of pain, he reported; the only thing he recalled of the surgery was the faint sound of a delightful music—"I believe it was the sawing of the bone."

Jackson's chipper attitude pointed toward an early recovery, and when he awoke on the morning of May 3 he felt vigorous enough to dictate a message to Lee, informing the commanding general of the circumstance that had forced him to relinquish charge of the Second Corps. That afternoon a courier brought Lee's response; Lieutenant Smith read the message aloud.

"General," it began, "I have just received your note, informing me that you were wounded. I cannot express my regret at the occurrence. Could I have directed events, I should have chosen for the good of the country to be disabled in your stead.

"I congratulate you upon the victory, which is due to your skill and energy."

In the lengthy pause that followed, Jackson turned his face from Smith. "General Lee is very kind," he said at last, "but he should give the praise to God."

In the days that followed, Jackson seemed to progress finely. By May 4 he was well enough to be transported the twenty-five miles to Guiney's Station, where he was to make his convalescence. He seemed in buoyant spirits and talked abundantly on a variety of subjects, but especially religion. "Many would regard [these wounds] as a great misfortune," he told Smith, "I regard them as one of the blessings of my life." Smith, a former seminary student, understood. The lieutenant quoted the apostle Paul: "All things work together for good to those that love God." Jackson nodded. "Yes," he said, "that's it, that's it."

At Guiney's Station someone brought him word of the fighting at Chancellorsville. Lee had pummelled Hooker's force, then turned east, driven Sedgwick's wing across the Rappahannock, and doubled back to confront Hooker again. Yet the Federal army was far from destroyed and Hooker had fortified himself in a strong position north of Chancellorsville. "That is bad; very bad," Jackson commented. On May 6 the Union army retired north of the Rappahannock, but Jackson never learned of this.

By the time word of the Federal retreat seeped into Guiney's Station, Jackson had contracted pneumonia. He may have had it since the night of his wounding, but the illness went undetected until it burst forth with fatal intensity. Dr. McGuire diag-

Mary Anna Jackson, the lieutenant general's widow. (Memoirs of "Stonewall" Jackson by Mary Ann Jackson, 1895; reprinted 1976)

nosed it at dawn on May 7, and by that time it had made serious inroads.

Later that day Anna arrived from Richmond. Just eight days earlier she had seen her husband at the peak of health, robust, vigorous; now his pale, clammy skin, mutilated arm, and rasping, half-suffocated breath pierced her to her soul. Jackson saw the anguish on her face. "My darling, you must cheer up, and not wear a long face. I love cheerfulness and brightness in a sick-room." He faded in and out, but whenever his mind was clear he attempted to reassure her. "My darling, you are very much loved," he would say. "You are one of the most precious little wives in the world."

By Sunday, May 10, 1863, the doctors knew he must die. They summoned Anna and told her so, and said she must tell her husband. Tenderly, she went to him, told him he would soon be in heaven. "Yes," Jackson murmured with slow conviction, "I prefer it, I prefer it."

Jackson now lived out his final hours. He told Anna he wished to be buried in Lexington, then greeted his infant daughter when little Julia was brought for a last look at her father. It was a visit she could not know the significance of, a last look at a father she would not remember.

By early afternoon it became more difficult for Jackson to speak. He had to fight for every breath. Helpless in the face of the disease that was killing his patient, Dr. McGuire could only offer the failing general a glass of brandy and water. Jackson refused it. "It will only delay my departure and do no good; I want to preserve my mind, if possible, to the last."

He slipped into delirium. His fevered mind roiled with thoughts of battle. "Order A.P. Hill to prepare for action," he rasped. "Pass the infantry to the front. Tell Major Hawks—" He grew quiet. There was a long silence, and then he said clearly, "Let us cross over the river, and rest under the shade of the trees."

Jackson's grave in Lexington, Virginia, near his home and the Virginia Military Institute. (Harper's New Monthly Magazine)

Recommended Reading

This listing of books on the strategy, tactics, campaigns, battles, and military leaders of the Civil War is divided into three parts:

1. General Works, including narratives, histories of particular armies or units, reference works, studies of strategy and tactics, naval history, and interpretive studies
2. Books on important military campaigns and battles
3. Biographies and other studies of important individuals

General Works
(Alphabetical by Author)

Adams, Michael C. C., *Our Masters the Rebels: A Speculation on Union Military Failure in the East, 1861–1865* (1978)

Beringer, Richard E., Herman Hattaway, Archer Jones, and William N. Still, Jr., *Why the South Lost the Civil War* (1986)

Boatner, Mark M., III, *The Civil War Dictionary* (rev. ed. 1989)

Brownlee, Richard S., *Gray Ghosts of the Confederacy: Guerrilla Warfare in the West, 1861–1865* (1984)

Bruce, Robert V., *Lincoln and the Tools of War* (1956)

Buel, Clarence C., and Robert U. Johnson, eds., *Battles and Leaders of the Civil War* (1888, reprint ed. 1982)

Catton, Bruce, Trilogy on the Army of the Potomac:
   Mr. Lincoln's Army (1951)
   Glory Road: The Bloody Route from Fredericksburg to Gettysburg (1952)
   A Stillness at Appomattox (1957)

Catton, Bruce, *The Centennial History of the Civil War:*
   The Coming Fury (1961)
   Terrible Swift Sword (1963)
   Never Call Retreat (1965)

Connelly, Thomas L., *Army of the Heartland: The Army of Tennessee 1861–1862* (1967)

Connelly, Thomas L., *Autumn of Glory: The Army of Tennessee 1862–1865* (1971)

Connelly, Thomas L., and Archer Jones, *The Politics of Command: Factions and Ideas in Confederate Strategy* (1973)

Cornish, Dudley T., *The Sable Arm: Negro Troops in the Union Army 1861–1865* (1956)

Coulter, E. Merton, *The Confederate States of America 1861–1865* (1950)

Davis, William C., ed., *The Image of War 1861–1865*, 6 vols. (1981–1984). A photographic history.

Donald, David, ed., *Why the North Won the Civil War* (1960)

Esposito, Vincent J., *The West Point Atlas of American Wars*, Vol. I, 1689–1900 (1959)

Faust, Patricia L., ed., *Historical Times Illlustrated Encyclopedia of the Civil War* (1986)

Foote, Shelby, *The Civil War: A Narrative*
   I. *Fort Sumter to Perryville* (1958)
   II. *Fredericksburg to Meridian* (1963)
   III. *Red River to Appomattox* (1974)

Freeman, Douglas Southall, *Lee's Lieutenants: A Study in Command*, 3 vols. (1942–44)

Gosnell, H. Allen, *Guns on the Western Waters: The Story of River Gunboats in the Civil War* (1949)

Griffith, Paddy, *Rally Once Again: Battle Tactics of the American Civil War* (1987)

Hagerman, Edward, *The American Civil War and the Origins of Modern Warfare* (1988)

Hattaway, Herman, and Archer Jones, *How the North Won: A Military History of the Civil War* (1983)

Jones, Virgil Carrington, *The Civil War at Sea*, 3 vols. (1960–62)

Jones, Virgil Carrington, *Gray Ghosts and Rebel Raiders* (1956). Guerrilla warfare in Virginia and West Virginia.

Linderman, Gerald F., *Embattled Courage: The Experience of Combat in the American Civil War* (1987)

Long, E. B., *The Civil War Day by Day: An Almanac 1861–1865* (1971)

McPherson, James M., *Battle Cry of Freedom: The Civil War Era* (1988)

McPherson, James M., *Ordeal By Fire: The Civil War and Reconstruction* (1982)

McWhiney, Grady, and Perry D. Jamieson, *Attack and Die: Civil War Military Tactics and the Southern Heritage* (1982)

Miller, Francis T., ed., *The Photographic History of the Civil War*, 10 vols. (1911, reprint ed. 1957)

Mitchell, Reid, *Civil War Soldiers* (1988)

Monaghan, Jay, *Civil War on the Western Border 1854–1865* (1955)

Nevins, Allan, *The War for the Union*
    I. *The Improvised War 1861–1862* (1959)
    II. *War Becomes Revolution* (1960)
    III. *The Organized War 1863–1864* (1971)
    IV. *The Organized War to Victory 1864–1865* (1971)

Nolan, Alan T., *The Iron Brigade* (1961)

Perry, Milton F., *Infernal Machines: The Story of Confederate Submarine and Mine Warfare* (1965)

Robertson, James I., *The Stonewall Brigade* (1963)

Sifakis, Stewart, *Who Was Who in the Civil War* (1988)

Thomas, Emory M., *The Confederate Nation 1861–1865* (1979)

Warner, Ezra J., *Generals in Blue: Lives of the Union Commanders* (1964)

Warner, Ezra J., *Generals in Gray: Lives of the Confederate Commanders* (1959)

Wiley, Bell Irvin, *The Life of Johnny Reb* (1943)

Wiley, Bell Irvin, *The Life of Billy Yank* (1952)

Williams, Kenneth P., *Lincoln Finds a General: A Military Study of the Civil War*, 5 vols. (1949–1959)

Williams, T. Harry, *Lincoln and His Generals* (1952)

Campaigns and Battles
(In Chronological Order)

Current, Richard N., *Lincoln and the First Shot* (1963)

Swanberg, William A., *First Blood: The Story of Fort Sumter* (1957)

Davis, William C., *Battle at Bull Run* (1977)

Hall, Martin H., *Sibley's New Mexico Campaign* (1960)

Hamilton, James J., *The Battle of Fort Donelson* (1968)

Davis, William C., *Duel Between the First Ironclads* (1975)

McDonough, James Lee, *Shiloh—In Hell Before Night* (1976)

Sword, Wiley, *Shiloh: Bloody April* (1974)

Tanner, Robert G., *Stonewall in the Valley* (1976)

Dowdey, Clifford, *Seven Days: The Emergence of Lee* (1964)

Stackpole, Edward J., *From Cedar Mountain to Antietam* (1959)

Murfin, James V., *The Gleam of Bayonets: The Battle of Antietam* (1965)

Sears, Stephen W., *Landscape Turned Red: The Battle of Antietam* (1983)

Frassanito, William A., *Antietam: The Photographic Legacy of America's Bloodiest Day* (1978)

Jones, Archer, *Confederate Strategy from Shiloh to Vicksburg* (1961)

McDonough, James Lee, *Stones River: Bloody Winter in Tennessee* (1980)

Stackpole, Edward J., *Drama on the Rappahannock: The Fredericksburg Campaign* (1957)

Stackpole, Edward J., *Chancellorsville: Lee's Greatest Battle* (1958)

Coddington, Edwin B., *The Gettysburg Campaign* (1968)

Hassler, Warren W., Jr., *Crisis at the Crossroads: The First Day at Gettysburg* (1970)

Pfanz, Harry W., *Gettysburg—the Second Day* (1987)

Stewart, George R., *Pickett's Charge: A Microhistory of the Final Attack at Gettysburg* (1959)

Frassanito, William A., *Gettysburg: A Journey in Time* (1975). A photographic history.

Shaara, Michael, *The Killer Angels* (1974)

Carter, Samuel, *The Final Fortress: The Campaign for Vicksburg* (1980)

Tucker, Glenn, *Chickamauga: Bloody Battle in the West* (1961)

Downey, Fairfax, *Storming the Gateway: Chattanooga, 1863* (1960)

Johnson, Ludwell H., *Red River Campaign: Politics and Cotton in the Civil War* (1958)

Steere, Edward, *The Wilderness Campaign* (1960)

Scott, Robert Garth, *Into the Wilderness with the Army of the Potomac* (1985)

Matter, William D., *If It Takes All Summer: The Battle of Spotsylvania* (1988)

Frassanito, William A., *Grant and Lee: The Virginia Campaigns 1864–1865* (1983). A photographic history.

Dowdey, Clifford, *Lee's Last Campaign* (1960)

Slotkin, Richard, *The Crater* (1980)

Sommers, Richard J., *Richmond Redeemed: The Siege at Petersburg* (1980)

Vandiver, Frank E., *Jubal's Raid* (1960)

McDonough, James Lee, and James Pickett Jones, *War So Terrible: Sherman and Atlanta* (1987)

Carter, Samuel, *The Siege of Atlanta, 1864* (1973)

Wert, Jeffry D., *From Winchester to Cedar Creek: The Shenandoah Campaign of 1864* (1987)

Lewis, Thomas A., *The Guns of Cedar Creek* (1988)

Davis, Burke, *Sherman's March* (1980)

Glaathaar, Joseph T., *The March to the Sea and Beyond: Sherman's Troops in the Savannah and Carolinas Campaigns* (1985)

McDonough, James Lee, and Thomas L. Connelly, *Five Tragic Hours: The Battle of Franklin* (1983)

Horn, Stanley F., *The Decisive Battle of Nashville* (1956)

Barrett, John B., *Sherman's March Through the Carolinas* (1956)

Lucas, Marion Brunson, *Sherman and the Burning of Columbia* (1976)

Patrick, Rembert W., *The Fall of Richmond* (1960)

Davis, Burke, *To Appomattox: Nine April Days, 1865* (1959)

Biographies
(Alphabetical by Name of Subject)

Williams, T. Harry, *Beauregard: Napoleon in Gray* (1955)

McWhiney, Grady, *Braxton Bragg and Confederate Defeat* (1969)

Strode, Hudson, *Jefferson Davis*, 3 vols. (1955–1964)

Henry, Robert S., *"First with the Most" Forrest* (1944)

Grant, Ulysses S., *Memoirs*, 2 vols. (1885; modern reprints)

Catton, Bruce, *Grant Moves South* (1960)

Catton, Bruce, *Grant Takes Command* (1968)

Fuller, J.F.C., *The Generalship of Ulysses S. Grant* (1929)

McFeely, William S., *Grant: A Biography* (1981)

McMurry, Richard M., *John Bell Hood* (1982)

Henderson, G.F.R., *Stonewall Jackson and the American Civil War*, 2 vols. (1898)

Vandiver, Frank E., *Mighty Stonewall* (1957)

Govan, Gilbert, and James Livingood, *A Different Valor: The Story of General Joseph E. Johnston* (1956)

Freeman, Douglas Southall, *R. E. Lee: A Biography*, 4 vols. (1934–35)

Connelly, Thomas L., *The Marble Man: Robert E. Lee and His Image in American Society* (1977)

Randall, James G., *Lincoln the President*, 4 vols. (Vol. IV completed by Richard N. Current) (1954–55)

Thomas, Benjamin P., *Abraham Lincoln: A Biography* (1952)

Oates, Stephen B., *With Malice Toward None: The Life of Abraham Lincoln* (1977)

Hanchett, William, *The Lincoln Murder Conspiracies* (1983)

Tidwell, William A., James O. Hall, and David Winfred Gaddy, *Come Retribution: The Confederate Secret Service and the Assassination of Lincoln* (1988)

Piston, William Garrett, *Lee's Tarnished Lieutenant: James Longstreet and His Place in Southern History* (1987)

Sears, Stephen W., *George B. McClellan: The Young Napoleon* (1988)

Cleaves, Freeman, *Meade of Gettysburg* (1960)

Lamers, William M., *The Edge of Glory: A Biography of General William S. Rosecrans* (1961)

O'Connor, Richard, *Sheridan the Inevitable* (1953)

Sherman, William T., *Memoirs*, 2 vols. (1875; modern reprints)

Lewis, Lloyd, *Sherman, Fighting Prophet* (1932)

Liddell Hart, Basil H., *Sherman: Soldier, Realist, American* (1929)

Reston, James, Jr., *Sherman and Vietnam* (1985)

Thomas, Emory M., *Bold Dragoon: The Life of J.E.B. Stuart* (1986)

Cleaves, Freeman, *Rock of Chickamauga: The Life of General George H. Thomas* (1948)

INDEX

Continued on next page

Continued on next page

Continued on next page

Continued on next page

Continued on next page

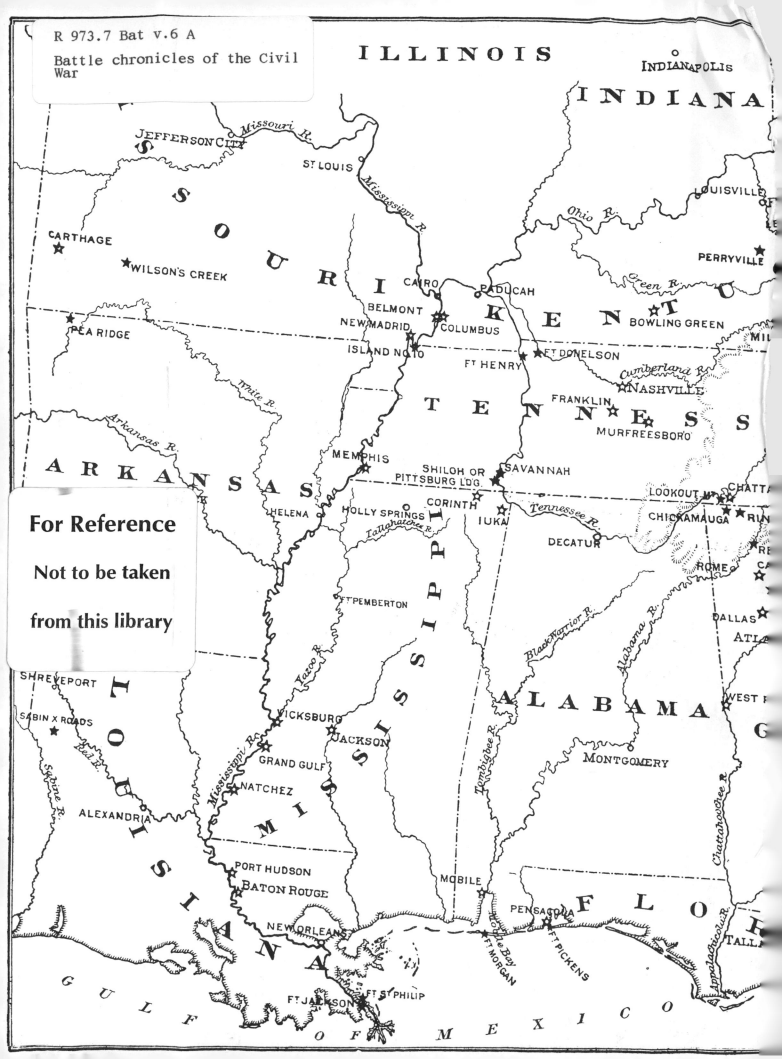

ILLINOIS

INDIANA

INDIANAPOLIS

LOUISVILLE

MISSOURI

JEFFERSON CITY

Missouri R.

ST LOUIS

Mississippi R.

CARTHAGE

WILSON'S CREEK

CAIRO

PADUCAH

BELMONT

NEW MADRID

COLUMBUS

Green R.

PERRYVILLE

KENT

PEA RIDGE

ISLAND NO 10

FT HENRY

BOWLING GREEN

MIL

FT DONELSON

White R.

ARKANSAS

Arkansas R.

TENNESSEE

Cumberland R.

NASHVILLE

FRANKLIN

MURFREESBOR'O

MEMPHIS

SHILOH OR
PITTSBURG L'DG.

SAVANNAH

LOOKOUT M

CHATTA

HELENA

HOLLY SPRINGS

CORINTH

IUKA

Tennessee R.

CHICKAMAUGA

RIN

Tallahatchee R.

DECATUR

RE

FT PEMBERTON

ROME

CA

DALLAS

ATLA

SHREVEPORT

Black Warrior R.

Alabama R.

ALABAMA

WEST

SABIN X ROADS

Red R.

LO

VICKSBURG

JACKSON

MISSISSIPPI

Yazoo R.

GRAND GULF

Mississippi R.

NATCHEZ

Tombigbee R.

MONTGOMERY

Sabine R.

ALEXANDRIA

IS

MI

PORT HUDSON

BATON ROUGE

MOBILE

Chattahoochee R.

ANA

NEW ORLEANS

PENSACOLA

FLO

Mobile Bay

FT MORGAN

FT PICKENS

Appalachicola R.

TALLA

GULF

FT JACKSON

FT ST PHILIP

G

OF

MEXICO